Inspired

JEWISH
LEADERSHIP

OTHER LEADERSHIP RESOURCES FROM JEWISH LIGHTS

Moses and the Journey to Leadership
Timeless Lessons of Effective Management from the Bible and Today's Leaders
By Dr. Norman J. Cohen

The Genesis of Leadership
What the Bible Teaches Us about Vision, Values and Leading Change
By Rabbi Nathan Laufer
Preface by Dr. Michael Hammer
Foreword by Senator Joseph I. Lieberman

The Spirituality of Welcoming
How to Transform Your Congregation into a Sacred Community
By Dr. Ron Wolfson

Rethinking Synagogues
A New Vocabulary for Congregational Life
By Rabbi Lawrence A. Hoffman, PhD

Spiritual Community
The Power to Restore Hope, Commitment and Joy
By Rabbi David A. Teutsch, PhD

Inspired
JEWISH
LEADERSHIP

Practical Approaches to
Building Strong Communities

Dr. Erica Brown

JEWISH LIGHTS Publishing
Woodstock, Vermont

Inspired Jewish Leadership:
Practical Approaches to Building Strong Communities

2008 Hardcover Edition, First Printing
© 2008 by Erica Brown

Library of Congress Cataloging-in-Publication Data
Brown, Erica, 1966–
  Inspired Jewish leadership : practical approaches to building strong communities / Erica Brown.
    p. cm.
  Includes bibliographical references.
  ISBN-13: 978-1-58023-361-3
  ISBN-10: 1-58023-361-9
  1. Jewish leadership—United States. 2. Jews—United States—Social life and customs—21st century. 3. Jews—United States—Politics and government—21st century. 4. Synagogues—United States—Organization and administration. 5. Leadership—Religious aspects—Judaism. I. Title.
  E184.36.S65B76 2008
  305.892'4—dc22

                                                                      2008027381

10 9 8 7 6 5 4 3 2 1

Manufactured in the United States of America
❀ Printed on recycled paper.
Jacket design: Melanie Robinson

Published by Jewish Lights Publishing
A Division of Longhill Partners, Inc.
Sunset Farm Offices, Route 4, P.O. Box 237
Woodstock, VT 05091
Tel: (802) 457-4000   Fax: (802) 457-4004
www.jewishlights.com

To Talia, Gavriel, Yishai, and Ayelet.

May God help you each grow in good deeds and wisdom so that one day you can assume the leadership of our people who need your energy, intelligence, creativity, and sweetness.

CONTENTS

PREFACE

Inspired Jewish Leadership: Practical Approaches to Building Strong Communities is for individuals—both professionals and volunteers—who seek a framework for working through important leadership issues and for boards to facilitate group leadership study. Its primary aim is to stimulate thinking about leadership from a Jewish perspective and to help discipline the generous impulse to lead with the skills to do so effectively. The anecdotes it contains are all true, even if some details have been changed to mask identities, and approximate rather than precise language has been used to re-create dialogue. The citations from individuals—culled from interviews, personal discussions, and class settings—are without attribution for reasons of confidentiality. The reflective questions, exercises, and recommended readings at the book's end are included to invite the reader into an interactive process of deliberation.

This publication grew out of a curriculum initiative of the Jewish Leadership Institute, a signature program that I direct at the Jewish Federation of Greater Washington. Leadership is a subject of constant discussion and concern in our nation's capital. The many memorials to great leaders throughout the city remind us that crisis and American history's most turbulent moments were managed by individuals of great wisdom, understanding, and vision. Looking inward, we can take similar pride in past Jewish leaders—the biblical heroes of old, the scholars who led medieval communities, and the Zionist thinkers who dreamed of a Jewish homeland. Given the challenges facing the Jewish community in Israel and the Diaspora today, it's clear that we need visionary leaders who are no less capable than the giants of our past.

I hope this book will be a valuable addition to Jewish institutional libraries and will help individuals and organizations act with greater professionalism and excellence. Of course, any inadvertent errors it contains are my responsibility alone.

In the words of Joel the prophet, let us all think expansively about our leadership potential: "Your old shall dream dreams, and your youth shall see visions" (Joel 3:1).

ACKNOWLEDGMENTS

Many people helped with this project. My thanks go to Misha Galperin and our many lay partners whose vision and commitment created the Jewish Leadership Institute (JLI) and began the conversations and classes that form the spine of this book. Special thanks to Vickie Marx, Sheryl Friedlander, Koranee Peppe, Michele Duchin, Adrienne Matthews, Daniel Lautman, Norman Goldstein, Michael Feinstein, Ric Fleischer, Sid Schwarz, and our advisory board. Each helped with some aspect of the Institute or the manuscript. Others who helped me in my thinking about leadership (among other things) are Rae Janvey and Rae Ringel and my good friends at the Wexner Foundation, United Jewish Communities, and the Mandel Leadership Institute. The hundreds of lay leaders and Jewish communal professionals who have taken our courses over the past five years have added so much to my understanding about leadership. I am grateful to Stuart M. Matlins, publisher of Jewish Lights, for his support, to Ira Rifkin for his careful editing, and to all those at Jewish Lights who brought this manuscript to light. Friends and colleagues who added their insights or were willing to read this manuscript added immeasurably to its contents.

I thank the editors at the *Journal of Jewish Communal Service* for permission to use excerpts in chapter 7 that originally appeared in "Making Inspired Leaders: New Approaches to Jewish Leadership Development" (vol. 81, 2006). I also thank those at the Wexner Heritage Foundation for granting permission to reprint paragraphs that originally appeared in the Wexner Leadership Library series, "Samuel and the Call to Leadership" (April 2000) in chapter 4.

Of course, my greatest thanks go to my friends and family for being who they are and giving me the time, space, and understanding to teach and write. I especially want to thank my loving husband, Jeremy, who has helped me think through these issues in the abstract and supported me when leadership issues were real and pressing. Talia, Gavriel, Yishai, and Ayelet have given me a wonderful leadership laboratory and are excellent teachers. My love and blessings are with you always. This book is for the many students, friends, and colleagues who have taken on the challenges of Jewish leadership. Stay on the journey. It took Moses forty years to get us to the Promised Land, but he got us there in the end. And that's what matters most.

INTRODUCTION

LEADING AND MEANING

The meaning of man's life lies in perfecting the universe. He has to distinguish ... and redeem the sparks of holiness scattered throughout the darkness of the world.

ABRAHAM JOSHUA HESCHEL

Great Jewish leadership has helped us survive slavery, guided us to the Promised Land, given us hope through exile and oppression, helped us enjoy membership in a nation of overachievers, and given birth to the State of Israel. Great Jewish leadership generates vision and, as a result, followers. It inspires us and helps us to stretch higher, see farther, and reach deeper.

But the converse is also true. Failed leadership causes any number of problems, missed opportunities, and crises. Professionals and lay leaders within Jewish nonprofits complain bitterly of a lack of vision, strategy, warmth, and guidance from those at their helm. A recurrent theme in failed Jewish leadership today is mediocrity. When did we become satisfied with so little when our history should point us continually in the direction of excellence?

These are not new problems. Just as Jewish tradition has left us with a legacy of outstanding leadership, so, too, has it left us

1

with a past riddled with leadership failures and mismanagement. The very last words in the biblical book of Judges—a tome about idolatry, political insurgency, and civil war—are "Everyone did what was right in his own eyes, since there was no king in Israel" (Judges 21:25). The many problems recounted in Judges are attributed to an astonishing lack of leadership.

These haunting words repeat themselves in a strikingly modern context. After Israeli novelist David Grossman lost his son in the final battle of the 2006 war in Lebanon, he gave a memorial speech for former prime minister Yitzchak Rabin on the anniversary of Rabin's assassination. Listen to the ancient resonances in his words:

> One of the toughest issues that the recent war has sharpened is the feeling that in these days, there is no king in Israel. That our leadership is hollow, our military and political leadership is hollow. I'm not even talking about the visible failures in the conduct of war … not about corruptions large and small. I am talking about the inability of Israel's current leaders to connect Israelis to their identity … to those parts of our identity, memory and founding values that will give us hope and strength. That will serve as antibodies to the weakening of mutual responsibility and connection to the land; that will give some significance to the exhausting, despairing struggle for survival.[1]

Grossman is talking not only about strategic planning and tactical maneuvering. He refers to the most primal aspects of great leadership: the ability to shape and inspire values and generate conversations about identity. The national exhaustion reflected in his words reveals the true ingredient behind extraordinary leadership—the power to communicate hope and purpose and to inspire mutual responsibility, particularly at times of crisis and vulnerability. Strategic planning and tactical maneuvering are relatively easy to manufacture in a leadership landscape. The human touch and the ability to muster in others genuine optimism and faith in the future are more difficult leadership characteristics to develop, but arguably, more important.

English novelist E. M. Forster may have offered us a simple formula about relationships in the epigraph to his 1910 novel *Howard's End*—"Only connect"—but nothing about that recipe is simple. Leadership is intensely complex. A popular news magazine defines outstanding leaders as those who motivate "people to work together to accomplish great things."[2] But the same article shares an ugly reality. Harvard University's Center for Public Leadership conducted a poll and concluded that "more than three-quarters of Americans believe that there is a leadership crisis in this country and that without better leadership in all sectors, the country will continue on a downward course."[3] Failing leadership is not only a Jewish issue; it is an epidemic of national and international proportions.

Some believe failure is an inevitable part of taking a public and principled stand on issues. A contemporary Jewish leader asks, "Why are the greatest so often haunted by a sense of failure?"[4] He concludes that within Jewish biblical models there are some common features of leadership that explain this phenomenon. Prophets have "a passionate drive to change the world, combined with a deep sense of personal inadequacy.... The very sense of responsibility that leads a prophet to heed the call of God can lead him to blame himself when the people around him do not heed the same call."[5] What prophets may have deemed personal failures, we look back on as majestic accomplishments. The combination of responsibility and humility, strength and struggle are intertwined in Jewish leadership—for individuals and also for us collectively as a people.

From the patriarchs of Genesis through David's kingship, from European Rabbinic giants of the medieval period to contemporary Israeli heroes, Jewish leaders share a long history of struggle. The children of Israel's wilderness journey to the Promised Land was replete with leadership lapses: crises of faith, the hostility of enemies, internal mutiny, and profound dissatisfaction. The desert backdrop presented additional challenges: uncharted territory, hunger, and a parched, unforgiving physical landscape in which the monochromatic scenery contributed to the people's ongoing sense of tedium.

Unable to see redemption on the horizon, the Israelites questioned Moses relentlessly and begged to return to the familiarity of their past oppression. Yet, in a survey of biblical verses using the Hebrew word for wilderness, *midbar*, the desert is not only a place that signifies peril but also a place of divine dependency, romantic longings, contemplative contact with nature, and expansive freedom. In the Hebrew Bible, the desert is often regarded as a place of refuge, where a large tribal group of slaves becomes a nation, receives the tablets of law, and builds a portable sanctuary.

Wilderness is an excellent metaphor for leadership because it takes us to the heart of a difficult place and asks us to find a way out. The wilderness itself was not our destination; it was a place of transition and transformation. Leaders traverse the wilderness when they run nonprofit institutions and movements. They may know the desired outcome but then have to strategize, plan, and inspire others to share their vision. To get there, leaders need skills, a moral compass of values, knowledge, and diverse fellowship to guide and advise.

In a fascinating Rabbinic observation from the early years of the Common Era, we learn that there are three ways to acquire Torah: with fire, with water, and with wilderness (Numbers Rabbah 1:1). Torah, a deep and abiding connection to the divine and to a code of ethics, can emerge from passion, from immersion, or as a result of a long trek through unknown places. The wilderness represents, on so many levels, the Jewish trials of leadership. In the words of author James Hanley, "You talk about walking in the wilderness, but what else *is* the world but that.... Aren't we all walking in one kind of wilderness or another?"[6]

Those who take on positions of leadership in the Jewish community know that like Moses, Aaron, and Miriam, they will have to make order out of potential chaos, forge a path for others to follow through unmarked terrain, and sustain a vision of the future in the face of skepticism. Jewish leaders, ever mindful of community needs, have to think about strengthening the committed, engaging the unaffiliated, and reaching out to those on the margins. Today's leaders have new challenges, but the base ingredients for good leadership seem universal; they rarely change over time, context, or location. Ancient Jewish models of leadership, when read carefully, remain relevant to modern challenges.

The lofty goals that most Jewish nonprofits set for themselves—truth, justice, and peace—have as their basis the words from *Pirkei Avot* (Ethics of the Fathers): "By virtue of three things does the world endure: truth, justice, and peace" (1:18). These goals are so often accomplished by virtue of good leadership. Yet, polls indicate that today we do not trust leaders—political, military, and religious—as we once did. Truth, justice, and peace seem to have taken a back seat to political prestige, clout, and popularity. We rarely believe what leaders say, and what they say often does not correlate with what they do. The honor once accorded leaders is waning, and it's no wonder it's become increasingly difficult to recruit new, competent leaders given the dark cloud the role now finds itself under.

It is time to return the honor to Jewish leadership that it deserves.

THE LEADER PERSONALITY AND THE FOLLOWER PERSONALITY

Since both Jewish sources and contemporary leadership literature stress the importance of the leadership personality, I always ask participants in the leadership seminars I conduct to give me a list of adjectives and verbs that they associate with leaders. What emerges is that leadership is both a state of *being* and a condition of *doing*. Here are some word associations I have collected:

- **Nouns:** change agent, ambassador, builder, speaker, organizer, dreamer, visionary, strategist, power broker, motivator, light, schlepper, actor, authority, face of an organization,

5

mover and shaker, planner, analyst, garbage man, rain-maker, role model

- **Adjectives:** flexible, patient, decisive, honest, inspiring, inclusive, empowering, selfless, charismatic, principled, goal-oriented, inclusive, responsive, compassionate, determined, strong-willed, thoughtful
- **Verbs:** delegate, dream, work, involve, engage, respond, inspire, listen, plan, organize, motivate, uplift, invigorate, create, commit, strategize, analyze, unite, educate, build, empower, change

These words demonstrate that being a leader is not only about who you are but about what you do and how you do it. For those on the outside looking in, a leader appears to be the one in the spotlight—the front person for an organization or movement. He or she wields power and authority within an organization and serves as a role model. But for those who have been in leadership roles, this perceived glory often appears illusionary. They often regard themselves as the target of criticism or the bearer of responsibilities no one else wants. They are the last to leave meetings and collect the garbage on the way out. In two stunning midrashim, ancient Rabbinic embellishments on biblical texts, we find that Joshua trained as Moses's successor by carrying buckets of water for his master[7] and rearranging the chairs in the house of study when everyone else had left.[8]

Does leadership mean being in the spotlight or cleaning up everyone's mess? In fairness, it is and always will be about both. Leaders need to be comfortable with both center stage and back stage to be change agents.

A key distinction in personality between leaders and followers is that leaders shape events through their active participation, while followers are shaped by events through their passive participation. At times of crisis or dysfunction, followers wait for someone else to solve problems and are often satisfied merely with complaining about their lot. Leaders, on the other hand, view crises as problem-solving opportunities and regularly put themselves in the center of that change. Most of the leaders I know *enjoy* problem solving and rarely look at a problem as intractable. They are energized by dilemmas. In *This I Remember*, Eleanor Roosevelt said of her husband, "I have never known a man who gave one a greater sense of security. That was because I never heard him say that there was a problem that he thought it was impossible to solve."[9]

This personality distinction between leaders and followers became apparent to me through my own board experience. I sit on a number of boards with varying degrees of involvement. One institution I was involved with was plagued by a culture of complaint. The institution seemed poised to be the place people loved to hate, the scapegoat for a host of communal problems. I would hear complaints regularly, sometimes to the point of verbal lynching. These individuals were not necessarily wrong in many of their assessments; many of them were sadly accurate even if they spoke in exaggeration.

I at first kept my mouth shut in the face of these complaints but after a while adopted a new strategy. "Why don't you do something about it?" I started to ask. People looked at me with wry amusement. "But isn't it important to you? Your whole family benefits from their services. It's your institution just as much as it's anyone else's." People naturally become defensive, but the bottom line is that most people do not see themselves as owners and stakeholders of communal institutions. They regard themselves as consumers. Stakeholders fix problems. Customers exchange, return, or complain. When customers are faced with an opportunity to problem-solve, they most often say things like:

- I tried once, and it was hopeless.
- There is no solution.
- It will never get better.
- It's been this way for so long, they don't even know how to get out of the problem.
- Nothing I can do will make a difference.
- I am so busy. I have a full-time job and kids. I don't have time for one more responsibility.

All of these excuses are really a way of saying, "It's not my problem." But in actual fact, if an institutional dysfunction is affecting you, your family, or your community, then it is your problem. You may choose not to solve it for any number of reasons, but you still have part ownership in the institution. In the leadership personality, individuals almost always regard themselves as owners and problem solvers. Followers do not see solutions, even when they are obvious, because they are not looking for them.

ESCAPING LEADERSHIP

What about those who run away from leadership even though they are natural leaders? The prophet Jonah is perhaps the best example of this phenomenon. He had the leadership personality but did not want the responsibility. Remember the story? He was tasked with reforming an ancient biblical city. Instead of going there, he hopped on a boat sailing in the opposite direction. Sometimes, the temptation to run away in the face of responsibility is overwhelming. In the Jonah story, no matter where Jonah runs, God uses the forces of nature to compel Jonah to confront responsibility.

At about the same time I was beginning my personal study of leadership, I had a curious encounter that spoke to the profound complications of responsibility. I was scheduled to speak in New York and took a cab from my Boston apartment to Logan Airport. The cab came early, and a rather portly gentleman with a trim gray beard and a flannel shirt that stretched across his stomach flashed me a good morning. I anticipated an extra half hour of sleep in the cab and was not prepared for the conversation that ensued.

"How are you today?"
"Fine, thank you. How are you?"
"Great. Going to Logan?"
"That's right."

*"No traffic this morning. We'll get you there in no time," he
said in a voice a little perky for me at this hour. "Where are
you flying to?"*

"New York."

"What are you doing in New York?"

The conversation was becoming a little too personal, and I won-
dered if I should stop it. After all, I was a woman alone in a cab at
an hour when hardly a soul was on the road. But he seemed nice and
harmless and rather than cut him off, I became annoyed at myself
for my suspicion. He was just being nice.

"I'm giving a lecture."

"On what?"

*"History," I blurted out, unsure if I should say something as
technical as "the history of biblical commentary."*

"What kind of history?"

"Jewish history."

"What period?"

I sat up in my seat. The language of this conversation was now
beyond polite exchange. This driver knew more than I had bar-
gained for.

"Sixteenth century," I replied.

*He turned his neck and smiled. "So, that means you've read
Gershom Scholem. Have you?"*

Scholem was the foremost scholar on Jewish mysticism of the last
century. I had never had a cabdriver who wanted to chat about the
writings of Gershom Scholem. I took out a pencil and began scrib-
bling down our conversation on the back of my checkbook. My husband will never believe this, I thought.

The driver proceeded to engage me in a discussion of some of the Jewish academic and spiritual lights of the twentieth century: Saul Lieberman, Abraham Joshua Heschel, Mordechai Kaplan. I no longer wanted to get to the airport quickly. I needed to get to the bottom of this.

"So let me ask you a question now. How is it that you are so widely read in these works?" Now, who's prying?

"Well, obviously I'm Jewish. I even studied to become a rabbi. I guess you could say that I really am a rabbi."

"No!" I said, surprise evident in my voice. This was just remarkable. A cabby rabbi.

"I went to HUC rabbinical school, and I loved the learning. I just loved my classes and my teachers. I studied with some of the greats and read the greats and thought I would be a rabbi as my career."

"What happened?" We were now at Logan, but I was not getting out of the car.

"Well, in my last year, we were supposed to intern in synagogues. I was given a small pulpit in New England, and I flew up there for Shabbat. I gave some sermons, like I was supposed to. But I just didn't feel comfortable as the leader of the congregation. I was nervous. After services, all these people came up to me to ask me questions about their lives: marriage problems, estranged kids, people who had lost loved ones. I felt afraid. What did I know? A kid from Chicago. I knew nothing about life. I just did not want this responsibility."

"So how did you become a cabdriver?"

"I got on a plane after Shabbat straight back to Chicago, and my best friend picked me up. I told him the story, and he asked me what I was going to do with my life. I had no idea. He was a cabdriver and said I should become one. It was decent money and a lot of freedom, and you meet interesting

people. One problem, though. I didn't know how to drive. So he taught me. He took me to empty parking lots, and I learned how to drive. I've been driving a cab ever since."

What a story. I would never have believed it had I not heard it myself. But it's true. A person who set out to lead a Jewish community feared the responsibility inherent in it and then, like Jonah the prophet, ran away. Or rather drove away—from a love and a calling—because it came with the enormous burden of leadership.

Our conversation had to be cut short, but in the moments before I ran to catch my flight I learned he was not currently a synagogue member. He married out of the faith. When he left New England that day, he left it for a totally different life. On the plane it dawned on me that I had learned so much about him but did not know his name.

Despite my cabby rabbi's successful escape, it is very hard to avoid leadership if you have a leadership personality. Problems fall in your lap and you want to solve them. You want to nurture, control, change things around you. It's a drive. For some, it's an obsession. But if you have a leadership personality and keep running away from leading, it may be time to reflect on that escape. What is holding you back? Can you learn what you need to know to confront the challenges of leadership and prepare for your responsibilities? Or will you run—or drive—away from what could be an incredible personal calling?

CAN LEADERSHIP BE TAUGHT?

Helping people come to terms with responsibility reminds me of a question I am often asked and a question that is sprinkled throughout leadership literature: Can leadership be taught, or is it a function of personality? We naturally assume that leaders are born, not made. We have witnessed, since our earliest days in school, that some children like to take charge and flourish as the center of attention. They know how to boss people about and have extroverted personalities. If we were able to track such children into adulthood, we might find that they follow a similar trajectory in their professional and home lives. We might also find that some of them use their innate leadership skills for good, while others become neighborhood bullies and magnets for negative attention.

The head of a large Jewish institution was sitting around a circle at a recent class on leadership for high-level Jewish professionals. She confessed to being unsure whether leadership could be taught: "I find that I go to conferences and seminars and hear some great speakers on leadership. I nod my head like everyone else and write notes furiously, and while I'm there, it all makes sense. But then I go back to work the next day, and to be perfectly honest, I lead the way I always have…. For me, I guess it all comes down to personality." As she spoke, I and others in the circle nodded.

It seems that we all have similar experiences. People in leadership positions seek out articles, books, and conferences where leadership is the topic. Everyone seems to have something to say about it, and everyone listening nods in agreement. But, at the end of the day, have we learned anything that makes us do things differently?

Someone suddenly challenged her: "I know what you're saying, but I find that the older I get, the more I am able to take pieces of what I learn and string them together. As I integrate these small pieces, I feel that I *have* changed over time. I am not the same leader that I was. Learning has made a difference." To this, a man across the room chimed in, "I agree. I like to think of leadership development as a course in sailing. You learn how to sail, and then the instructor just adds little hints so that the course becomes smoother, and you feel more competent over time."

Leadership can be learned, but it is a slow and incremental process of absorption and integration. It is not the instant result of study, but the consequence of experience coupled with gentle mentoring.

Warren Bennis, one of the early and influential writers on the new "science" of leadership, supports this view because he believes that leadership cannot be taught. It must be learned. According to a report he cites called "No Limits to Learning: Bridging the Human Gap,"[10] there are two principal modes of conventional learning. One is maintenance learning, which is "the acquisition of fixed outlooks, methods and rules for dealing with known and recurring situations." This kind of learning helps us maintain an established way of life. The second mode is shock learning, events that overwhelm us by their enormity, tragedy, or beauty and, in the process, impart life lessons. This form of learning can be limited, since the education it brings in the form of crisis is not always applicable to situations that are not as extreme.

These two ways of learning are meant to present a balance between the management of ordinary events and systems and those that are out of the ordinary. But they both still represent conventional styles of learning. The authors of this report contend that these two ways of understanding the world alone will not prepare us for the global complexities we now face. Instead, they advocate innovative learning.

Innovative learning is characterized by three emotions or behaviors:

- **Anticipation:** being active and imaginative rather than passive and habitual
- **Receptivity:** learning by listening to others
- **Participation:** shaping events rather than being shaped by them

Leaders are touted for their vision, which is just another way of saying anticipation. Leaders anticipate the danger zones ahead and prepare their followers to meet the challenge. They check their vision by listening to the insights and complaints of others, and they participate in creating solutions. Innovative learning can be taught as long as individuals are receptive while learning.

This does not mean that a class, a degree, or even on-the-job training will make a shy person into an extrovert or a nervous public speaker into a radio and television personality. What it does mean is that when people are given the time, materials, reflective training, and a helpful network of people, they will be able to think more about the way leadership and fellowship work, understand how institutions operate, and be able to implement change more successfully.

Leaders in the midst of their responsibilities should make the time for training, despite their hectic schedules, because it will actually save them time and aggravation and give them a circle of like-minded individuals with whom to think and strategize. Often, we will get a call about our leadership course from someone who asks about the time commitment and then says, "Sounds like a great idea, but I'm just too busy." My answer is always the same: "We're only looking for people who are too busy to do the course!" Every time we run it, I am amazed by the attendees. They have very full lives, often juggling professional and domestic responsibilities while putting in the equivalent of a part-time job volunteering. But they also need a place to think about leading while they are in the thick of it. Without it, burnout is just around the corner.

Leadership is not only about personality, although the influence of personality is impossible to ignore. Leadership is also about transformation and outcomes, and individuals of all types can create changes in institutions and attitudes. Conscious, deliberative thinking about leadership is not accomplished through one avenue. We learn it, read it, live it. Leadership is not a copyrighted science; it is an art form that demands public conversation.

Lastly, leadership development is not a difficult or esoteric subject of study. In his pioneering work *The Path of the Just*, Rabbi Moses Chayim Luzzato claims that none of the truths in his book are original but are obvious to anyone who reflects on them:

> I have written this work not to teach men what they do not know, but to remind them of what they already know and is very evident to them, for you will find in my words only things which most people know, and concerning which they entertain no doubts. But to the extent that they are all well

known and their truths revealed to all, so is forgetfulness in relation to them extremely prevalent.... Its benefit is to be derived, rather, through review and persistent study, by which one is reminded of those things which, by nature, he is prone to forget and through which he is caused to take to heart the duty that he tends to overlook.[11]

Likewise, the leadership advice offered in this book is self-evident, but as Luzzato reminds us, we all need to be reminded of what we already know. Leadership is not a grand discipline that requires years in a degree program. The best training is on the job. And even the best leaders need to be reminded of the obvious.

1

Guilt and Pleasure

Putting the Jewish in Jewish Leadership

It is good that in our generation, one person should have stood firm in opposition to every one else to proclaim the sanctity of man and of human life whether people listened to him or not. Such a one was Abraham.

Rabbi S. Zevin

Seven habits. Twelve steps. Eight ways. Five theories. Just follow the neatly packaged program. It sounds so clean and easy. But in reality, leadership is rarely so simple. It is messy and unpredictable. One of the expressions we use to describe complicated leadership situations is "swamp problems." This description takes us into a thick, murky, uncomfortable place where we feel ourselves constantly sinking. There is no stable ground in a swamp. It is for this reason that leadership training cannot be reduced to basic steps or by-the-book skills. It needs to generate attitudinal changes that prepare individuals to embrace the messiness and become resourceful problem solvers.

One of the most complicated biblical stories of leadership—a veritable ancient swamp—involves Joseph. In Genesis chapters 37–46, we watch a father's favorite, scorned and reviled brother, and one-time prisoner turn into a courtier through a complex set of circumstances. Joseph, one of the few biblical leaders we observe from birth to burial, makes his way in the world by dreaming big, paying a steep price for his confidence, and finding creative ways out of crisis. When we encounter him in Genesis chapter 41, Pharaoh is so pleased with Joseph's dream interpretation that the Egyptian leader offers him a special place in his court; he will become second in command to Pharaoh, and as a result, Pharaoh gifts him with a new wardrobe, name, and wife:

> Pharaoh ... said to Joseph, "See, I put you in charge of all the land of Egypt." And removing his signet ring from his hand, Pharaoh put it on Joseph's hand; and he had him dressed in robes of fine linen and put a gold chain about his neck. He had him ride in the chariot of his second in command, and they cried before him, "Bow." Thus he placed him over all the land of Egypt. Pharaoh said to Joseph, "I am Pharaoh; yet without you, no one shall lift up hand or foot in all the land of Egypt." Pharaoh then gave Joseph the name Zaphenath Paneah, and he gave him for a wife Asenath daughter of Poti-phera, priest of On.
>
> (Genesis 41:41–45)

Joseph is given all of the external signs of leadership: a new name, fine robes, a signet ring and chain, a chariot, and a trophy wife. He is to be escorted around Egypt in his chariot and paraded in the streets with public aplomb. Everyone will bow to him and acknowledge that he is second in command.

As the chapter continues, we find that Joseph is so taken by his new leadership role that he names his children both for his current success and for abandoning the false hope for success that he nursed growing up at home, where his leadership dreams were regarded as arrogant imaginings of a self-absorbed adolescent:

> Thus Joseph emerged in charge of the land of Egypt. Joseph was thirty years old.... Before the years of famine came, Joseph became the father of two sons, whom Asenath daughter of Poti-phera, priest of On, bore to him. Joseph

named the first-born Menasheh, meaning, "God has made me forget completely my hardship in my parental home." And the second he named Ephraim, meaning, "God has made me fertile in the land of my affliction."

(Genesis 41:45–46, 41:50–52)

At thirty, Joseph becomes a great leader, but he is not a great *Jewish* leader. He works for Pharaoh, enhancing Pharaoh's coffers as he plans for a national famine. His time, his energy, and profits are all directed at a royal treasury. Only one generation later, Joseph's descendants in Egypt will become slave laborers, exploited by the economic machine that Joseph himself helps create. Something goes wrong, very wrong.

When Joseph becomes a leader, he covers up some aspects of his Jewishness. He takes on a new, Egyptian name. He wears different clothes. He speaks a different language, and most tragically, he names one of his sons after his own sense of personal abandonment in his father's house. However, bestowing a name on a child that's designed to help us forget our own childhood wounds never works. With each mention of the child's name, the pain or the nostalgia returns. These outside changes pierce the existential question of Joseph's personal leadership identity. Who do I serve? How do I serve? Who am I?

Joseph has a watershed moment when his royal and religious identities converge, forcing him to confront his past and his future. Joseph's brothers come down to Egypt seeking bread during famine. After testing them, Joseph observes that his brothers have matured in their notions of familial responsibility. Swept up in the emotion of this realization, Joseph can no longer withhold his emotion. In Genesis chapter 45 we read:

Joseph could no longer control himself before all his attendants, and he cried out, "Have everyone withdraw from me!" So there was no one else about when Joseph made himself known to his brothers. His sobs were so loud that the Egyptians could hear, and so the news reached Pharaoh's palace.

(Genesis 45:1–2)

Joseph tries to separate his family identity from his life in the palace. He demands that all the Egyptians in his midst leave the room when he reveals his real identity to his brothers. But the text tells us that all of the Egyptians hear his sobs; the news quickly reaches Pharaoh's palace. He can no longer play his game of doubles and hide his real self.

Like this biblical hero, we need to consider what is uniquely Jewish about our leadership and how different and sometimes competing values can merge together in a more integrated and authentic way. We live in an age that respects ethnicity and does not force our spiritual identities into hiding in order to compete in corporate or academic settings. Neither does Joseph. Pharaoh respects Joseph's Jewishness and invites Joseph's family to live in the best land that Egypt has to offer. There are no recriminations. Joseph only becomes more whole as a result of his confession and the integration of his former and current selves. Coming to terms with our Jewish identities is one of the first acts of great *Jewish* leadership. It is an internal calibration that only we can undertake.

As an important side leadership lesson, we find many external signs of leadership success in Joseph's narrative—a nice chariot, leadership jewelry, and prestige. Joseph merits these external signs as a result of his esoteric and practical wisdom. Joseph not only dreams himself, he is a person of big dreams who can interpret the dreams of others and even turn nightmares into promising realities. His dreams and visions, once recognized, offer him status. Wisdom first. Nice chariot later. Today, we often give leadership positions to those who have nice chariots and signet rings. They have money, status, and prestige and, by virtue of these, are offered a place on a board, sometimes a presidency. Only later are their actual leadership skills questioned. But status in the biblical text comes not from money but from intelligence and divinely inspired leadership.

Money and its ability to influence come as a result of wisdom and not the other way around.

WHAT IS JEWISH LEADERSHIP?

In our Jewish Leadership Institute classes, I always ask our participants what specific Jewish values are reflected in the way they lead. They rarely mention that they are following a biblical or Talmudic tradition of leadership, well established by ancient heroes and heroines. Some of them simply confess to there being nothing intrinsically Jewish about their leadership. In their professional roles, they may supervise, manage, direct, and delegate, but these activities are not informed by Judaism in any way. But in every course, after chewing the question for a few minutes, one person will chirp up and discuss a family tradition of communal service or philanthropy that, for them, feels distinctly Jewish: "Now that I think about it, my grandmother volunteered for decades, and I always looked up to her." Others reflect on what they observed every day in their childhood homes: "My parents were always serving on some board or another. They taught me without saying anything that being a member of a community is taking responsibility for it."

A torrent of Jewish responses follows: "When I was a kid, my parents took me to Soviet Jewry rallies all of the time. They told me that we have a responsibility to help Jews wherever they are to achieve basic freedoms. I remember the signs that stretched across the podium that said 'Let my people go.' That's from Exodus, and it is the reason I am a social activist today." How about this classic? "My father used to do my taxes every year. One year he sat me down and said, 'You're earning so much money. How come you don't give more to charity?' That moment changed everything. I started to give more money to charity but also began to get more active in social justice and community issues."

In a recent class, I asked this question, and a woman shot up her hand instantly. "So what makes *your* leadership Jewish?" I asked as I turned to her. "Guilt," she answered with confidence.

The class laughed but then quieted down as she explained herself: "I've always associated guilt with being Jewish. When you're in school, your grades aren't good enough. When you're a parent, you never feel that you're doing enough. When you give charity, it's never enough. Even when you do something good for someone else, it's not enough. Maybe Jewish leadership is about saying it's never enough." Around the room, there were nods of recognition, as if a group of engaged participants all felt the same way.

When this young woman, who is on the executive committee of a synagogue, defined guilt as a hallmark of Jewish leadership, she did not consider guilt to be a negative emotion. In fact, she acknowledged its motivational power and its pervasive grip. It's not that guilt does not exist in other cultures or religions, but for Jews, it feels like home. Ruth Andrew Ellenson introduces her anthology *The Modern Jewish Girl's Guide to Guilt* with her personal observations about guilt that impact on Jewish leadership:

> Between the ideal of who you should be and the reality of who you are, lies guilt. And when you're Jewish, there seems to be no shortage of people who are willing to point out just how guilty you should feel. Families, rabbis and communities happily, but not always so helpfully, are all too eager to bring it to your attention, or you can agonize over it yourself. For me, it takes the form of the following internal reprimand: "Jews have barely managed to survive for thousands of years, and you, you little *pisher*, are going to screw it up for everybody." As soon as I hear those words, the guilt works its way down into my chest and hooks my heart. It happens every time I'm faced with a decision that questions my Jewish loyalties, or whenever I've flat out failed to live up to the prodigious expectations of my people.... I have heard the siren's call of Jewish guilt throughout my life. I have tried rejecting the voice, laughing at it, and sometimes even accepting it with a heavy heart—but I always stop when I hear it speak.[1]

In other words, even when guilt is a constriction in the chest, it still speaks to our hearts. Guilt is often the symptom, not the problem, of the high expectations we have of ourselves. Without question, the Jewish leaders I have studied with feel a deep sense of personal responsibility for others that is often driven, in part, by guilt. Here is a sample of the "guilty" questions they ask themselves:

- If I do not take this leadership role, who will?
- What is my responsibility as a role model?
- What is the right thing to do?
- When will I get this done if I do not do it now?

For those of us who read *Pirkei Avot* (Ethics of the Fathers), a book of Rabbinic wisdom in the form of wise and pithy sayings, we hear resonances of the great Hillel's words: "If I am not for myself, who am I? If I am only for myself, what am I? If not now, when?" (1:14). These self-reflective questions force us to look carefully at our responsibilities to ourselves and to others. These are not questions to generate guilt as much as they are questions that help us shape our lives with intentionality.

So what makes guilt emotionally toxic? Guilt ceases to be a motivator when we are driven to lead *only* by a gnawing sense of responsibility and experience none of the personal pleasure, reward, or goodness that comes with purpose-driven activities. Without the emotional bank deposit, to quote Steven Covey, we continue to finish our tasks out of an over-attenuated sense of commitment. In the extreme, this leads to burnout. Burnout is pervasive in Jewish leadership. But it is not, I believe, simply a result of overworking.

Work offers the opportunity for immense gratification coming from feelings of accomplishment and pride. Burnout is the result of working too hard out of guilt without experiencing the benefits of accomplishment. In the words of a consultant on leadership, "Burnout happens, not because we're trying to solve problems but because we've been trying to solve the same problem over and over and over."[2]

Teaching Leadership from a Jewish Perspective

As close as Judaism is to our hearts, it may not be integrated into our leadership. It takes deliberate consideration to tie our Jewish identities into our leadership. What does this mean? Does it mean teaching a group of Jews about leadership? Does it mean using Jewish texts to teach leadership? Does it mean using sociological and demographic research on the Jewish community to teach leadership? Yes, yes, and yes.

By Jewish perspective, I mean principally a set of Jewish values that guides our behavior as leaders. Jewish perspective also refers to the inclusion of Jewish texts in leadership development, be they biblical, Rabbinic, medieval, or modern philosophy and history, as a resource for study and discussion. This also includes the growing body of contemporary scholarship on Jewish sociology and demographics. Teaching from a Jewish perspective involves a profound understanding of the Jewish cultural and community norms, traditions, and practices by which we identify and shape our institutions.

Many courses on leadership that currently serve the Jewish community bring in experts and consultants who address agenda setting, advocacy, and changing demographics. In this scenario, leadership boils down to a particular set of practical skills, usually presented by multiple experts. However, bringing in an expert on fundraising, for example, who has no knowledge of Jewish day schools or synagogue life is shortsighted because so many of our giving patterns are entrenched in cultural contexts. Active participation may be encouraged, but the next step of processing the information learned into the very real contexts of institutions is rarely accomplished. There isn't enough time. The consultant must make his or her flight; institutional politics cannot be mastered in two hours. What is Jewish about the session is that Jewish people attend or Jewish institutions sponsor such seminars. People leave satisfied because offering some reflective consideration of leadership issues is better than nothing. They are impressed by the titles that experts bring to the lectern. They rarely consider that education is predominantly about integration and how you process the ideas you learn. The information that is passed on has no Jewish flavor; it is just delivered to Jewish audiences.

Ideally, leadership is taught from a Jewish perspective for the following five compelling reasons. Please feel free to add your own reasons:

1. We are blessed to have a textual tradition with leadership wisdom spanning thousands of years. From the legendary tales of King David to Talmudic advice and medieval legal treatises, our Jewish scholarly tradition is replete with discussions of leadership. We have no sainthood genre of religious writing. Mistakes are included to role model responsibility and accountability.

2. Jumping out of the texts are the chronicles of Jewish history. They demonstrate our ambitious will to survive in the face of persecution and the vicissitudes of everyday living. This proud history of survival was contingent upon effective leadership. Whether we read historical testimonies of medieval rabbis and community leaders or the biographies of early Zionists, we are aware that we must honor the leadership of the past by becoming the Jewish leaders of the future. Jewish historical sensitivity leads us to the conclusion that mastery of leadership is pivotal for tomorrow.

3. We expect our political leaders to master the language, history, values, and cultural traditions that formed their respective countries. It is time to expect that Jewish leaders also possess basic knowledge of their own religious and ethnic traditions and history. Today, perhaps more than in any other period of Jewish history, there are so many educational outlets for Jewish adult education that Jewish literacy should be a requisite for Jewish leaders.

4. The study of Jewish texts and values can provide a wonderful template for leadership development. The study of a

complex biblical narrative can help forge a safe passage through group discord. I know of a board that studies two laws of *lashon ha-ra* before each meeting to elevate their discourse. Some institutions have extensive rules of ethical governance or mission statements that emerge out of Jewish values. Judaism informs, frames, and guides leadership documents and decisions.

5. Many leadership courses and readings often fail to inspire. Their sole focus is practical outcomes. They rarely ask participants to reflect on *why* they aspire to positions of leadership and how that core motivation is critical in moments of despair and conflict. Religion has been a traditional source of inspiration since the dawn of humanity. When people study Jewish texts or participate in Jewish rituals, they feel connected to a past and future greater than themselves. It is this powerful sense of belonging that inspires them to lead. Tapping into that inspiration energizes people to sustain high levels of leadership and to motivate others.

Every volunteer joins a nonprofit for a reason; often those reasons are tied to faith or family commitments. For Jewish communal professionals, their career choice is also tied to issues of identity and inspiration. Take time to explore the personal Jewish journeys of those on your board or your staff.

THE STRENGTH OF JEWISH LEADERSHIP

To be a member of the Sanhedrin, the highest legislative court in Jewish law during the Talmudic era and earlier, the Talmud came up with certain criteria. Maimonides codified these in one of his books of law:

> Every conceivable effort should be made to the end that all members of the Sanhedrin be of mature age, imposing

> stature, good appearance, that they be able to express their
> views in clear and well-chosen words and be conversant
> with most of the spoken languages, in order that the
> Sanhedrin may dispense with the services of an interpreter.[3]

These requirements may be regarded as ancient image management. How others view leaders is a significant factor in Jewish leadership. There are harsh Talmudic words reserved for Sages who had stains on their clothes, wore tattered sandals, or appeared in public with people of dubious character. These requirements beg the question of what role internal values play in grooming a leader if external factors are so strongly considered. In the very next set of laws, Maimonides points us to these requirements for every judge, in a small or large court:

> It is essential that every one of its members possess the following seven qualifications: wisdom, humility, fear of God, disdain of financial gain, love of truth, love of people, and a good reputation.[4]

These seven values are distilled from the *mitzvot* (commandments) in the Torah that require a highly developed allegiance to God and to humanity. For Jewish leaders, they are essential requirements. These are more than seven "habits"; they are qualifications and standards of excellence and integrity.

Returning to the question we asked earlier—are leaders born or made?—we find that this list of qualities is not innate. You can be smart, but it is life experience rather than pure intelligence that makes you wise. Humility, fear, disdain of financial gain, love of truth, and love of people are all "acquired" behaviors. We are not born humble. Our attitudes toward money, truth, and people develop over time and through experience. The love of truth and the love of people sound like natural and obvious qualities. Yet, when you pause to think about it, people who love truth are often impatient with human fallibility. They are exact, precise, and unbending. People who love people are often just the opposite.

They negotiate and bend because human happiness and relationships are more important than being "right." The fact that Maimonides did not separate these qualities means that leaders must find a balance between being principled and being compassionate, being driven and being patient, being honest and being forgiving. There is nothing easy about this balancing act, and just like a scale, it is all too easy to become weighted to one side.

It is this careful calibration—am I being fair, am I being honest?—that generates the good reputation that concludes Maimonides' statement. It is hard to know if Maimonides saw this last quality of a good reputation as something distinct from the others and causally related or another behavior in and of itself. The creating of a reputation is essentially dependent on other people. Others will comment, observe, praise and share our reputations. We cannot control how others see us. But we can care about the way that we present ourselves. Great leaders are exquisitely careful about the way others see them and are attuned to the need to create and sustain an image of integrity.

A good example: I was speaking to a rabbi who was a little older than myself. When I called and addressed him as rabbi, he said, "Please call me Sam" (not his real name). I felt uncomfortable because "rabbi" is a hard-earned title, and I grew up respecting titles. "OK, Sam. Thank you. Do your congregants call you by your first name?" "No," he replied. "It's not that I don't want them to. When I left rabbinical school, I wanted to be a friend to everybody. I said that I was going to be the rabbi they could call by his first name. I thought that would change the way my congregation would relate to me. I didn't want to be one of those long-distance rabbis, high on the *bima* and remote from everyone with robes and airs. So, I would tell people, 'Just call me Sam.' You know, it didn't work. I realized that they didn't want to call me Sam. When I was doing a funeral or a wedding, people didn't want a friend. They wanted a rabbi. They were right to want a rabbi. That is my job, and the way that they need to see me. Maybe I was being selfish in asking them to address my need for popularity instead of their need, at times, for authority. It took me years to realize that I could be a friend and a rabbi and still be called 'rabbi.'"

TWO CHALLENGES TO JEWISH LEADERSHIP

Finding individuals with the right leadership personalities—that combination of problem-solving skills and sense of mission—is not easy. The problem is enhanced today by two obstacles: board homogeneity and too little Jewish literacy. Boards of many Jewish organizations today are simply too homogeneous in composition. The *Washington Post* recently discussed the problem of "homophily"—the natural need of people to talk to others who remind them of themselves.[5]

We gravitate to people who think like us, vote like us, send kids to the same schools and synagogues, and even give to the same causes. We do this to affirm our own sense of self. Being around other people who think and talk as we do is a great way to secure and shore up our own views on the world. Technology has contributed to this international phenomenon. The iPod allows us to customize the music we listen to, and the Internet enables us to read the opinions of only those with whom we agree. We can get the word out to friends and family via blogs and personal websites. We don't have to listen to others when there are so many ways of expressing ourselves.

But boards represent the collective voice and, as such, need to be composed of a range of individuals with diverse opinions, personalities, and ways to contribute. Today, one of the main—and sometimes only—selection criteria for board membership is giving ability. There, I said it. One of the dirty secrets of Jewish leadership today is that we have allowed boards to become lopsided by selecting only or mostly individuals with deep pockets rather than creating boards that are representative of the diverse constituencies in our communities.

Buying power rarely makes for an inclusive and intellectually expansive leadership team. Jewish leadership should be marked by a level of commitment to the Jewish community, an ability to mobilize people for a cause, and a content-rich bank of ideas and actions to bring about paradigm shifts. Leaders can use money as a form of manipulation or allow the fiscal support of an institution to mask personal difficulties in consensus building.

Financial resources are critical and necessary to leadership efforts, but they alone do not make a man or woman a leader. Jim Collins, in his monograph *Good to Great and the Social Sector*, helps outline the relationship of money to nonprofits eloquently:

> In business, money is both an input (a resource for achieving greatness) and an output (a measure of greatness). In the social sectors, money is *only* an input, and not a measure of greatness.... In the social sectors, the critical question is not "How much money do we make per dollar of invested capital?" but "How effectively do we deliver on our mission and make a distinctive impact, relative to our resources?"[6]

Moreover, we must begin to insist that those in positions of Jewish leadership, and in particular those in the upper echelon, take steps to become Jewishly literate if they are not already. Jewish leaders should know what the Mishnah is, when Maimonides lived, and the Jewish position on major ethical dilemmas. Jewish leaders are rarely asked if they know Hebrew or have a working knowledge of Israel's history. Moshe Dayan was once asked what the American Jewish community could do to help Israel. Dayan replied, "Just be Jewish.... Jews know what to do when Jews are in trouble."[7]

Just be Jewish. To be fully Jewish is to be aware of Jewish values, history, and tradition. The importance of Dayan's pithy insight cannot be overstated.

—∞—

2

DEFINING LEADERSHIP

For the essence and greatness of man do not lie in his ability to please his ego, to satisfy his own needs, but rather in his ability to stand above his ego....

ABRAHAM JOSHUA HESCHEL

Leadership for Dummies defines leadership as "the set of qualities that causes people to follow."[1] This definition is very basic and perhaps a bit simplistic. In contrast, the *Oxford English Dictionary* defines the verb "to lead" in many ways. Leading can refer to the head of a band or the head horse in a wagon-drawn team. It can refer to the head of parliament or another governing body, and it is also used in fishing to refer to the line that is first thrown forward. Each of these definitions can be understood literally or metaphorically. Leadership involves the front line and the limelight. It may require risk taking and managing a team cooperatively. The definition that may best suit the Jewish community is a "lead" as a small vein that carries blood to a larger vein. Those actively engaged in Jewish life—volunteers and professionals—are all carrying the lifeblood of a Jewish community together—individual, small voices contributing to the larger collective voice of caring and compassion.

What happens, however, when these leads—these individual veins—are not functioning properly to keep the organ of Jewish life working at its best? There are obstructions along the way. Pathways forward get clogged with incivility, poorly run meetings, or fiscal mismanagement. Volunteers lack direction or are not vested with meaningful roles. Difficult board members prevent important motions from being passed. Every year, I meet hundreds of people from around the country who care profoundly about the Jewish community but feel stymied by the poor leadership of individuals at the helm of institutions that are important to them. We stand in a conference room or the parking lot after a lecture, and I hear their frustration and anger. They want the Jewish community and those who serve it to work optimally. They want to replace mediocrity with excellence. They do not understand why it is so difficult to achieve leadership excellence.

According to a recent study on American Jewish leadership:

> Jewish leadership is a subject often discussed but rarely understood. Controversy frequently centers on the degree of democracy in Jewish communal life. Many criticize actions and decisions taken by Jewish leaders as unrepresentative of their constituency or uninformed by Jewish learning or tradition. Still others criticize the growing influence of professionals in Jewish communal life and claim that volunteer leaders have conceded too much authority to a growing Jewish civil service.[2]

How can we change this reality? Re-engineering a corporation may involve downsizing, getting the "wrong people off the bus," or another metaphor or euphemism that masks the cold reality of dismissing workers to cut expenditures. Jewish nonprofits, however, rarely benefit from this kind of language. This attitude applied wholesale to a volunteer organization would be calamitous. We are in the "business" of bringing people *into* the vibrant life of a community. We need leadership that is fiscally responsible but also warm-hearted; leadership that not only relies on innovation but is also anchored firmly in tradition. We want to *keep* people on the bus and expand our notions of community and belonging exponentially.

But leadership is not for everyone. Not everyone can handle the demands or manage others well. If everyone is a leader, then no one is a real leader. Another myth relevant to Jewish nonprofits is that people who get to the top are leaders. People often get to the top of Jewish organizations because of their financial support of institutions, their sustained commitment to an organization's mandate, or their political savvy. For people to stay at the top and have an impact, we have to raise the expectations of leadership. We need leaders who can deliver results and do not merely sustain the status quo once they get to the top of an organization. We need leaders for whom leadership is a discipline and who have invested time in reflective thinking and exploring leadership theories.

LEADERSHIP THEORIES: GREAT MEN AND CONTINGENCY THEORIES

The most popular and idealized theory of leadership is called "the great men theory" of leadership. It is just as its title suggests. We learn about leadership from reading about the trials and tribulations of great individuals, most often men because of society's history of male domination. These icons typically served as leaders in a military, political, or religious setting and imparted their wisdom in letters, journals, or actions that have given rise to imitation. When we read about their tests of fate and faith, we may be inspired to demand more of ourselves or face crisis with equanimity, perseverance, and determination as they did. But inspiration is not instruction. It is nearly impossible to translate the historical context of one leader's setting into another person's reality. I may read a biography of Abraham Lincoln and the fractiousness he faced in trying to keep the United States together and feel powerfully inspired by his tenacity. But that alone will not impart the skills to help me manage a conflicted board at a time of rupture. The circumstances and ramifications are vastly different.

Steven Covey, the best-selling author of *The 7 Habits of Highly Effective People*, took on the challenge of describing humane leadership culture in another of his books, *Principle-Centered Leadership*. Covey believes that there is more to leadership than is typically portrayed in magazines that highlight successful, aggressive businessmen and -women. He argues that "real leadership power comes from an honorable character and from the exercise of certain power tools and principles."[3] Most leadership discussions, he argues, focus on "great men" theories, personality trait theories, or behavioral style theories.[4] The problem with such theories is that they have "more of an explanatory value than a predictive" one. We may use these theories when we look back on the leadership tenure of a particular individual, but it is nearly impossible to use them to train and cultivate new leadership. Books like *Leading Minds* by Howard Gardner offer compelling portraits of world-renowned leaders that help us understand them and the contexts in which they led.[5] We can extract qualities and commonalities of their leadership, but we can hardly train future leaders using such descriptions. Instead, we have to focus on how leaders understand and use their power with humility and dignity, how they expand their spheres of influence responsibly and ethically. We have to stimulate conversations about vision and management, mentoring and succession.

Leadership is rarely personal; it is usually situational. It speaks to how we run meetings, how we manage difficulties, and how we persuade others to adopt an agenda. Leadership always takes place within a very specific culture and context. This type of leadership model is called "contingency theory." Unlike the "great men theory" of leadership, this model minimizes the individual role and instead emphasizes the particular situation in which leadership is demanded.

In *On Becoming a Leader*, Warren Bennis suggests that we are all "creatures of our context" and that understanding and mastering context is essential to being effective.[6] Subsequently, we have to understand ourselves within that context and through consultation with the team of people who help us run an institution. Nonprofit leadership and certainly Jewish leadership never take place in a vacuum. To create long-lasting social change in an institution, or even to function capably every day, requires a team of committed individuals. Leadership conversations take place *with other people.* One problem with the contingency theory of leadership, according to Robert Goffee and Gareth Jones in "Leadership: A Small History of a Big Topic," is that "given that there are endless contingencies in life, there are endless varieties of leadership ... the beleaguered executive looking for a model to help him is hopelessly lost."[7] Contingency theory as a model of leadership must be based on enduring but flexible principles to sustain the permutations that situational leadership presents.

The biblical model for the contingency theory lies in the "career path" that almost every significant biblical leader assumed, from Abraham to Rachel to King David. Each of these leaders, along with Isaac, Jacob, Joseph and his brothers, Moses, and onward, spent time as a shepherd before or parallel to having a leadership role.

The shepherd is an outstanding metaphor for the leader because of the skills required, the tasks and responsibilities undertaken, and the nature of the flock. In order to be a shepherd, you need to be flexible and adaptable to changes in terrain and weather. You need to be possessive and territorial to protect your sheep from enemies and account for them—each of them—at all times. And you need to be nurturing.

As a successful shepherd you need to be comfortable wandering in search of better pastureland and unafraid of the unexpected. You also need the inner resources to cope with solitude and isolation. Ideally, and in keeping with the biblical model, you use your time alone to contemplate the world, to feel your insignificance in the universe, and to praise God for the majesty of your natural surroundings. Your solitude is not a source of angst but a font of spirituality.

The contingent leader, like the shepherd, has both the skills and the fortitude to cope with change and even welcome the unexpected. He or she has no "manual" to follow but allows the exigencies of leadership to sculpt a way forward. Contingent leaders learn from their mistakes and their successes, crafting their leadership role on the run. In the Bible, our most famous leaders were shepherds not because their followers were empty-headed flocks who went wherever directed. The Jewish people are called a "stiff-necked" nation precisely because they did not follow aimlessly or without question.

If you have ever watched a shepherd and his flock, you probably noticed that the shepherd leads from behind, standing at the rear of his flock. This counterintuitive position actually allows the shepherd to see his entire flock clearly. From this vantage point, he can gauge the direction and external conditions that will determine the course. He can see which sheep require added vigilance and protection. Most importantly, it prevents the distance that many leaders have from their followers. Those who lead from the front often don't turn around to see who is behind them. They are so remote or their ideas are so distant from their constituents that they fail to service the very people they lead. If a shepherd did that, he would not only endanger his flock, he would risk losing them altogether.

The shepherd is such an important biblical metaphor for leadership that one of our most famous psalms describes God as a shepherd:

> The LORD is my shepherd. I lack nothing. He makes me lie down in green pastures; he leads me to waters in places of repose. He renews my life; he guides me in right paths as befits His name. Though I walk in through a valley of deepest darkness, I fear no harm, for You are with me; Your rod and Your staff comfort me.
>
> (Psalm 23:1–4)

In this psalm, because God is a shepherd, we, God's flock, have nothing to fear. We are directed to places that benefit and renew us.

We are protected, and even in our darkest hours, we are comforted by the shepherd's tools of authority and leadership: the rod and the staff. From the perspective of the flock, the shepherd keeps everyone alive.

This powerful metaphor indicates, along with the skills required for contingent leadership, just how responsible a leader has to be for—and to—his or her followers. If a flock is entirely dependent on the shepherd for life and protection, then the shepherd must be fully accountable for his sheep. Many leaders want power. They want to lead from the front. They desire followers and want control without ultimate responsibility for those they lead. Leading from behind offers a complete perspective on the role of everyone within an organizational structure.

Jim Collins, in his monograph about moving from good to great for the social sector (his term for nonprofits), concludes that "every institution has its unique set of irrational and difficult constraints, yet some make a leap while others facing the same environmental challenges do not.... Greatness is not a function of circumstance. Greatness, it turns out, is largely a matter of conscious choice and discipline."[8] In other words, it is not that companies and institutions face irrevocable problems that determine their inability to succeed. It is that great leaders have made a choice to succeed despite the problems that are inevitably there and have the discipline to carry out their missions. The shepherd is a sensitive and disciplined leader.

SERVANT-LEADERSHIP: A MODEL OF NONPROFIT LEADERSHIP

Moses and Joshua, his successor, are called God's servants in the Bible and personify servant-leadership. This is not a demeaning title suggesting a subordinate position. This is high biblical praise; it means that the leader in question was filled with humility and valued a lifetime of service to others. It means that rank was not about ego, power, or authority. It was about generosity, modesty, and giving.

37

Moses is regarded in mystical literature as a "vessel of God." This visual image helps explain his modesty. A vessel has form and shape with strong sides or a resilient outer casing, yet its interior is empty. In that empty space, there is room for God. The emptying process, far from disempowering, offers a leader an important glimpse into his priorities and his ego. It is a mechanism for great self-discipline and personal maturity. When we are filled with our own egos, it becomes hard to listen to others, but when we approach others as empty vessels, we make room for them. Servant-leadership is a powerful framework to achieve this level of humility as a leader.

In the Jerusalem home of Rabbi Abraham Isaac Kook, the first chief rabbi of Israel, visitors can see letters that he signed as "Servant of Israel." Following the Mosaic tradition, the highest religious authority in Israel regarded himself as a simple servant of his people.

Servant-leadership is the name of a popular theory of non-profit leadership coined by Robert Greenleaf in his 1970 essay "The Servant as Leader." Greenleaf had a lengthy career in management research that took an unusual turn in the 1960s. After reading Hermann Hesse's novel *Journey to the East,* the story of a mythical, spiritual journey, Greenleaf came to the conclusion that great leaders are primarily great servants who have a deep desire to help others.[9] Greenleaf's model became very influential precisely because it tapped into issues of personal inspiration:

> Servant-leadership begins with the natural feeling that one wants to serve, to serve first. Then conscious choice brings one to aspire to lead. The difference manifests itself in the care taken by the servant—first to make sure that other people's highest priority needs are being served. The best test is: Do those served grow as persons; do they, while being served, become healthier, wiser, freer, more autonomous, more likely themselves to become servants?[10]

One of Greenleaf's disciples, Larry Spears, developed a list of ten qualities embodied by a servant-leader based on Greenleaf's writings:

1. **Listening:** The servant-leader seeks to identify the will of a group and helps clarify that will. He or she seeks to listen receptively to what is being said.
2. **Empathy:** The servant-leader strives to understand and empathize with others.... He or she assumes the good intentions of co-workers and does not reject them as people, even while refusing to accept poor behavior or performance.
3. **Healing:** One of the strengths of servant-leadership is the potential for healing oneself and others. Many people have broken spirits and have suffered from a variety of emotional hurts.
4. **Awareness:** General awareness, and especially self-awareness, strengthens the servant-leader.
5. **Persuasion:** The servant-leader seeks to convince others, rather than coerce compliance.
6. **Conceptualization:** Servant-leaders seek to nurture their abilities to "dream great dreams."
7. **Foresight:** Foresight is a characteristic that enables the servant-leader to understand the lessons from the past, the realities of the present, and the likely consequences of a decision for the future. It is also deeply rooted within the intuitive mind.
8. **Stewardship:** "Holding something in trust for another," servant-leaders play significant roles in holding their institutions in trust for the greater good of society.
9. **Commitment to the growth of people:** Servant-leaders believe that people have an intrinsic value beyond their tangible contributions as workers.... The servant-leader is deeply committed to the growth of each and every individual within his or her institution.
10. **Building community:** The servant-leader senses that much has been lost in recent human history as a result of the shift from local communities to large institutions as the primary shaper of human lives.[11]

The servant-leader model has been adopted in many different leadership circles but has particularly resonated within religious communities because its principles reflect values that are central to faith-based communities. The *New York Times* notes, "Servant leadership deals with the reality of power in everyday life—its legitimacy, the ethical restraints upon it and the beneficial results that can be attained through the appropriate use of power."[12] A careful review of the ten characteristics of the servant-leader suggests major adaptations in our views of power and authority. The servant-leader model can help us reconsider uses of power and influence.

Servant-leadership also means listening to the needs of those we serve in the broadest possible way. Staying with one specific institution for too long or in one board position for too long can stunt our ability to see the bigger picture of Jewish life, rather than move people to other positions of influence. Those of you using this book will, no doubt, see your primary responsibility as becoming the best board member or Jewish communal professional for your current institution. So you should.

But being in a specific leadership role should also obligate us to look at the Jewish community more holistically. Learning about group homes, for example, might make you more sensitive to special needs within your Jewish day school or supplemental Hebrew school. Appreciating synagogue life may make you understand the spiritual needs of the community even if you're busy at the JCC making sure the sports equipment is working properly. Not only does a "think globally, act locally" attitude help you create a stronger mission for your specific organization; it also pushes you to think about future steps and long-term plans. It helps individual leaders appreciate the competing demands for scarce human and financial resources.

The fact that multiple definitions, myths, and theories of leadership exist tells us that there is no right way to lead and no quick formula for effective leadership. Instead, situations call for different and varied approaches. We have used three visual images—the staff, the shepherd, and the vessel—to communicate leadership theories that depend largely on skills and styles: the authoritarian or heroic style, leadership from behind that is ready for life's crises, and leadership as an act of service. In the ideal sense, we have to analyze our own leadership styles and combine theories to make sure that a leadership approach is appropriate for a given situation. There are many personality tests and evaluative mechanisms for those interested in understanding their own leadership style, and I highly recommend using evaluating tools before assuming an involved position of leadership, professionally or personally. These self-assessment tools can be a helpful mirror to the self that also guide us in how we can use our gifts and manage our deficiencies when responsible for others.

⧬

3

WHO ARE WE LEADING?

Age, Ethnicity, and Community

Let all those who occupy themselves with the business of the community do so only for the sake of heaven, for the merit of their ancestors will sustain them and their devotion, too, will endure forever.
PIRKEI AVOT (ETHICS OF THE FATHERS) 2:2

Leaders who understand their followers naturally stand the best chance of motivating them. However, gaining this understanding requires more than simple observation alone. It requires listening and keeping up with the latest research and current events. Most of all, it requires constantly asking: Just who am I leading, and what is the nature of the fluid, dynamic entity that we call community?

This reading and introspection do not always come naturally to leaders. A lot of leaders are better talkers than they are listeners. They may care more about being at the center of attention and self-promotion than genuinely serving others.

I recall an interview I conducted with a community leader who was applying for a job. It felt like a bad date. He asked me nothing about our organization or about my own work. He talked for the better part of a half hour, entertaining me with stories, jokes, and anecdotes that he believed revealed his charm and charisma. When he finally asked me about my own work, I noticed his distraction when I was speaking. He looked around the room at the objects in my office and barely made eye contact. Afterward, I asked him only one question: "Do you consider yourself a good listener?" He smiled broadly, looked straight at me, and replied, "'People tell me that I'm a wonderful listener."

Being a good listener and observer are key to understanding the Jewish community and central to engaging others. An attentive ear and laser vision are critical, both of which I'll say more about in a chapter 4.

We can only move people and change the culture of institutions that we understand, and the Jewish community today is extremely complex. Membership is more permeable than ever before: Being Jewish for some is a matter of birth; for others it is a matter of choice. For some it is about feelings, while for others it is about obligation. Some link their Judaism to their ethnicity; for others the link is to personal history. If our task is the management of a nonprofit entity that serves the Jewish community, then engagement must begin with a firm understanding of today's Jewish community. But defining and understanding community are never easy.

"Community" is an "essentially contested concept."[1] In the words of Joel Westheimer, author of *Among School Teachers: Community, Autonomy and Ideology in Teacher's Work,* "The idea of community is ... elusive. There appears to be no clear consensus as to its central meaning."[2] Is it a moral entity or does it have geographic constraints? Some thinkers believe that the word "community" is used to divert attention from the schisms within a group and present a more unified picture than really exists.[3] In addition to these problems, today's media capabilities have changed the way that we think about communities. Internet chat rooms, university courses, and even religious services have raised new questions about what constitutes true communal membership.

A popular exercise in our leadership classes is to ask people to come up with a list of positive and negative associations with the word "community" encapsulated in a word or phrase. The following are some of the words I've collected over the years:

- **Positive associations:** shared values, unity, membership, support, safety net, understanding, laughter, education, activities, mutual fund, peoplehood, belonging, familiarity, pride, trust, guidance, responsibility, obligation, networking, friendship, history, empowerment, comfort, sharing, continuity, commitment, traditions, closeness, ritual, togetherness, communication, roots, cohesion
- **Negative associations:** exclusiveness, convention, stifling, friction, gossip, segregation, tribalism, obligation, responsibility, prejudice, pressure, judgment, barriers, expense, cliques, politics, rules, forced membership, lack of privacy, guilt

For many Jews, community may mean a limited population, such as their neighborhood or the individuals they regularly pray with at synagogue. But community can also extend to those we do not normally encounter face-to-face, such as Jews in distress in other parts of the globe to whom we feel a responsibility and a sense of collective destiny. In this sense, the word "peoplehood" may be substituted for "community," since it extends beyond the boundaries of those in our immediate geographic or historical reality.

Peoplehood may describe a group of individuals who share a sense of history and fate expressed as culture, faith, language, law, customs, goals, and obligations. In the case of oppression or racism, it may also be externally determined by those outside such groupings.

THE PROBLEM WITH PEOPLEHOOD

Recent sociological studies of the American Jewish community have found, not surprisingly, that community takes a back seat to individuality for many Jews today. This is not a Jewish problem alone but is endemic to Western culture and worth investigating. Some sociologists credit the American emphasis on diversity and pluralism with slowly pulling individuals away from the expected conventions of community living.

Tolerance and diversity are American values and as such have been largely accepted by the American Jewish population. America's greatness has always been in the multiplicity of religious, ethnic and racial groups that claim adherence to the same national identity. The price of this pluralistic diversity, combined with a lack of persecution is a fluidity of personal commitment and a subsequent weakened and/or symbolic sense of minority or group identity.[4]

In *The Jew Within: Self, Family, and Community in America*, qualitative interviews led Steven Cohen and Arnold Eisen to come up with some defining characteristics of American Jews today. They term these characteristics "the sovereign Jewish self."[5] The term implies a certain distance from communal obligations. The following are some of the characteristics they identified as the sovereign Jewish self:

- A sense of inalienability (I'm Jewish regardless of what I do or do not do)
- An orientation toward volunteerism
- A supposition of personal autonomy
- A highly developed sense of personalism
- An aversion to judgmentalism
- A sense of journey without commitment to a particular stance or belief

Think about how each of these statements influences notions of community. While an orientation toward volunteerism is critical in maintaining vibrant communities, virtually every other aspect of the sovereign Jewish self can have a negative impact on Jewish peoplehood. For example, a sense of inalienability is a paramount break from Jewish tradition where religious authorities are charged with determining membership and preserving a shared language of ritual and law. If anyone can be Jewish by feeling and not necessarily by birth, deed, or commitment, then the parameters of Jewish peoplehood may become stretched beyond recognition. While Cohen and Eisen conclude that modern American Jews loathe judgmentalism, it does remain an important mechanism for keeping people within a set of collectively accepted boundaries and shared norms. Personalism and autonomy are, obviously, individually determined and, when regarded as supreme Jewish values, diminish from the impact of a collective Jewish inner language. The glue that held the Jewish community together historically—shared language (Hebrew, Ladino, Yiddish), shared texts, and shared practices—has lost its hold without any replacement.

It is not surprising that people, both Jews and non-Jews, have often regarded anti-Semitism as a means to create a sense of Jewish peoplehood. Sadly, this leaves our unity to the random whim of those who hate us. The ramifications are enormous.

The shift from reliance on religious authority to personal authority means that individuals are no longer dependent on the writings or pronouncements of a religious hierarchy, either for their spiritual interpretation of Scripture or for guidance on the right way to live. The resulting individualistic approach to religious practice and belief makes it much more difficult to achieve and sustain a shared understanding of what it means to be Jewish.[6]

What does all of this mean for Jewish leaders today? For starters, those who were charged in the past with raising funds for communal projects or maintaining high levels of social or educational services must add a preliminary step to their engagement. They must convince nonaffiliated and moderately involved Jews that they *need* to be part of the Jewish community. We can no longer assume membership or a sense of belonging and communal obligation. Where once the pillars of the Jewish community were involved almost exclusively with Jewish concerns, today's strongly committed Jews often spread their allegiances and charitable giving across multiple overlapping communities, be they political, environmental, educational, or civic. Notions of community have changed dramatically, and we ignore those changes at our own peril. Jewish institutions are reinventing themselves or bending over backward to attract members.

> Institutional vitality is a burning practical issue in contemporary American-Jewish life. Numerous organizations are engaged in self-evaluation and re-definition, as they attempt to meet new challenges, such as attracting and retaining members, volunteers and philanthropists in order to maintain established infrastructures and programs. In addition to internal institutional anxiety, Jewish organizational participation is currently a crucial concern not only for the institutions involved but for the entire Jewish community.[7]

Demographic studies show that even institutions designed to bring Jews back into the folds of Judaism, such as burgeoning Jewish spirituality/mystical study centers, have not engendered commitments to the community at large. The emphasis again is the self at the center. While personal growth is an excellent stimulus to inspire people to look first or again at their Jewish heritage, Jewish leaders have to ensure that personal journeys are connected in some way to community building.

How do we transform this profound sense of individualism into an awareness of community needs? How do we reach out to those who are moving further away? There is no one-size-fits-all solution. These are questions that every Jewish institution has to ask and create a strategic plan to answer. Every Jewish leader today is faced with the dramatic changes of the past century in our notions of community.

One first step is to understand the importance of language that joins us together with a sense of unique purpose. In the second chapter of Exodus, the Jewish people move from a loosely knit amalgam of tribes to a nation. That process begins, according to Rabbi Joseph Soloveitchik, with an articulation of the Israelites' collective pain. Early books of the Hebrew Bible do not address the Israelite anguish regarding slavery. Only when Moses enters the scene do the children of Israel begin the slow process of speaking of their pain. Without a leader, a redeemer, it was useless to cry—much the way little children look for their parents after a fall. If no one is watching, then the tears are wasted and withheld. These slaves finally cry out about their oppression. Suddenly, they realize that their collective voice is stronger than their individual complaints. That voice grows greater and more assertive until it turns into a clarion call for freedom. It is this collective voice of communal identity that begins primitively but that develops that we need to encourage today.

THE IMPACT OF THE GENERATION GAP ON JEWISH LIFE TODAY

In addition to changing notions of membership and community, we are today more aware of the impact of generation gaps on Jewish peoplehood. In recent years, numerous studies have been done on the relationship of Generations Xers and Millennials (or Generation Y) to religion, community, and communal institutions. A birth breakdown is helpful in knowing whom we are discussing:

- Traditionalists (1900–45)
- Baby Boomers (1946–64)
- Generation Xers (1965–80)
- Millennials (1981–99)

Without an understanding of the latter two segments of the Jewish community, it is very difficult to lead effectively and to mentor younger Jewish leaders. What emerges from contemporary studies is a generation with radically different notions of connectivity, given technological advances and a sense of multiculturalism that challenges traditional concepts of peoplehood.

Here is what one study tells us:

The twenty something generation has moved away from the idea of rigid boundaries that separate people from one another. For a generation that has come of age in a global society, permeated by technology, media and diverse cultural influences, boundaries have become much more porous. This generational cohort seeks out a broad spectrum of social environments and composes their identity from multiple sources—ethnically, culturally, and professionally.... Moreover, because of their preference for multiple, overlapping social circles, this generation challenges or rejects situations and organizations that define, exclude or marginalize people because of their gender, race, financial status or professional rank.[8]

Another well-known study of this generation, done from a general rather than Jewish perspective, states that young people are more religiously pluralistic and generally disconnected from institutions but also feel a "genuine attachment to religious life" and have strong ideological leanings.[9]

This general disconnect from institutions bears out in Jewish sociological studies. In a study done for Synagogue 3000, a nonprofit organization dedicated to revitalizing congregational life, Steven Cohen reported that only 19 percent of singles and 28 percent of couples under forty-five are members of a synagogue. With this rate of membership, the next generation of Jews will not be serviced by as many or as vibrant congregations; shrinking membership means diminished material support for these institutions. Millennials seek something else from synagogue membership. In "What Do They Want?" Tobin Belzer speaks out for this population:

What we found is that young adults in our survey did not attend worship services out of a sense of obligation or guilt. Instead, members of this generation are keenly attuned to their likes and dislikes, and see their attendance as part of a larger spiritual journey. Across faiths, research participants reported there were a few key factors determining their attraction to a particular religious institution. They were open and pluralistic, encouraged a non-judgmental atmos-

phere, and offered opportunities for community involvement, creativity and leadership beyond the four walls of the
sanctuary.[10]

Belzer urges Jewish leaders to examine the changing needs of the
twenty- and thirtysomethings and to rethink synagogue attendance
as a marker of Jewish identity for this population. This group simply
will not join synagogues as a statement of Jewish identity when not
interested in services (as did many members of the Baby Boomer
generation). "However, when they do decide to join, they participate as active, invested members."[11]

Many Baby Boomers and Traditionalists struggle with these
trends. They do not understand why they should cater to a generation that has not paid its dues—literally as members and
figuratively as volunteers. Anecdotally, executive directors and
presidents of Jewish organizations bemoan young Jews who want
programs directed at them to be fully funded but do not want to pay
membership fees to cover salaries and other fixed costs. Giving
money to what serves your constituency directly may put the "fun"
in funding, but the lights and heat have to stay on, and someone has
to pay for these services.

"I don't know what to do," complains the president of an area
JCC. "We get traffic from Millennials for our literary and film festi-
vals and occasionally the gym. But most don't want to pay membership. I still have to make sure the pool is clean and the theater is
renovated. This isn't someone else's community that you're a guest
in where the host covers all of the expenses. This is your community as much as it belongs to anyone else. If you don't take care of it,
it won't be here for your kids."

The analogy to a guest-host relationship is critical. When we
visit a friend for a long stay, we imagine that they will pay for the
food, clean the sheets, prepare our room, and welcome us with open
arms. We are there to enjoy the friendship. When it is time to leave,
we go. Someone else will clean up after us or, if we are well-
mannered, we will do it ourselves. But the expectation is that

because we are in someone else's home, the primary responsibility for our stay lies with our hosts. This gift of gracious hosting is undertaken with the implicit understanding of reciprocity.

Now imagine that you are a guest about to leave. You say thank you and assume that you have been sufficiently polite and grateful. Instead, the host turns to you in dismay and says, "Wait, you are not a guest. This is not my house. It's *our* house. Where do you think you are going? We need to stock up the fridge, wash the blankets, and—wait, wait—there's a pile of dishes in the sink that have to be washed. This is our house. You and me together. It's *our* responsibility."

The custodial feeling of taking care of the house—the Jewish community—while someone else gets to enjoy it on his or her terms frustrates and angers Traditionalists and Baby Boomers. It leads them to question the meaning of ownership, continuity, and responsibility. This contributes to the generational divide.

To this, Generation Xers and, more so, Millennials, are saying that they feel misunderstood. They have high expectations about the quality and interest of programs and institutions and are not willing to settle, as their parents did, for signing on to a Jewish life that is meaningless as an empty marker of just being Jewish. They care more about meaning than they do about duty and responsibility. They are tired of faceless charitable giving that does not involve them or allow them to designate a gift or help in a direct and unmediated way. They believe in the power of technology to help people keep in touch in constant rather than sporadic ways and feel undermined and undervalued when judgments are made about their preferred reliance on e-mail, text messaging, and other current technologies.

To use another analogy, they view Jewish institutions as formal parties run by an older generation out of touch with their needs. They are not consulted about the location or theme of the party. They are not asked to make choices and decisions about the events and entertainment, yet they are asked to help defray the costs and pay the bills for someone else's idea of a good time. "We're happy to drop by if we have nothing better to do, but please don't charge us for the food. We would have served something else."

This might be countered with a word from a Baby Boomer about how long it took to earn enough money to pay most of the costs of the party and how this generation has been shouldering a lot of expenses. In the words of one Baby Boomer who was disappointed by a synagogue campaign that Generation Xers and Millennials did not contribute to in any significant way, we detect resentment and even confusion about contemporary values:

> I gotta tell you, I am really worried about tomorrow. When I was married and putting my kids through a Jewish school and paying tuition and my shul asked me for a donation for a new building, I got a second mortgage on my house. That wasn't just me. That was me and most of my friends. We gave to elder care even though it wasn't on our radar screens. It was what you did because you were part of a community. It wasn't just about me. It was about us. We were all in this together. Today, I can't get anyone in their twenties or thirties to give a real donation to the shul. They are renovating kitchens and paying for school. What, we didn't do that? I have college tuition to pay now; it's not like your personal expenses go away. Mine just got worse, but I never stopped thinking about the community. Not for a second.

Another kink in the generational divide is longevity. Research and trends on the Baby Boomer population show that their lives are being shaped by their own higher standards of income and health, and by the need to take care of both elderly parents and adult children.[12] They often feel financially extended and want the younger generation to assume more responsibility for itself and our collective future. A recent study of the Baby Boomer population by the United Jewish Communities shows the impact of these trends to be significant for North American Jewry.

In fact, according to the United Jewish Communities, "Jewish umbrella organizations like Federations are likely to see greater demands for Jewish social services for the chronically ill and a larger number of volunteers needed to join the system. We will be caring for more Jewish elderly and trying to keep them in their own homes and communities for as long as possible."[13] A senior executive in an agency that cares for the elderly notes how the definition of "senior citizen" has evolved as people live longer. "I have a seventy-five-year-old woman who is worried about her fifty-six-year-old son and her ninety-three-year-old mother. By definition, our agency considers all of them seniors. We have an agency responsibility to them all, but this requires many more resources than we banked on, even twenty years ago."

All of this fragmentation, resentment, and division have to be understood by Jewish leaders so they can create venues for intergenerational interaction. We cannot afford as a people to break the link in our chain of tradition in any one place. This directive is more than personal; it is historic. None of us can afford to turn away from a history and a people so ancient that have survived persecution and oppression and have contributed in any number of ways to Western civilization. This is not an invitation to guilt as much as a plea for more expansive, historic thinking.

I am reminded of a ritual I witnessed many years ago. My now teenage son was then six years old and receiving his *Tanakh*, Hebrew Bible, from a Jewish day school. The children acted out the receiving of the Torah at Mount Sinai (my son got the lead part as Moses—never neglect an opportunity to share *nachas*, parental pride!). When the play ended, each child was called up with diploma-awarding seriousness to receive his or her very own Bible. Many of the children, even those who gingerly walked up to shake the principal's hand, took the book with zeal and planted a firm kiss on its covers. As I watched one child after another, I felt that another generation was being inducted into the language of tradition while taking personal ownership of a text that had influenced generations before them. With this ritual, a shared language of values was advancing yet again.

When the children finished the ceremony, they took a very long paper chain and encircled the audience, singing songs that glorified the Torah. The children continued their march until the whole group—siblings, parents, grandparents, and friends—was encircled, underscoring that what they were doing was not just personal but entailed an entrance into a community of people who are all bound by the same text. It was a living celebration of the People of the Book that reminded participants and observers alike that we jump from the text to life and back again over the course of a lifetime *together*.

Whether you sit in a community professional seat or on a board of an institution that handles specific needs, you will encounter all or a variation of most of these challenges. It is incumbent for all leaders to let go of the insider language and assumptions they have and listen to those they are leading and even those who refuse to be led.

Trying to lead in a vacuum prevents us from hearing the disenfranchisement of those on the margins, those affected by the generation gap, and those who are too ignorant to be aware of these issues. The fours sons of the Seder table remind us that no matter how you define your Judaism—from the highly engaged to the ignoramus—you have a place at the table and are obliged to hear the Jewish story of redemption. If we all deserve a seat at the table, we had better make sure that there is room for everyone.

—⦷—

4

VISION AND MENTORING

O God, You have appointed me to watch over the life of Your creatures. Here I am, ready for my vocation.

MAIMONIDES

Leaders can sometimes identify the moment when a sense of urgency moved them to get involved with an organization or make a personal contribution to a cause.[1] Some feel an affinity toward a movement or group of people who are trying earnestly to effect changes through their nonprofit work. They experience an "ah-hah" moment and know they must respond to their inner voice. Others are drawn in by an alternative feeling. They look around at the indifference, the materialism, or the cynicism that surrounds us all and decide they cannot sit on the sidelines any longer.

Take Jonathan as an example. Jonathan was explaining to a classroom of like-minded Jewish communal professionals that he reached a turning point in his arid law career after a series of visits to a senior partner in his firm. Before computer-generated billing tabs, this elderly partner recorded all of his billable hours in thick, bound books. Proudly, he displayed his life's work in forty-five books of billable hours. Surveying the monotony of those bindings, Jon concluded that his life was going to record something else, something more personally meaningful and colorful than professional "receipts." Jonathan was able to hear the still, small voice inside and magnify it until it led him to different professional choices. He remembers the exact moment the shift in perspective took hold of him. If we, like Jonathan, tap into these moments of transformation, we can begin to understand the significant role that inspiration plays in authentic leadership.

Religious thinkers and spiritual texts sometimes refer to this experience as a "calling" or a "vocation." The word "calling" used within a religious context signifies a specific moment when an individual has been summoned to exhibit leadership. This term has enjoyed more serious regard in Christian literature than in Jewish writings.[2] It is common for an individual to describe a midlife change to take a leadership position within the church as answering "the call."[3] However, the term "calling" has a more formal definition in the scholarship of religion, as this definition from the *Encyclopedia of Religion and Ethics* indicates:

> A divine call or election, of a revelatory character, [is] addressed to religiously gifted or charismatic personalities. It forms the first phase of their initiation into an often unwillingly accepted intermediary function between human society and the sacred world.[4]

The Rabbis understood the significance of call texts and drew our attention to them in a fascinating midrash, or Rabbinic teaching, dating from the first centuries of the Common Era. It shows the connection that calling has as a literal or symbolic communication between humans and the divine.

> The Rabbis said: You find that when God gave the Torah to Moses, He gave it to him after "calling." How do we know this? Since it is said, "And the LORD called Moses to the top of the mount; and Moses went up" (Exodus 19:20). Also Moses our teacher, when he came to repeat the Torah to Israel said to them: "Just as I received the Torah with 'calling' so too will I hand it over to God's children with 'call-

ing.' "From where do we know this? From what is written in the context: "And Moses called to all of Israel, and said to them."

(Deuteronomy Rabbah 7:8)

Moses received the Torah "with calling" (in fact, the book of Leviticus in Hebrew is *Vayikra*, "And He called," referring to God's calling of Moses), and decided that the children of Israel should share this important preliminary stage of responsibility. What the midrash conveys between the lines is that just as an outstanding leader experiences a call to leadership, so too should he inspire others to hear this call. In other words, the preparation for the receipt of a mission, be it individual or collective, is in both hearing the call and generating the call for others. The midrash communicates a sense of personal invitation to the Torah and its demands. Great leaders invite people into responsibility, imparting both the warmth of communion and belonging with the confidence in another that they may not have in themselves. When God invited Moses up the mount, Moses understood that he was to give the Torah by imitating the same method: calling.

A calling is not always comfortable. Notice the powerful symbolism in the midrash that likens a calling to an invitation to scale a mountain. A calling is an upward propulsion that requires great inner and sometimes physical strength, endurance, and perseverance. We may feel impelled to do something for which we have no formal training or experience. We may feel guilt-tripped into taking a role. Compulsion can generate a calling; it is rare for guilt to create a calling, because with guilt, we often hear someone else's voice in our heads rather than our own. What makes a responsibility a calling is that we can intuit it—it comes from deep within, not from without. Sometimes our lives are so busy that we fail to hear the still, small voice because of all of the distracting ambient noise. Sometimes, we allow and even encourage the distraction to spare us from the demands of our inner voice.

The famous psychologist Abraham Maslow used the term "Jonah complex" to describe the cluster of emotions of people who run away from their calling in life. Jonah the prophet heard God calling him to a mission and ran in the opposite direction. A conversation I overheard at an Ivy League Hillel illustrates Maslow's complex perfectly.

A young man in a position of senior professional leadership in Hillel was walking the head of his local Federation through the Hillel cafeteria, praising its offerings. I was sitting at a table, innocently eavesdropping as I waited for a class I was to teach to begin. The Federation CEO said, "I thought you said you were never going to work for the Jewish community."

> *"You're right. I did say that. What with my dad and my mother and my siblings so involved, I told myself to create some distance."*
>
> *"So, what happened?"*
>
> *"I guess it's the Jonah complex. Whenever I tried to run away from it, it just followed me. I realized at some point to just follow my calling instead of running away. Since then, I've never looked back."*

Another friend who was a committed volunteer told me she decided to do something that wasn't Jewishly related for once. She signed up for a pottery class to meet new people and do something remote from her work with the Jewish community and her deep attachment to all things Jewish. "I realized that that strategy wasn't going to work when my first project in this ceramics class was a *Havdalah* set." Both of these vignettes, told as they were in jest, suggest a sense of fate and destiny that seems inescapable.

A call, as it is usually understood today, is an inner voice that stirs a person to action or transformation. When people describe work as a calling, they usually mean that it has more than financial benefits; it is personally satisfying and ennobling. Elizabeth Jeffries believes that "a calling requires certain preconditions. One is talent.... For a calling to be right, it must fit our abilities."[5] Finding professional work or volunteer opportunities that match our inspiration to our talents can take a long time, even a lifetime.

What does a calling have to do with leadership? Leaders who can identify and be reflective about their own transformative moments will be more attentive and able to create those moments for others. They will usually be more attuned to the role of wonder and inspiration in leadership in general and are able to tap into their own resources when needed. Recruitment and retention are a central focus of research today for Jewish communal professionals and volunteers. We need to know what will engage more people and offer them a sense of purposeful connection to the Jewish community. Even though the process of calling is internal, Jewish leaders should be able to generate enough sparks of interest to create inspired moments for others.

A middle-aged woman in a large East Coast city shared with a group of women that she was looking for meaning in her life. Her search led her to meetings of a Jewish organization. There, she met a woman who never failed to inspire her. This leader would get up and tell the stories of her organization and mesmerize the room. "I felt held in some magnetic force field when she spoke," this woman shared. For years, our middle-aged friend inspired others to get involved by "borrowing" the stories she heard this great female leader tell. "It wasn't until I took my first trip to Israel that I realized it was time to tell my own stories. You can only borrow inspiration for so long." This reinforced an important leadership lesson for me. We each have to own our own calling.

THE CALLING IN BIBLICAL TEXTS

In sacred texts, it is not the inner voice that stirs us or initiates changes but the voice of the divine. Our own sacred Scriptures are replete with "call texts," passages that convey defining moments for our biblical leaders. Abraham was called in Genesis chapter 12, and he immediately accepted his task. Moses and Jeremiah responded to the call with humility and initial refusal. Jonah fled from the call, and Esther was prompted to leadership not by God, but by Mordechai. An exploration of these texts can inspire our own reflections on how we respond to leadership requests and can better equip us to hear our own inner stirrings. How does a prophet hear and respond to God's call to leadership? How do we?

In Genesis 12:1–4, Abraham is called upon to go to a new land and start a new nation on the foundation of monotheism. A careful look at the text shows that Abraham responds to the call with a silent "yes":

> The LORD said to Abram, "Go forth from your native land and from your father's home to the land that I will show you. I will make of you a great nation, and I will bless you; I will make your name great, and you shall be a blessing.... Abram went forth as the LORD had commanded him, and Lot went with him.
>
> (Genesis 12:1–2, 12:4)

Abraham goes without question and—throughout the many chapters of his struggle—without complaint. Other biblical leaders respond to a call with the profound single word that shows preparedness for the challenges ahead: *Hineni*—"I am here. I am ready." But the Bible is a varied text with a large and diverse cast of characters. Not everyone responds affirmatively to a call. In one of the most famous rejections, in the third chapter of Exodus, we find Moses flummoxed by God's request to lead the Jews out of slavery:

> "Now the cry of the Israelites has reached Me; moreover, I have seen how the Egyptians oppress them. Come, therefore, I will send you to Pharaoh, and you shall free My people, the Israelites, from Egypt." But Moses said to God, "Who am I that I should go to Pharaoh and free the Israelites from Egypt?"
>
> (Exodus 3:9–11)

And then Moses adds a further hesitation: "What if they do not believe me...?" (Exodus 4:1). Finally, Moses refuses one last time:

> Moses said to the LORD, "Please, O Lord, I have never been a man of words, either in times past or now that you have spoken to Your servant; I am slow of speech and slow of tongue." And the LORD said to him, "Who gives man speech? Who makes him dumb or deaf, seeing or blind? Is it not I, the LORD? Now go, and I will be with you as you speak and will instruct you what to say." But he said, "Please, O Lord, make someone else your agent." The LORD became angry with Moses, and He said, "There is your brother Aaron the Levite. He, I know, speaks readily.... You shall speak to him and put the words in his mouth—I will be with you and with him as you speak, and tell both of you what to do—and he shall speak for you to the people. Thus, he shall serve as your spokesman, with you playing the role of God to him, and take with you this rod, with which you will perform the signs."
>
> (Exodus 4:10–17)

Moses's stubborn hesitation earns him God's help and God's anger. God gives Moses a staff to speak louder than words, his own divine presence as support, a brother as a spokesperson, and a lesson in destiny. God created Moses's handicap and bestowed him with a life purpose. Who is Moses to refuse?

SAMUEL'S CALLING

One of the strangest call texts of the Hebrew Bible appears in the first book of Samuel. I use the text of Samuel to stimulate thinking on how to inspire leadership because more than most other biblical writing, it parallels the modern-day condition of indifference.

The story of Samuel really begins with his pious mother, Hannah. She makes frequent pilgrimages to the Temple at Shiloh to pray for a child because she is anguished by her infertility. Her prayer achieves such intensity that the high priest, Eli, accuses her of being drunk. In her prayer, Hannah negotiates with God and offers to give her child back to God should God grant her plea: "If You will grant Your maidservant a male child, I will dedicate him to the LORD for all the days of his life" (1 Samuel 1:11). Hannah's deepest wish comes true; she has a son and names him Samuel. After weaning him, she brings him to the Temple.

Eli, already an old man, must mentor this young man, despite the fact that he has not done well educating his own sons. In chapter 2 of 1 Samuel, we learn that Eli's two sons have exploited their positions of leadership and have corrupted the priesthood. Samuel is Eli's last chance to leave behind a positive legacy of leadership for the future. Chapter 3 of 1 Samuel opens with two introductory statements: "Young Samuel was in the service of the LORD under Eli. In those days the word of the LORD was rare; prophecy was not widespread" (1 Samuel 3:1). Samuel's name means "to hear God," and his introduction at this tense juncture indicates that help is on the way. Someone is really listening.

The first part of the verse tells us about Samuel's relationship with Eli, his mentor; the second part of the verse informs us that prophecy was rare in the days of Eli. The priesthood was active; prophecy was not. This verse foreshadows the change of leadership from priest to prophet that will take place through the agency of Samuel. A new type of leadership is about to emerge. It is within this context that Samuel first hears the call, as we read in the biblical text:

> One day, Eli was asleep in his usual place; his eyes had begun to fail and he could barely see. The lamp of God had not yet gone out, and Samuel was sleeping in the temple of the LORD where the Ark of God was. The LORD called out to Samuel, and he answered, "I'm coming." He ran to Eli and said, "Here I am; you called me." But he replied, "I did not call you; go back to sleep." So he went back and lay down.
>
> (1 Samuel 3:2–5)

This passage is rich in symbolism. Eli, the old man, is at the end of his life. We are told this directly, but it is also hinted at with several images. Eli was asleep; even when awake his eyes were failing him, and he could barely see. At the same time, the lamp of God was about to go out. In only a few lines, the text has created the twilight of a man's life, the pending darkness of eternal sleep. The image of dimming eyes harkens us back to Deuteronomy 34:7, where we are told that Moses's life was taken while "his eyes were yet undimmed and his vigor yet unabated." These are sure signs of able leadership: vision and strength. But Eli is old and his eyes fail him. His vision is gone. Dim eyes remind us of Isaac and his failure to detect deception because of his blindness. What will Eli fail to see because of his dim eyes? In a rather ironic twist, it is not that Eli fails to see but that he fails to hear. It is hearing, that which is heard and that which has yet to be heard, that calls for the reader's attention.

Samuel is given a prime place to rest his head, near the Ark. Again with wonderful symbolic imagery, Samuel is placed there to make sure the lamp of God that is nearly extinguished does not go out. It is Samuel who will keep the flame alight; his job will require vision, a watchful eye. The Rabbis of the Talmud also understood this wonderful imagery and compared this verse to Ecclesiastes 1:5: "And the sun rises and the sun sets." Before God brings the sun to set on the life of one leader, he raises the sun of another. Before Moses's sun sets, Joshua's sun rises. Before Eli's lamp goes out, Samuel is there to light it.[6]

God calls Samuel directly, but novice that he is, he confuses the voice of God with the voice of his mentor. The chapter opens with young Samuel in "the service of the LORD under Eli," but at this juncture it is the voice of Eli and not of God that Samuel recognizes. As a faithful apprentice, Samuel runs to Eli's side with the weighty biblical word *"Hineni"* on his lips—"I am here to serve." His zeal is rewarded with the most ironic repeated phrase of the chapter, "Go back to sleep." God calls the prophet, yet the prophet's mentor tells him to go back to sleep. Samuel's mentor has failed him.

A MOMENT ON MENTORING

Mentoring is a serious business. The responsibilities of taking some-one under your wing and supervising him or her to achieve personal growth are great. Mentoring takes time. John Gardner, in his well-regarded book *On Leadership*, likens the mentor to the farmer:

> Mentors are "growers," good farmers rather than inventors or mechanics. Growers have to accept that the main ingredi-ents and processes with which they work are not under their own control. They are in a patient partnership with nature, with an eye to the weather and a feeling for cultivation. A recognition that seeds sometimes fall on barren ground, a willingness to keep trying, a concern for the growing thing, patience—such are the virtues of the grower. And mentor.[7]

Notice the emphasis Gardner places on being watchful, not domi-neering. The mentor nurtures the ripe conditions for growth with-out coercing change. In "Mentoring as Partnership," Chip Bell argues that the traditional definition of a mentor as a person of sen-iority conversing with a young recruit is insufficient:

> A mentor is simply someone who helps someone else learn something that he or she would have learned less well, more slowly or not at all, if left alone. Notice the power-free nature of this definition! Mentors are not power figures. *Mentors are learning coaches—sensitive, trusted advisors....* Mentoring from a partnership perspective means, "We are fellow travelers on this journey toward wisdom."[8]

Very few people seek out mentors in either their professional or vol-unteer commitments. Yet those who do often describe a pivotal relationship and credit much of their accomplishments to someone who pushed them beyond what they thought themselves capable of achieving.

Gardner also mentions the importance of novices being exposed to "seasoned leaders and exemplary figures so that they can perceive and understand those dimensions of leadership that cannot be put into words."[9] Not every aspect of leadership is spelled out clearly; since so much of good leadership involves good judgment, it is important to observe the subtleties of leadership up close. Laurent A. Daloz suggests three main purposes of mentoring: (1) offering support, (2) creating challenge, and (3) facilitating vision.[10]

Offering support for a disciple or novice creates a firm relationship of caring but does not necessarily advance someone. A mentor has to take active steps in helping his or her charge develop a personal vision and take steps, even risks, to reach an objective. One guide describes six roles for a mentor:

1. Providing time for the mentee
2. Creating a safe space to share
3. Simple, emotional, and respectful listening
4. Sharing personal and professional experiences
5. Sharing information and materials
6. Celebrating successes of the mentee[11]

BACK TO SAMUEL

God calls Samuel three times, and each time Eli fails to understand the momentous drama of this call and translate it for the uninitiated Samuel. Each time, Eli advises Samuel to return to bed. The text itself explains why Samuel keeps making this serious error: "Now Samuel had not yet experienced the LORD; the word of the LORD had not yet been revealed to him" (1 Samuel 3:7). Samuel is young and does not know the voice of God. The third time, however, Eli understands the profundity of the night's restlessness. He tells the boy to lie down but this time adds, "If you are called again, say, 'Speak, LORD, for your servant is listening'" (1 Samuel 3:9). That small word "if" reveals all the failings of Eli. Perhaps after calling Samuel three times, God will not bother again. Perhaps Eli's failure to recognize this leadership moment will mean that Samuel's calling will never take place. On Eli's shoulders rests the burden of leadership that he may have failed to pass down. As both Eli and Samuel return to their respective places, one senses that neither will rest. The night has been too interrupted. The stakes are too high for sleep.

But Samuel is vindicated; the fourth time God calls him twice, "Samuel, Samuel" (1 Samuel 3:10). There is a persistence in the repeated calling of his name. In Genesis 22:11, we read, "Abraham, Abraham." In Exodus 3:4, it is, "Moses, Moses." In 1 Samuel 3:10, it is Samuel who is called twice. With a parental love, God awakens the slumbering child. He is a child no more. In just one evening, Samuel will go from boy to man, from novice to prophet. Samuel answers as he has been told, "Speak, for your servant is listening" (1 Samuel 3:10). Samuel, in one line, has transitioned himself from being the servant of Eli to being the servant of God. However, Samuel has left out one word, perhaps the most critical word, from what his mentor told him: "LORD." He forgot to say, "Speak, LORD, for your servant is listening." Just as Samuel did not hear God's call, he does not yet know God well enough to call God by name. Yet we have confidence in Samuel's answer. Finally, someone is listening.

The reader expects that Samuel will be consecrated and will join the prophetic ranks. Instead of being assigned any responsibility, however, Samuel is told that his mentor has failed and is held accountable for the failure of his sons. Eli's house will perish. "The LORD said to Samuel: 'I am going to do in Israel such a thing that both ears of anyone who hears about it will tingle. In that day I will fulfill against Eli all that I spoke concerning his house, from beginning to end'" (1 Samuel 3:11–12). Where the word of God was not sufficiently audible earlier for Samuel to recognize God's voice, it will now tingle in the ears of all. No more will Eli's leadership and that of his sons be tolerated. It is the young apprentice who is burdened with this news. He is not told about the leader that he will become, only about the leadership that will cease to exist.

After this momentous revelation, "Samuel lay there until the morning" (1 Samuel 3:15). No more does Samuel run to Eli; he has finally surpassed his mentor. Eli is told about God's revelation and accepts the harsh message with equanimity: "He is the LORD; He will do what He deems right" (1 Samuel 3:18). This, too, is an important lesson of leadership: know when it is time to hand over the reins to the next generation and accept the change with maturity. The transfer of leadership from Eli to Samuel is not conveyed by some public pronouncement, as one might expect. Instead, "Samuel lay there until the morning, and then he opened the doors of the House of the LORD" (1 Samuel 3:15). He is no longer the child who waits to ensure that the lamp of God is not extinguished but is now the one who opens the doors to the sanctuary.

The chapter closes with the early success of young Samuel:

> Samuel grew up and the LORD was with him, and none of his words were allowed to fall to the ground. All of Israel, from Dan to Beer-sheba, knew that Samuel was trustworthy as a prophet of the LORD. And the LORD continued to appear at Shiloh: the LORD revealed Himself to Samuel at Shiloh with the word of the LORD.
>
> (1 Samuel 3:19–21)

Where prophecy was not widespread before, the presence of it was now spreading throughout Israel, "from Dan to Beer-sheba." Where before "the word of the LORD was rare" (1 Samuel 3:1), now it is "the word of the LORD" (1 Samuel 3:21) that closes the chapter; it is with Samuel continuously. Where the leader garnered little respect earlier, now the leader is regarded as trustworthy throughout Israel. How does this sea change in both leadership and followship take place? The text offers a hint in the ambiguous words "And none of his words were allowed to fall to the ground" (1 Samuel 3:19). This beautiful expression communicates a dedication to Samuel's very words. Rather than fall on the ground, his words are lifted high and heard.

As Samuel grows up, others realize that he has been gifted not with a particular prophecy but with the mission of leadership. This special child called by God from his sanctified place near the Ark is cared for and singled out for special treatment by the priests and the rest of the community. He grows into a leadership role in full view of the community. As such, his words are guarded and watched. He is encouraged to grow into the kind of leader who inspires confidence by the confidence others have in his words: his words are not allowed to fall to the ground. The chapter closes with the message that it is not only Samuel's call that makes him into a leader but also the commitment of the community to care for and nurture its new leadership.

It is clear from these passages that hearing and seeing—attentiveness and vision—are critical components of responding to the call of leadership. Humanity must imitate a God who is sensitive to sight and sound. Images of seeing and hearing are present in God's response to Israelite oppression in Egypt:

> The Israelites were groaning under the bondage and cried out; and their cry for help from the bondage rose up to God. God *heard* their moaning and God remembered His covenant with Abraham and Isaac and Jacob. God *looked* upon the Israelites, and God took notice of them.
>
> (Exodus 2:23–25)

The first stage of leadership is attentiveness: a sharp ear and a quick eye. In the book of Samuel, the failure of leadership is characterized by an inability to hear and to see. By the end of chapter 3 of 1 Samuel, we are convinced that for Samuel to redeem Eli and his household, he will have to have both attentiveness and vision. One of the keys to having a personal mission is to recognize a calling. We need to train ourselves to hear that call, especially if we intend to mentor others to positions of leadership. Some people in the volunteer world have "call waiting." They hear calls that resonate all of the time; these are the voices that help our compassion surface. But to be good leaders, we also have to train ourselves *not* to answer every call but to focus our leadership activities productively. For others, it is caller ID that counts: who is asking us to take on a position of leadership?

REVISITING VISION

Perhaps no single word is bandied about more in discussions of leadership than "vision." Vision is not only what we see but what we would like to see, a future direction for ourselves and our nonprofit institutions. In order for "vision" to be a word of practical importance and not only poetic flair, it should be based first on what we see around us in the moment. Being visionary involves not only reflecting on the future, but also on taking a sharp, sometimes painful look at what currently exists. In order for Samuel to change the predominant leadership paradigm, he had to be made brutally aware of the current state of leadership. In Abraham Joshua Heschel's majestic tome on prophecy, he describes the prophet's gifts, highlighting these two qualities in this form of ancient Jewish leadership:

> To a person endowed with prophetic sight, everyone else appears blind; to a person whose ear perceives God's voice, everyone else appears deaf. No one is just; no knowing is strong enough, no trust complete enough. The prophet hates the approximate; he shuns the middles of the road. Man must live on the summit to avoid the abyss. There is nothing to hold except to God. Carried away by the challenge, the demand to straighten out man's ways, the prophet is strange, one-sided, an unbearable extremist.[12]

The prophet as a leader is a lopsided being who sees and hears too much. He is exquisitely sensitive to injustice and does not let crime and inhumanity go ignored. The prophet as a model for Jewish leadership today tells us the importance of speaking truth to power and not turning away from that which we do not want or are afraid to see. This laser vision and honesty are at the heart of seeing a community for what it really is, rather than as an idealized portrait. In Samuel's first encounter with revelation, God forces him to confront all that is wrong with his mentor.

In *Good to Great*, Jim Collins creates a leadership ranking of the kind of qualities that make for outstanding leadership of companies. He contends that level-five leaders—his highest level of leadership—are individuals who can face the "brutal truths" of their institutions. See what lies before you; only then can you envision what lies ahead of you. In Heschel's terms, "In speaking, the prophet reveals God. This is the marvel of a prophet's work: in his words, *the invisible God becomes audible.*"[13] Sound and sight are heightened in the prophet's experience of the world. He uses these senses to see and hear what others shut out and then inspires changes that allow others to open their senses. This ability is a hallmark of prophetic leadership.

Vision and attentiveness—hearing and seeing—form the foundation for strong biblical leadership. As we move from text to life, we find that the same criteria apply. John Kotter, in writing about why transformation efforts in business fail, acknowledges the importance of vision and the difficulties that arise without it:

> Without a sensible vision, a transformation effort can easily dissolve into a list of confusing and incompatible projects that can take the organization in the wrong direction or nowhere at all.... In failed transformations, you often find plenty of plans and directives and programs but no vision.[14]

Vision might be the basis for strong leadership, but to make good on the vision the leader must be attuned to the complexity of the situation and the possibility of crisis. In a serious attempt to understand the needs of leadership today, one contemporary writer on leadership suggests that "in a crisis we tend to look for the wrong kind of leadership. We call for someone with answers, decision, strength, and a map of the future, someone who knows where we ought to be going—in short, someone who can make hard problems simple."[15]

Strength and direction seem to be good leadership qualities on the surface. But we have to be wary of opting for simple answers to escape confronting complex problems. Sound bites and slogans are just that—words. They should not be mistaken for problem solving.

TURNING A CALL INTO A MISSION

Earlier, we defined the call as a mission "addressed to a religiously gifted or charismatic personality." We have explored several gifted biblical personalities. We have examined the role of seeing and hearing in responding to the call. But we have not yet demonstrated how to hear the inner call today. In the absence of divine revelation, we cannot identify with certainty the charismatic personalities within our midst who will be tomorrow's visionaries. The most we can do is to sharpen our own faculties of vision and attentiveness to hear an inner calling to action.

This self-awareness in leadership also makes an appearance in one of the most beautiful and moving call texts. It is captured in only a few words. The prophet Isaiah recounts his moment of election. He has a vision of God on a throne and the angels as they are cry out, "Holy, holy, holy" (Isaiah 6:3). Isaiah, feeling himself unworthy of the divine presence, professes his inadequacy in front of God. Yet it is then, in Isaiah 6:8, in that moment of unworthiness, that Isaiah hears the call that will change his life and the prophetic history of Israel: "I *heard* the voice of the Lord saying, 'Whom shall we send and who will go for us?' Then said I, 'Here I am; send me.'"

Isaiah is not answering a call, he is answering a question. God does not assign Isaiah to a task. It is Isaiah who hears God asking a question, a general question: who will be a leader? Isaiah attunes himself to this voice and directs the question to himself.

The question of who will assume leadership is expressed loudly in every generation, "Who will go for us?" We are always reframing God's question, "Whom shall we send?" in religion, education, and politics. Few are those of us who stand up as Isaiah did and answer the call with that unique combination of humility and bravery, modesty and spiritual audacity: *Hineni*—Here I am. Send me.

❧

5

AUTHENTIC LEADERSHIP

Full deployments, engagement, hone and sharpen all of one's gifts, and ensure that one will be an original, not a copy.
WARREN BENNIS

A small room in Kibbutz Merhavia in Israel has been preserved as Golda Meir's first home after she immigrated to Palestine. The room is only sixty-five square feet in size and records a materially modest life: a bed, wall hooks, a table, a chair, and a small desk. This petite woman who lived large started her life in Israel with very humble beginnings. In fact, the kibbutz initially rejected Golda and Morris Meyerson when they arrived there in September 1921. The kibbutz members looked upon Americans as "spoiled" and poorly suited for the tough kibbutz lifestyle, but they eventually overturned their decision. The Meyerson's entry ticket was a curious and sought-after object they brought from home: a gramophone. The kibbutz did not own one and so let the young couple join to benefit from this cultural treasure.[1]

Kibbutz Merhavia soon learned to benefit from the industry of the "American" woman who would become the first female prime minister of Israel. It was leadership from very strange and humble beginnings, which took a few lucky and unexpected turns but always returned to the theme of a passionate ideology coupled with hard work and profound humility. Golda was not going to give up on something she wanted and was not looking for an easy life; she wanted to make a difference. The rest is history.

Authentic leadership is the product of introspection and painful honesty about what we want in life and the sacrifices we are willing to make to achieve it. Leaders who only respond and react to others are not leaders at all. They are either followers with more power than others, or frauds and wannabes. They may have a visual picture of what a leader *should* look like and try to dress the part. They may have pre-prepared speeches that sound like what a leader *should* say. They deliver them and find that they get a lukewarm reaction because the words do not ring true. At these moments, leaders defy themselves, and their leadership may be insincere and short-lived. In the words of a writer on leadership:

> Leaders are all very different people. Any prospective leader who buys into the necessity of attempting to emulate all the characteristics of a leader is doomed to fail. I know because I tried it early in my career. It simply doesn't work. The one essential quality every leader must have is to be your own person, authentic in every regard. The best leaders are autonomous and highly independent. Those who are too responsive to the desires of others are likely to be whipsawed by competing interests, too quick to deviate from their course, or unwilling to make difficult decisions for fear of offending. My advice to the people I mentor is simply to be themselves.[2]

How do we measure authenticity? I believe that authentic leadership comes from closeting ourselves in our own inner spaces and working out our needs, desires, deficiencies, aspirations, and strategies. It is not about how others see us as leaders; authentic leadership is about how we see ourselves. Without this self-knowledge, leaders can burn out or find themselves compromising their per-

sonal integrity and wondering how it happened, or feel disconnected from their ideological or emotional core. Sometimes it takes
someone else to notice it: "You're not acting the same lately.
Everything OK?"

Leaders who are not being themselves may find accompanying
visceral reactions; they feel anxious, confused, tired, or weary.
Keeping up appearances can be exhausting. Inauthentic leaders
may also show signs of depression: sadness, despondency, unusual
weight gain or loss, disorientation. They are compelled to be someone they think they *should* be rather than answering their inner
voices. They are slowly nursing an identity crisis.

John Gardner, in his book *Self-Renewal*, discusses the importance of self-knowledge and the easy way we run away from it:

> Human beings have always employed an enormous variety
> of clever devices for running away from themselves, and the
> modern world is particularly rich in stratagems. We can
> keep ourselves so busy, fill our lives with so many diversions,
> stuff our heads with so much knowledge, involve ourselves
> with so many people and cover so much ground that we
> never have time to probe the fearful and wonderful world
> within. More often than not we don't want to know our-
> selves, don't want to depend on ourselves, don't want to live
> with ourselves. By middle life most of us are accomplished
> fugitives from ourselves.[3]

Are you an accomplished fugitive from yourself? What a terrifying
question. We know that self-knowledge may exact a steep price.
When I am alone with myself, I may have to ask if I am in the
right job, am with the right spouse, have the right peer group, or
am living a life of integrity. We also have dependents and financial responsibilities that we cannot easily avoid. We need not
question every aspect of our lives to arrive at authentic leadership.
But it does require solitary time to sort through how we lead, how
we balance the demands of leadership with our family commitments, how effective we are, what are our leadership weaknesses,

and how we invest our time and money. We may not be happy with our conclusions, but the self-awareness is invaluable in forging new directions.

A lay leader I met in my travels was burning out in his volunteer board position. He invested hours of time each night answering phone calls, defending his institution at a time of fiscal difficulty, and trying, at the same time, to get all the books in order. His family was becoming fed up with his absence and his mood swings. He confided his feelings to me in words I will not soon forget:

> I took this position because I wanted to change things and believed I could. Others put me here to do that. At least, that's what they said. But who are they kidding? They didn't want me to change anything.... I want to be creative, but I can't do that in this position. I feel so trapped by the expectations of others that I am just not myself anymore. I'm even finding it hard to have an internal conversation about what I want. I don't know anymore. I just don't know.

As painful as this conversation was, it helped him come to terms with the ambiguity of his leadership. He did not know where he stood anymore because he had failed to match his ideology and creativity with the realistic limitations of working with others and the politics of his nonprofit. Realizing that he was trying too hard to accommodate everyone and making no one happy in the process, he began making key decisions about how he would measure the months ahead. How could he fulfill his role more meaningfully? How much could he compromise on issues and still retain a strong sense of self? He realized that he had never communicated his own need for autonomy and creativity to his board and that stating it could help them understand him better. The honest conversation he had with me about his feelings led him to a process of self-questioning that helped reenergize and redirect him before he gave up altogether. For the first time, he gave himself the gift of personal clarity.

A HASIDIC APPROACH TO AUTHENTICITY

Martin Buber, the great Jewish philosopher and another pioneer émigré to Israel, analyzed a powerful Hasidic tale in his slim collection *The Way of Man: According to the Teaching of Hasidism*. Hasidic stories are a repository of hidden wisdoms, usually centered on the rebbe or *tzaddik*, the former being one's personal rabbi and the latter referring to a very righteous person. Because Hasidism is based on the notion that certain individuals have a special link to the divine, the role of the rebbe or *tzaddik* is particularly interesting from a leadership perspective. Rebbes are not only consulted about matters of faith and doubt; their guidance is also solicited on business transactions, marriages, and a host of other personal matters. The rebbe is the patriarch of a Hasidic court or dynasty. With loving care and concern, he is responsible, in large part, for shaping the lives of his Hasidim, his disciples.

For Buber, Hasidism has a wonderful way of unifying inner human contradictions or simply offering the license to live with multiple and conflicting pulls in a state of accepted balance. Rather than berating ourselves for having a soul and a body that often move in opposing directions, Hasidic tradition searches for ways to sanctify the mundane aspects of our lives and make sacral what others consider base, unwanted temptations. In many ways, this attempt at creating personal harmony helps individuals find their authentic selves within a community that places great value on adherence to tightly prescribed convention. In the words of Buber:

> The man with the divided, complicated, contradictory soul is not helpless; the core of his soul, the divine force in its depths is capable of acting upon it, changing it, binding the conflicting forces together, amalgamating the diverging elements—is capable of unifying it. This unification must be accomplished *before* a man undertakes some unusual work.[4]

Buber writes convincingly of the need for profound self-awareness before taking on any "unusual work." His suggestion is powerful when applied to the art of leadership. Leaders, perhaps more than other individuals, need to know the conflicting forces that lie within themselves that drive and inspire them before taking positions of authority that involve directing others.

Leaders can be very insecure and thin-skinned. They may be driven by ambition, envy, jealousy, or the competitive need to be first and best. They may have grown up with a strong need for approval that spills over into their adult, professional lives. They may have adopted a patina of indifference to protect themselves against criticism or try too hard to accommodate out of a desire to be popular. Many leaders confess to serious bouts of depression that alternately motivates them to squeeze meaning out of every day or prevents them from being as effective as they want to be. Sometimes one wrong decision that impacts others in a major way—a general's decision to go to war, a personal affair, or the extortion of funds—can create a ripple effect so significant that it destroys the faith people have in them or their institution. Leaders who do not confront their inner demons and find mechanisms to control them for the communal good can influence others so profoundly that they bring about tragic outcomes. Think only of Melville's Captain Ahab, who, out of a desire for personal vengeance for the loss of his leg, imperiled the lives of all of his sailors in pursuing Moby-Dick.

In Buber's writings, the Hasidic conception of humanity is the need to bring these conflicting drives into check by careful self-examination: "Real transformation, real restoration, at first of the single person and subsequently of the relationship between him and his fellow-men can only be achieved by the comprehension of the whole as a whole."[5] To this end, Buber tells the story of Rabbi Yitzchak of Vorki, who was discussing the value of good household servants with a group of prominent men he was hosting. Rabbi Yitzchak tells them that he once thought that a good servant was of prime importance but had come to understand that it was really the master who mattered. He relates how his teacher, Rabbi David of Lelov, once scolded him when he came to him with some domestic problems. His rebbe asked him, "Why do you speak to me? Speak to yourself!"

Rabbi Yitzchak took these powerful words to heart. "My teacher showed me that everything depends on the master of the house." It was upon him to sort out the issue by listening to his own inner voice. The rebbe was suggesting that the problems of a servant in a house are really a metaphor for the body and the soul. If your dependents and subordinates are having problems, understand that you are their master. You determine their direction and you guide them. You are in charge. If you do not understand yourself, then that which is subordinate to you will control you.

We find this in all walks of life. Parents are controlled by children. Students control teachers. Bosses are controlled by their assistants. Housekeepers control householders. Why? Because those in leadership positions are not listening to their inner voices that tell them to lead. They may have perceived leadership in terms of authority, but without authenticity, the "real" authority lies with someone else.

The difference between real and perceived leadership lies largely in the neglect of leaders to be their authentic selves. In Hasidic thought, human relationships and conflict are not someone else's problem. The expression "It takes two to tango" is counter to the way Hasidic thought operates. All conflict starts not with two but with one:

> The practical difference is that in Hasidit man is not treated as an object of examination but is called upon to "straighten himself out." At first a man should realize that conflict situations between himself and others are nothing but the effects of conflict situations in his own soul; then he should try to overcome this inner conflict, so that afterwards he may go out to his fellow-men and enter into new, transformed relationships with them.[6]

Hasidic teachings suggest holding up a mirror to the self at a time of conflict and understanding the unique role that you yourself play in the problem. It is a compelling piece of advice for leaders who often merit their positions because of certain innate qualities but develop a "leadership personality" as a second skin that covers their real selves.

Leaders can acquire "personalities" to be responsive to those they lead in ways that do not come naturally to them. For example, a CEO may have risen to the top of his professional game as a result of long hours and careful analysis, but once at the top, a new persona is called for that involves image making. Whereas hard work and intellect got him to where he is, new traits are required to keep him there. He may need to motivate or inspire employees; he may need to adapt himself to social situations that do not come naturally to him now that he holds an ambassadorial role. He may need to manage unfamiliar crises. Many new executives find that they worked years to achieve success only to ask themselves, "Can I survive my own promotion?"

For some, the answer is a resounding "no." Additional perks and benefits notwithstanding, such individuals are simply unable to make the transition. Others make a conscious decision to succeed and will develop adaptive mechanisms to handle the unfamiliar new territory. Expanding the personal shell of leadership is nothing short of a conscious choice to succeed.

For the new leadership persona to emerge holistically, leaders need to (1) see the value of the changes, even if they experience personal difficulty in the learning trajectory, (2) have feedback mechanisms in place to measure success or failure, and (3) be able to cite examples that demonstrate real, internal change.

For example, a leader may not be technologically savvy or well organized; these two factors may have been deterrents to promotion, either in a professional or volunteer capacity. The person is so committed to becoming a board president that she finds ways to compensate for these difficulties and shows a willingness to learn. She may opt for a seminar or an executive coach. She does not resist the change but is honest about her deficiencies and, more importantly, realizes the benefits of being a well-organized person. She does not put this trait down because she does not possess it. With a few courses under her belt, she appoints a friend, colleague, or board member as a peer mentor and asks discreetly for feedback as she runs her first meeting and all subsequent meetings. At first, she stumbles with some dates and facts but catches her old behavior and remembers some good tips from her coach. She checks in later with a friend and is told that she was much improved. She may not see it at first, but later in the very same year, she looks back on situations and wonders how she could have ever let herself get in such a bind. Her former self is unrecognizable. By this, I do not mean that she forgot her old behaviors, but that they are so distant from her current self that she almost wonders who that other person was that inhabited her body and soul for so many years.

At this stage, she has developed an important piece of a new leadership persona that has become part of an authentic self. She is not paying lip service as so many politicians do—telling you what you want to hear. Through the help of others, she was able to recognize a problem within herself and make the critical decision to change because *she* valued the change and wanted to be different. Many a leader will say that they cannot be other than they are. This is a smoke screen. What they really need to say to be honest is "I don't want to be other than I am."

Knowing yourself and being candid about your inadequacies is not something that can or should happen in public. For Buber, it occurs in the hours when we are utterly alone. It is difficult to face ourselves with this level of honesty but impossible not to. Buber uses language powerfully to capture the pain of isolation as we move beyond "the fiery jaws of collectivism" that consume the self.

Who is the real leader—the person in the office or in the bedroom? The conference room or the living room? Authenticity, according to some experts, is really about creating consistency, where possible, between the public and private selves of a leader.

> A psychological term, *authenticity*, means pretty much what you might guess: you're real, not a fake. Your outer person is much the same as your inner person, not a mask you put on.

Who you are is the same as what you do and say. Only authenticity builds trust, because sooner or later people spot the fakers. Whatever leadership ethics you may preach, people will watch what you do. If you're cutting corners, the best will lose faith in you. The worst will follow your footsteps. The rest will do what they must to survive in a muddy ethical environment. This becomes a pervasive barrier to getting things done.[7]

William James, the famous psychologist who tried to analyze religious experience, understood that the authentic self is not only the most productive self, but the happiest one as well.

I have often thought that the best way to define a man's character would be to seek out the particular mental or moral attitude in which, when it came upon him, he felt himself most deeply and intensively active and alive. At such moments, there is a voice inside which speaks and says, "This is the real me."[8]

James's insight is contingent on one thing: we have enough inner silence to hear the voice within us speaking, telling us that we have identified the real person within the layers of identity that we each embody.

I was with a friend at a retreat and spent part of a long Saturday night in discussion with him about some personal aspirations. I was stymied about next steps and felt the kind of confusion that can only be likened to dense fog. No path seemed clear or apparent. I turned to him and said, "What do you think I should do?" He said, "I know what you'd tell me if I asked you. You would say, 'Listen to your inner voice.' You've told me that before, and it was very important advice at the time." What could I say to this? He had thrown back my own advice, but now, in hearing it and not saying it, I suddenly realized how much static there is between the voice of reality and the choice of decision making. I, who had given this advice to others, had trouble hearing my own voice. The static was too great.

If we do not actively create inner silence, then we cannot hear the thin voice of authenticity speak.

One of my favorite biblical verses is from the book of Exodus following God's revelation at Sinai. The ancient Israelites are terrified by the thunder, lightning, and threatening voice of God. They beg Moses to say the Ten Commandments because they are afraid to hear God speak. Moses tells them not to be afraid, but they ignore him. And although they refuse to budge, Moses is prepared to take risks, to step into uncertain places: "So the people remained at a distance, while Moses approached the thick cloud where God was" (Exodus 20:18). Leaders are willing to go where others are not, even if it means stepping into the fog to get to the other side.

How do we begin the process of self-exploration, take the first step into the unknown? First of all, we have to schedule time with ourselves. Calendar it in. It may mean fifteen minutes of journal writing a day. It may mean solitary walks on a regular basis. It may involve going away on a personal retreat every few months. You may need to employ a therapist or a life coach who will help you hold up a mirror to yourself and help you nurture your own questions. Alternatively, you may ask a person you respect to mentor you by meeting with you on a monthly basis or choose a peer mentor and give each other mirroring time. There are a lot of ways to grow the voice of self and hear it somewhere in the static of life. Self-knowledge, however, is not a gift. It is a choice. We each decide as leaders if we will hear an inner voice or if we will ignore it.

6

THE OPTIMISTIC LEADER

Optimism is not anything to be commanded or ordered. One cannot even force oneself to be optimistic indiscriminately, against all odds, against all hope.

VIKTOR FRANKEL

In Exodus 2:2, there are two words that sum up Jewish leadership: *ki tov*—"it is good, it will be good." Hope and the ability to see a better future and create it have been the underlying strength of Jewish leadership for millennia. *Hatikva,* "The Hope," is the title of the Israeli national anthem. It references thousands of years of Jewish history and a contemporary list of wars and hatred that are transcended by one value that supersedes all others: hope.

To be a Jewish leader means to believe that whatever circumstances befall us, we will endure and as a result grow stronger. So sure are we that Jewish leadership is centered on the hope that we will survive that Mordechai tells Queen Esther at a time of Persian persecution, "If you keep silent at this time, relief and deliverance will come to the Jews from elsewhere" (Esther 4:14). Mordechai has no doubt in Jewish relief and deliverance; his only question is whether Esther wants to be part of the story or not.

Whose story do you want to be in? Are you a Jewish leader or not? Do you have faith in the eternal survival of the Jewish people? Or do you prefer sitting on the sidelines while someone else makes history?

Mordechai inspires Esther through a series of personal questions that she must confront. One might say that Mordechai uses emotional intelligence to frame his argument. Emotional intelligence is a recently coined phrase in psychology that describes the capacity to understand, analyze, and manage one's own emotions and those of others. In a recent study on the impact of emotional intelligence on leadership, two researchers concluded that hope was one of three key ingredients in resonant leaders. Resonant leaders are those who are able to connect deeply with others through personal mindfulness of themselves, others, and situations, through compassion and through the ability to communicate hope. Such leaders are attuned to their own needs and competencies, are attentive to others, and are also able to direct them to higher ground through their leadership: "Hope enables us to believe that the future we envision is attainable, and to move toward our visions and goals while inspiring others toward those goals as well."[1] At a time of cynicism, corruption, and suspicion in the political arena, we know all too well how valuable it is to inspire others with a vision of a better world.

Our two Hebrew words of abiding hope—*ki tov*—were not uttered in Exodus at a time of joy but in the most trying of circumstances. Exodus begins with a tragic pronouncement that can only be mitigated by a completely new vision of Jewish peoplehood. Pharaoh declares that all male children be thrown into the Nile River in an attempt to reduce the number of Jews in Egypt and eat away at the centrality of family in the Jewish tradition. Jewish leadership was critical, but no one was up to the task. Then, Exodus chapter 2 records the birth of a male child, an event that seems only worthy of mourning given Pharaoh's dictate. But the mother of this child sees what others cannot. She sees hope where others see only despair. She sees new life. She sees a future. She, too, makes a pronouncement about the birth: *ki tov*—it "is good" (Exodus 2:2).

That child is Moses, future savior of the Jewish people, who *does* create a new vision of Jewish life. Through his leadership, Jews move from being a tribal slave entity to being a free nation with their own homeland. That creation is presaged by two words of hope at a time of persecution: *ki tov*. Moses's mother, unnamed in the text, is recognized not by a personal identity but by the small and potent words that she mouths over the birth of her male son. She could have cried. She could have wailed. She could have mimicked the pessimism of other mothers of newly born sons. Instead, she finds pleasure in her young son, a pleasure so profound that she declares against all rational odds that this child will bring good into the world. And he does.

The biblical words *ki tov* are initially found four times in the Hebrew Bible during another creation narrative: the creation of the universe in Genesis chapter 1. God speaks the world into existence and then declares four times that His creations are good. Genesis chapter 1 culminates in an even stronger expression of pride: "And God saw all that He made, and it was very good" (Genesis 1:31). The rhythm of Genesis chapter 1 is highly patterned; God precedes creation with words, creates, and then evaluates creation as each day unfolds and closes. God determines a pattern for all of creation: intention, action, and evaluation.

Every leader must assess their efforts, their creation. Every leader must be able to find the good in their work and share their assessment with others. However, in our Exodus story—a small, family-centered narrative about the birth of one child—a human being takes this evaluation one step higher. She declares the birth of her son good when on the surface it appears to be anything but. Moses's mother begs the question: why do Jewish leaders embrace an almost irrational belief that life will always get better?

If you have ever been a leader in any community—a school council president, the head of your civic association, the president of the PTA, or a middle manager at work—you know what it means to navigate negativity. Leaders are always surrounded by naysayers who insist things will never change for the better. They can be very loud and convincing. They cite countless examples of failure. They criticize people, institutions, and initiatives. They minimize good-will and are suspicious of good intentions. They sit across from each other at Shabbat tables and meetings pinpointing the errors of Jewish institutions and their leaders. They communicate a sense of little hope in the future.

Take a recent participant in one of our courses. In exasperation she shared the frustrations that emerged in her boardroom:

> There is one person on our board—I think she's been there forever—who always has to take the opposite opinion of everyone else. I mean, she's entitled to her own opinion and everything, but it's like she just needs to be different. She is always the one who pipes up and says something bad about our shul, and I know that she doesn't keep her feelings to herself. I just can't figure out why she's been a member of the shul for so many years and why she serves on the board. It's strange. She hates the place and can't stop talking about it. Why not go somewhere else? There are three synagogues in our area that she could go to. Why us?

Why do people who are so negative choose to stay within an organization? The answer, quite simply, is that they crave attention. If all they can muster is negative attention, well so be it. They'll gladly take it. Like children, they come across as vehement, indignant, or resentful because that's what it takes for them to get what they desperately need. They hunger for intense emotion and may need small dramas to hold their interest. Alternatively, these individuals may need to focus on the negative in an institution or on a leader as a scapegoat for their personal problems; it's safer than confronting the real subject of their emotional pain.

A mother of a young, well-adjusted child in a Jewish day school kept complaining to anyone who would listen about her conflicts with certain teachers and the school in general. She told person after person that she was going to take her daughter out of school—she did it within earshot of her daughter and her other kids, whom she planned on keeping in the school. She failed to recognize how pernicious this was for her own children, who day after day had to balance their mother's strong negativity with their own happiness. She did not earn a reputation as a problem solver, only as a resident complainer. Unintentionally, she tarnished her own image more than the image of the institution she was targeting.

I am no psychologist, but I do believe that when negativity reaches certain heights (or should I say lows?), the anger expressed may be a sign of deep emotional trauma or personal baggage that's better served by getting professional help.

Regardless of its cause, all leaders must learn how to navigate negativity and ultimately transcend it. You may inherit a particularly negative board member who simply will not go away. You may be on the receiving end of pent-up scorn only because you're new to the job. One new senior-level leader confessed to wrangling with just this issue:

> There were a few people who came up to me in my first weeks of work with a laundry list of everything that they thought was wrong with this organization. I guess it's good I didn't meet them before I took this job or I never would have accepted! This would usually happen on the weekends or in a supermarket. No space or time was safe and neutral territory. I think they felt that I was here to eliminate every one of the problems they perceived and wanted to make sure I had the whole list. Looking back on it now, I should have seen the signs not to invest that much time in these conversations, because the laundry list kept changing and getting longer. After a while, when I saw that there was nothing I could do to make them happy, I pulled away. They probably just think I am now part of the problem, and I have to let go. I am not going to make everyone happy. If I cannot live with that admission, I am not going to be able to do this job.

In my experience leading Jewish leadership workshops, I have come across extreme negativity as the silent killer of potentially good leadership. I have watched dozens of people in volunteer and professional leadership positions become exhausted by the demeaning negativity of others. The situations discussed in this chapter are extreme cases of negativity rather than run-of-the-mill issues that come up periodically. It is extreme negativity that is particularly corrosive in volunteer-driven organizations, where a leader may give the equivalent of a part-time job in charitable hours only to spend much of their time dealing with people who have little hope and even less gratitude. In the exasperated words of one ex officio board president: "I never took this one complainer seriously, but at the same time, it wore me down. I just didn't have the patience. And it was always the same story. Again and again. It's like you give a person a bad piece of gefilte fish in 1967, and they just can't let go."

I have come to realize that only those individuals who can shield themselves and hover above the negativity can truly influence others.

In *Principle-Centered Leadership*, Stephen Covey writes that one of the qualities necessary for leadership is the ability to radiate positive energy. The attitude of such leaders, he writes, is optimistic, positive, upbeat:

> Their spirit is enthusiastic, hopeful, believing. This positive energy is like an energy field or an aura that surrounds them and that similarly charges or changes weaker, negative energy fields around them. They also attract and magnify smaller energy fields. When they come into contact with strong, negative energy sources, they tend either to neutralize or to sidestep this negative energy. Sometimes, they will simply leave it, walking away from its poisonous orbit…. Be aware of the effect of your own energy and understand how to radiate and direct it. And in the middle of confusion or contention or negative energy, strive to be a peacemaker, a harmonizer, to undo or reverse destructive energy.[2]

Covey asks us to be mindful of our own energy and aware of its impact on others. If you look around you, you will notice that the best leaders tend to be more upbeat. They may walk with a heightened bounce in their step, smile more often than others, and use humor to bring people out of their negative thinking. They *do* radiate positive energy, and other people feel good in their presence. They have an aura of specialness, as if God graced them with a different force field. They are able to be self-renewing when they do not get the support they need from others. Leaders respond to negativity by increasing this aura so that it is able to neutralize tension and hostility.

We should all be able to identify naysayers in our immediate orbit. I once had a professor in graduate school I referred to as Dr. No. He rejected any paper idea that did not conform to his recommendations. All suggestions made in class were met with an instant frown. Students learned a lot in his class. They learned that any idea that conflicted with the professor's should be relinquished. Since saying good-bye to Dr. No, I've met hundreds of other such characters: Mr. No and Mrs. No, Rabbi No, Principal No, Executive Director No. They, too, have their own special aura. It says implicitly: No Trespassing. Go away. I'm not interested.

We may pity such people. We may feel compassion for them. We may even try to win them around on a sunny day. But it is best to avoid them wherever possible. Radiate positive energy and surround yourself with others who do the same. Stay strong and be hopeful. Place yourself in locations of peace and beauty. Reenergize yourself by thinking of what inspires you about your volunteer or professional commitment. Be carried by the love of others. Hardcopy e-mails with compliments and keep them a box of positive letters. Store up the praise, because you will need it when the kvetchers come around. I know too many Jewish leaders succumb to an avalanche of negativity. They spend so much time reacting to criticism that they do not do enough to affirm their positive personal or institutional mission.

And here is the line that no leader who believes in change can handle: you will not change the complainers. You can fix the world. You cannot fix them. You should not try to fix them. It's energy poorly spent. Tell them that you have a different opinion, smile broadly, and walk away. Transcend them. As they are speaking, keep a two-word biblical mantra in your mind: *ki tov*. It will get better. It has to.

In his exegesis of the Exodus story, a Talmudic Sage concluded that only one-fifth of the Jews in Egypt left when they had an opportunity to do so. Only 20 percent of a slave nation pursued freedom. How this number was arrived at is pure speculation. We have no idea who stayed and who left Egypt. It is not written in any biblical text. What charged the Rabbinic imagination to arrive at this dismal percentage? This Sage understood that redemption is not for everyone. Not everyone has the hope that life will change, that it can get better—that it can be good, even very good. There are people who are locked into an abysmal portrait of today and cannot envision a hopeful tomorrow. They are stuck. They are paralyzed by negativity and do not move forward. Moses called to them, but they refused. They paid a price in sweat and tears for their choice. The 80 percent are people we still recognize today. They are not Jewish leaders. In essence, they are not even followers.

I say this not as Ellen Porter's Pollyanna who makes everything negative into something positive. It is critical to receive honest feedback and to ask for it often and explicitly. But honest feedback is also balanced feedback. Leaders should be able to make judgment calls after a few encounters to determine if those who are issuing the criticism are also issuing the praise. Here are a few questions for an inner dialogue on that assessment. They can assist you in silently evaluating the critic. Look for signs that tell you this encounter is worth pursuing or worth dropping:

- Does this person have loyalty to me or to the institution in question?
- Does this individual care about a positive outcome, and can he or she be counted on to be part of a solution?
- How much time (add it up in actual minutes) are my conversations and communications with this person taking?

- Does the same issue come up again and again without an opportunity to move beyond it?
- Have I been able to demonstrate any turnaround of any of this person's opinions?
- Do I feel that this person is listening as well as talking?
- Have there been any demonstrable changes in behavior, attitude, or responsiveness of the actual leader or the institution that may have precipitated tensions?
- Why do I continue this relationship if it is not creating any gain? Am I continuing it for financial, political, or social reasons, and if so, are the gains worth the price?
- What emotions do I feel toward this person generally and specifically in the moment he or she expresses a complaint?
- Does this individual express himself or herself with dignity and respect for me and others? What other relationships may be compromised if I continue to associate with this critic?
- What is the worst thing that could happen if I were to confront or push back against the criticism?

Make no mistake. These are difficult questions that may lead to some uncomfortable conclusions, but we delay asking them at our own peril. Adding malcontents to an already busy schedule is a singular and ill-advised waste of time. When your own optimism is compromised, you may find it difficult to inspire others. Sometimes, respectfully pushing back really helps. Complainers often respect you more for taking a principled stand; they realize that you are not a pushover.

A board vice president of a West Coast Jewish institution received long letters and e-mails containing personal tirades and complaints about the institution she helped run. She at first took them seriously and spent hours researching and responding to each issue raised. It did not take long to realize that she was getting nowhere and only feeling increasingly exasperated. So, in response to lengthy e-mails, she began responding with a one-sentence friendly reply: "Thanks so much for your e-mail. I hope you are well." Her complainers got the message and stopped writing. One complainer, she shared with me, was angrier than ever because she was not getting the attention she craved, but this vice president was no longer worried. She was protecting herself.

> I felt like I needed a shower every time I got off the phone, because I just couldn't move her and hated to hear so many bad things about the place I care so much about, that is doing such good work. I didn't want to go down into the mud with her, so I made a decision. I will just be polite and keep it brief. That way—whatever happens—I will still like myself.

At the same time that leaders have to sustain and bolster their optimism, they run the risk of being too dismissive and unbalanced. If you are so much of a cheerleader for your institution that you are not receptive to *any* negativity, then people will stop giving you constructive feedback that can help advance your leadership and your institution. You get pegged as someone who just promotes the status quo and not as a change agent. There are many valid complaints that do not get a proper hearing because leaders stick their heads in the proverbial sand. Balancing optimism with a dose of realism is a hallmark of a great leader.

Not everyone has the belief, the energy, and the patience to fight their way through the thorny wilderness to get to the Promised Land. But such people do exist. Mature leaders appreciate that obstacles are also opportunities for growth. They can manage negativity while preserving dignity. Those who are able to strike this balance—and it can take years—may find hope in the two words uttered by the ordinary, unnamed mother of an extraordinary Jewish leader: *ki tov*.

7

LEADING FOR TRANSFORMATION

Deep knowledge about yourself enables you to be consistent, to present yourself authentically, as you are.
RICHARD BOYATZIS AND ANNIE MCKEE

We hear a lot about inspiration and transformation and the absence of it in the arena of political leadership today. But what do the pundits and commentators mean? What does inspiration mean? How can we get to transformation without inspiration? If we don't know what it is, it's going to be very difficult to explain why leaders should have it and dispense it generously.

Let's turn to a reliable source for our answer: the Miriam-Webster Dictionary.

> Inspire (n-spr) *v.* in·spired, in·spir·ing, in·spires: 1. To affect, guide, or arouse by divine influence. 2. To fill with enlivening or exalting emotion. 3. To stimulate to action; motivate; to affect or touch. 4. To draw forth; elicit or arouse. 5. To be the cause or source of; bring about. 6. To draw in (air) by inhaling. 7. To stimulate energies, ideals, or reverence. 8. To inhale.

If I asked you to circle the definition of "inspire" that best describes your leadership, what would you choose and why? Notice the emotional resonances in these definitions and how someone or something is responsible for helping arouse, motivate, or touch someone in a deep and highly affecting manner. It's not easy, even with the definition right in front of us, to understand the process of inspiration. But one thing is certain; if we feel uninspired, it is hard to inspire others. Conversely, if we feel inspired, how can we share it and help others feel that sense of exaltation and transcendence?

Harris Collingwood concluded in a recent *Harvard Business Review* article, "Leadership is autobiographical. If I don't know your life story, I don't know a thing about you as a leader."[1] During the third class in our Jewish Leadership Institute seminar, we give leaders a chance to tell their stories in a class on inspiration, vision, and mentoring. There are lots of skills involved in leadership training, but the real work of leaders begins not with skills but with these stories. Our discussion on inspiration begins by tapping into these stories and figuring out what has helped transform and motivate us.

Think of a moment that transformed your leadership or commitment to a cause. One man became a synagogue president because he heard his grandfather's voice stir within him, asking him to take care of the Jewish community after he died. A breast cancer victim might share the empowerment she felt when she ran a marathon for the first time. We heard this from one day-school parent:

> I think the turning point for me in my commitment to the school was the time my then first-grader had an assignment to describe what he would want if he could have anything he wished for. He said, "I'd make sure there was school every day." How many kids say that? It was then that I really started to pay attention to what he was doing and learning, and when they asked me to serve on the board, it was a big "yes" without hesitation.

Every time I do this exercise with a group I feel deeply touched by the stories that people share, sometimes moved to tears. I understand the power of these personal narratives and the importance of articulating them as a way to inspire more people to leadership roles. Each time, I feel that participants have given themselves a gift; they have reenergized their nonprofit work by coming into touch with what brought them there in the first place. For a few moments, they transcend their organization's politics and conflicts and realize that they need to do this more often—and need to help others do it as well.

Our next task is to take a piece of this narrative and sculpt it into the story of their organization. Inspiration is not only important to recharge our own batteries; it is critical in expanding the membership of our organizations, retaining those who are loosing energy, and keeping active members committed to an institution's core values. The leadership expert John Kotter claims that leaders who fail to inspire have difficulty creating and sustaining a vision for their institutions: "Achieving a vision requires *motivating* and *inspiring*—keeping people moving in the right direction, despite major obstacles to change by appealing to basic but often untapped human needs, values and emotions."[2]

John Kotter begins one of his latest works on leadership with the following observation: "People change what they do less because they are given *analysis* that shifts their *thinking* than because they are *shown* a truth that influences their *feelings*."[3] The noncognitive aspect of inspiration that goes beyond analysis is what we are trying to understand and bottle. Daniel Goleman, author of the book *Emotional Intelligence*, says of inspiration:

> Great leaders move us. They ignite our passion and inspire the best in us. When we try to explain why they are so effective, we speak of strategy, vision, or powerful ideas. But the reality is much more primal: Great leadership works through the emotions.[4]

To be inspiring, Goleman recommends that leaders become more reflective and deliberative in their use of emotion, handling their own emotions and understanding and improving the way they handle the emotions of their constituents:

Leaders typically talked more than anyone else, and what they said was listened to more carefully.... Because the leader's way of seeing things has special weight, leaders "manage meaning" for a group, offering a way to interpret, and so react emotionally to, a given situation. But the impact on emotions goes beyond what a leader says. In these studies, even when leaders were not talking, they were watched more carefully than anyone else in the group.... Indeed, group members generally see the leader's emotional reaction as the most valid response, and some model their own on it—particularly in an ambiguous situation, where various members react differently. In a sense, the leader sets the emotional standard.[5]

Whether or not leaders are conscious of their emotional responses, their followers may be acutely aware of them. Goleman's observations force us to ask two critical questions: what kind of emotions does a Jewish leader need to exhibit in order to tackle a crisis of inspiration, and once we identify these emotions, can we teach them as a tool in leadership development?

We do talk about the emotions of leaders all the time, but not usually their positive emotions. We might point out when a leader loses control, loses patience, or expresses unreasonable anger. Barbara Kellerman's recent work *Bad Leadership* is a character study of many living leaders today who use negative and often destructive emotions to lead others.[6] These include callousness, insularity, and intemperate behaviors. Kellerman challenges her readers to consider bad leadership and its emotional undercurrents because of the influence such leaders have in our society. We make a mistake when we think that "leader" always implies "good" rather than bad traits and behaviors. Some of the most influential leaders in history drove their followers to inexcusable, immoral behavior. If it is true that emotionally toxic leadership creates followship, then the reverse must also be the case: emotionally resonant leadership should generate inspiration.

Teaching emotions may not be possible. Creating awareness of emotions is very possible. I'd like to suggest two ways that leaders can tap into inspiration and share it. The first is related to the personal work discussed in the previous chapter. Leaders need to create multiple avenues for self-awareness. People need to know their leadership styles and be able to look within at how they manage or handle difficult leadership moments. Journaling can be an excellent method to articulate your personal leadership challenges and the high and low points you experience. There are also many standard tests to measure and evaluate leadership styles today. This may also involve reflecting on the emotional ways that leaders have been led—both good and bad—to understand how they should lead. Case studies, reflective exercises, and conversations with friends and colleagues can all help. My second recommendation for leaders is to get a lot of honest feedback.

It is hard to inspire and transform if you, as a leader, do not know how well you are doing. Goleman points out that "leaders have more trouble than anybody else when it comes to receiving candid feedback, particularly about how they're doing as leaders."[7] This is particularly true the more leaders advance in their organizations. We are afraid to tell our leaders that they are out of touch with their constituents or lack the courage to confront someone with power and authority over us. We may feel intimidated by our lack of knowledge and regard the leader as an expert. Goleman contends that top executives get the *least* reliable information about how they are doing:

> An analysis of 177 separate studies that assessed more than 28,000 managers found that feedback on performance became less consistent the higher the manager's position or the more complex the manager's role.... While most people tend to overestimate their own abilities to some extent, it's the very poor performers who exaggerate their abilities the most.[8]

Goleman and his colleagues believe that leaders do not ask for this feedback not because they are infallible or vain, but because they believe that they are unable to change. This often

translates into the same belief about the leader by those who
work for him or her. People will not give leaders feedback if they
are not encouraged to do so and if they do not believe that their
feedback will make a difference. Problems like this seem
intractable, but Goleman asks that we suspend judgment: "Old
leaders can learn new tricks. Leaders can and do make significant, in some cases life-altering, changes in their styles that ripple into their teams and trigger important changes throughout
the entire organization."[9]

Jewish organizations do not always have mechanisms by
which their most senior professional gets regular and constructive
feedback in a disciplined way. Senior lay leaders often get less
because of a fear that negative feedback about their leadership will
translate into a loss of philanthropic support, a loss of pride, or a
loss of interest in the institution. We need, however, to reconsider
the price we pay for not helping leaders become more emotionally
self-aware and more encouraging and open to feedback. Today,
with more coaching and mentoring options available, we no longer
have the same excuses for keeping our leaders in the dark about
their effectiveness. If leaders can be better at what they do, then
we are morally remiss if we do not provide the support they need to
become more inspiring and more emotionally mindful of their
constituents.

A distraught congregant approached me about her rabbi,
whom she felt was not touching the lives of his congregants. He had
poor pastoral skills. She lost her mother and felt that the spiritual
guide she needed in her life was simply not there for her. I asked her
if this was something that only she felt and experienced or if it was
something that fellow congregants identified as a problem.

> *"I'm not the only one, if that's what you're asking. People are
> always talking about this because there are so many people
> going through death and divorce, marriage and babies. I just
> can't believe that you can go to rabbinial school and not like
> people."*

"Do you know if your rabbi is evaluated on an annual basis? Do you think he ever hears this feedback?"

"No way. I once asked our president privately that same question, and he looked at me as if I just insulted the rabbi. He said that the rabbi would be very hurt if we instituted that policy.... He also told me that they just renewed the rabbi's contract."

One of the principal board responsibilities of any nonprofit is to evaluate the CEO, executive director, or president in an ongoing and comprehensive fashion. It is not only because charitable funding covers the salary of those in these professional leadership positions (although that would be enough of a reason and is true in virtually any other professional context), it is also and primarily to help the leader of an institution be a better, more effective, more inspiring leader. If you are in such a position, you need to make sure that you invite feedback and create safe mechanisms to achieve this. If you are on a board of a nonprofit, you need to make sure that such a policy becomes a regular part of your institutional culture. The more instruments of evaluation there are, the less threatening feedback is.

There is one other factor that I believe is critical in "teaching" leaders to inspire and transform. And it deserves its own section and consideration: personal warmth. Leaders with personal warmth are inclusive and create loyalty and trust. Leaders without personal warmth often communicate that they care more about ideas than people, but it is people and not ideas that are followers.

INSPIRATION AND PERSONAL WARMTH

Jewish leaders today struggle with the indifference and alienation that so many Jews feel toward the organized Jewish community. This, in turn, obligates leaders to communicate inclusiveness, warmth, caring, and encouragement. I have heard "charisma" defined as a quality that makes everyone touched by it feel special. Every once in a while we hear a master speaker who may be addressing hundreds, if not thousands, of people and yet we feel that he or she is actually speaking to us alone. We not only feel inspired; sometimes we even feel loved. We feel like we belong.

Chaim Nachman Bialik, one of our greatest Jewish poets, offers a hint at this alienation and subsequent need for belonging in an observation he made as a lonely child, yearning to reconnect to family and community:

> The misery at home, the bitter orphanhood, weighed heavily on me. I was invited by relatives to a wedding party. The light and music filled my heart, which thirsted so badly to feel joy again. Like a madman I danced barefoot to feel joy to the music. I forgot myself, but my heart longed to join the circle, to cleave to something, to belong.[10]

Even without Bialik's impoverished youth, we all long, as he did, to join a circle, to connect to something larger than ourselves, to feel that sense of belonging. The image of the dance circle as a metaphor for community is very powerful. A circle is a space defined by an uninterrupted line; every point that radiates from its center is equal and equidistant. The circle as a dance allows entry to each person and expands the circle while retaining this inherent sense of equality. Everyone in a circle dance can see one another, no matter how far apart.

Today's Jewish circle is a bit of a challenge. There are those who refuse to hold hands and those who stand apart, looking at the circle with suspicion. And then there are those, perhaps the majority, whose backs are turned and do not even know that a circle exists that welcomes their participation. Unpacking the metaphor, we look at today's Jewish community and struggle to find the connective embrace of that circle for which Bialik pined. The circle seems broken in too many places.

Rabbi Judah Lowe of Prague, the Maharal of sixteenth-century fame, wrote a brief discourse on the circle dance and its ability to stretch and expand to accommodate more people without losing its essential shape. The circle, like the Jewish people, is an unbroken image no matter how large or small it gets. The circle is expansive and, at the same time, promotes and sustains equality. While it is true that a visual image cannot create a narrative, it can stimulate a different way of viewing a traditional structure.

The circle as a dance is a place of joy and belonging, not a place of hierarchy with sharp corners and support scaffolding. The circle as a dance is a place of intense activity and membership regardless of stature and means. We cannot create, in a few pages, a compelling new narrative to bridge the many schisms of our Jewish community. What we can do is hold up and promote a new visual image that can inform the way leaders connect with others and make room for participation. The circle—a Jewish circle—maintains a consistent center as it invites expansiveness.

If we use the circle as a physical image of inclusivity that creates emotional bonds and connects fellow Jews to each other, then what emotions does the leader need to engender to bring others into the circle? Primarily, the leader has to *create* the circle and inspire people to join it while allowing the impact of "membership" to do its own work.

At Jewish weddings and happy occasions, watch the group psychology of the circle dance. There are some people who need to be at the center if there are multiple concentric circles. Some shuffle about in the middle, happy to be part of the fun with no need to attract attention. Others hover at the margins and will not join. They just want to watch. And on every dance floor there is a person in the circle who looks around the room identifying those on the margins, outstretches his or her arm, and invites person after person to be part of the circle. That's the leader.

Leaders are responsible for expanding the circle through outreach. Leaders have to understand the power of the personal invitation. People are drawn to friendliness and warmth and a leader's ability to be persuasive without being overbearing. The leader has to welcome people into the circle, make room, spread the circle out wider, be more inclusive, and maintain the stability of the shape. The leader must be friendly, open-minded, inviting, welcoming, and nurturing. These are all attributes that inspire others to join the circle of community.

8

NURTURING WOMEN'S LEADERSHIP

Strength and dignity are her clothing.... She opens her mouth with wisdom.

PROVERBS 31:25–26

Talking about the circle as a symbol of inclusiveness behooves us to consider who has traditionally been kept out of the leadership circle: women. Women may have played leadership roles in the Hebrew Bible, but other than that they appear without any notable frequency for most of Jewish history. In an ideal world, we would not have a chapter exclusively devoted to women's leadership in a general book on Jewish leadership. Women would advance to senior lay and professional roles within the Jewish community in equal measure with their male counterparts. Professionally, they would receive comparable opportunities, salaries, and benefits and be taken under the wings of veteran leaders to be mentored. In a volunteer context, they would be groomed and positioned to move up a trajectory of leadership based on merit and proportional to their numbers. Sadly, we are not there yet. In Jewish schools, social service agencies, and synagogues, women are still hitting the stained-glass ceiling.

In terms of women's participation on Jewish nonprofit boards, a broad consensus agrees that gender inequity still exists at the top ranks. More serious than its expected existence is an almost dismissive attitude about the problem. It is seen as a problem that will work itself out as women advance in other areas rather than an issue that must be tackled in deliberative and conscious ways.[1] It will fix itself. Yet, we know that most objects that are broken do not "just fix themselves" but require thoughtful repair and attention. Nurturing women's leadership is no different. Until it is a community priority expressed in bold terms and underlined with visible actions, women will not achieve all that they can as Jewish leaders.

Returning to the Bible, we find that women played either a backstage role in decision making or a front and center role in leading. Our image of Sarah is of a woman staying behind her husband Abraham's tent flaps. Rebecca was feeding the camels in an act of kindness that merits her marriage to the patriarch Isaac. Rachel and Leah's arguments over fertility again show the woman as the domestic rather than national force. In each of these biblical narratives, women played a behind-the-scenes decision-making role that had important consequences for the shaping of future Jewish leadership. These biblical women had a background role commensurate with the social expectations of their historical context. Women today do not have to stay behind tent flaps to shape the Jewish future. The fact that they do is often no fault of their own.

Did the biblical woman have a tent of her own, or did she always remain in the shadow of a man? There is no one answer to this question. Women are not a monolithic group in the Bible, or elsewhere, for that matter, who act based solely on a single gender-driven expectation. The women of Genesis did largely wield influence from behind the scenes, but the role of women in the Bible shifts beginning with Exodus. The move from the Genesis to the Exodus narratives shows a larger biblical transition from family to tribe to nation. Noticeably, the book of Exodus has few family stories. The transition from family to nation diminishes our interest in the founding fathers and mothers as we try to parcel together the making of a people moving toward a homeland. The few family stories we have seem arrested midway. Moses's marriage and the birth of his children are told with distinct brevity; our interest in Moses has now taken on a greater national significance.

Not surprisingly, we begin to find another type of heroine developing when the biblical stories hit national proportions. This "new" woman is embodied in the character of Miriam. When Miriam is first introduced in Exodus chapter 2, she has no name or identity. She is merely a protective appendage to her younger, vulnerable brother Moses: "And his sister placed herself at a distance to learn what would befall him" (Exodus 2:4). Miriam is her brother's sister and protector. No more, no less. Once again, the female in the story occupies an emotional and physical station away from the center of the story. But after Moses is found by maidens in Pharaoh's daughter's cortege, something remarkable happens to Miriam. She initiates a move out of the reeds and into the foreground of the story. She brazenly asks the princess if Moses can be nursed by a Hebrew woman—the child's natural mother. In this one act, Miriam propels herself to the center and nurtures the future redeemer while, at the same time, becoming a savior herself.

When you think about what Miriam did in approaching royalty as both a slave and a child, you cannot but conclude that she was—what I affectionately call—a hutzpah lady.

As Miriam's story and the Exodus from Egypt unfold, a new female persona emerges. Miriam places *herself* at the center of the narrative again when Israel is victorious. After Moses sings his song of triumph in Exodus chapter 15, Miriam gathers the women together, in a text made famous by Jewish feminists, to sing and play musical instruments. Miriam will once again be the center of another story, that of Numbers chapter 12, in a less flattering way. In conversation with Aaron, her brother, she speaks ill of Moses and the superior leadership role he has assumed. In this exchange, Miriam makes an astounding claim. She is not blinded by gender in her statement about leadership. She is blinded by power and does not understand why Moses has more power than she and her brother. How refreshing it is that Miriam never questions or limits herself because she is a woman.

Gender and power are not the same thing. To be blinded by gender means that we cannot evaluate a person's leadership capabilities because his or her gender forces a biased blind spot. When someone assesses a leader's ability by color or gender rather than speech or actions, they cannot see beyond the blind spot. We do not measure a person's worth or capability beyond what gender signals. The wrong question is "Can a woman do this job?" The right question is "Does this *individual* have the talent, background, temperament, and experience to do the work?"

When Miriam questions Moses's leadership and equates all of the siblings, she does not assume that being a woman holds her back. She wants equal power, and God explicitly tells her that she and Aaron are not on the same level of prophecy. There is no mention made of her gender. This fascinating encounter reveals that even among ancient Israelites, there was no question about Miriam's capabilities as a person. We do not even know the name of Miriam's husband. That information is irrelevant. We are no longer in the midst of family stories. We are enmeshed in the making of Jewish history writ large. In the text, family life pales in comparison to nation building. Leadership counts. Male or female.

On the way to nationhood, something else happens to women: They stop—for the most part—being singled out as individuals. They now act as part of a collective. This represents an important move that minimizes individual accomplishment or gender bias. Individuals are in service to a larger goal: the endurance and strengthening of a people. It is Deborah who wields an army. It is Yael who kills Sisera in this national story. Ruth gives birth to the ancestors of King David, and Bathsheba ensures that her son Solomon will become heir to David's throne. From Miriam onward, the women who make critical inroads in leadership put themselves in the center of history. They do not wait to be asked. And in each narrative, women make a difference in advancing the national agenda.

MOVING TO THE CENTER

Advancing a national agenda by pushing and pressuring the center is still an issue for female Jewish leaders. We highlight individual women, but this kind of attention often underscores how few others are influencing the center. Magazines and newspapers regularly tout ten, twenty, or fifty "women to watch." Articles on female industry leaders, media personalities, and social activists show photos that visually document success while discussing the obstacles these women faced on their way up. Some of the challenges they confronted were formidable, and yet they had the courage, the force of personality, or the audacity to succeed. We watch these women soar. We do not have to watch *over* them; we just have to watch them. They will get to where they are going whether we watch over them or not.

But there are, within every Jewish organizational structure, women we *do* have to watch over, whose leadership we have to nurture. These are women who can grow into senior managers or agency presidents given the right blend of expectations, encouragement, and support. Without active mentoring, however, they may never be ready or confident enough for top positions. Unless we showcase them, others may not see the strength and capabilities of these female leaders who are emerging from behind the tent flap. The Jewish community needs to watch over them and make room for them.

Studies that were done of both female rabbis in the Conservative movement and of Jewish Community Center professionals show gender-related disparities that cannot be ignored.[2] There is a noticeable absence of women in the top ranks of Federation professional leadership, accompanied by "a steady increase in the proportion of females as one moved down the professional hierarchy."[3] In other words, even where the majority of positions in a Jewish organization are held by women, the senior leadership of such organizations is predominantly male. In Federations women constitute roughly 70 percent of the staff.[4] The larger the city, the less likely it is for the top Federation professional to be a woman. As of 2008, not one of the twenty largest federations is or has ever been headed by a woman.[5]

A recent study identifies three reasons that women do not move into senior leadership positions within Jewish organizations:

- An insufficient number of women are in the leadership pipeline.
- Male decision makers have been slow to recognize women as possessing equal vision, political acumen, and financial skills.
- The perception that women place family needs above their career commitments and leadership advancement is not spoken of and thereby challenged. It is merely assumed.[6]

These conclusions assume that men have not acknowledged or "discovered" talented women to lead and that women have contributed to this leadership dearth by voluntarily opting out of senior positions. While women may choose *not* to pursue high-powered careers, it is not clear that this is their choice alone. Current research in the corporate sector found that 55 percent of women in senior corporate roles would like to be but are not being considered for a CEO position.[7]

Statistics are never the whole story. There is almost always an accompanying narrative to the story told by numbers. There are undocumented assumptions and prejudices. There are unstated insecurities. I've spoken with dozens of women and have heard the same laments over and over. A senior leader in a Jewish nonprofit who came from the corporate sector says she feels Jewish nonprofits do not do enough to groom women actively for senior posts and that more efforts are made in the for-profit sector:

When I worked in a corporate setting, they made an enormous push to get women into senior positions. They had women-only meetings for senior leaders and major recruiting programs that specifically targeted women. They also made an effort to retain women and brought in many female speakers. They almost had to tell the men and women of the organization that women could be successful and make money for the company.

She recommends that Jewish nonprofits make strategic, consistent, and deliberate efforts to reach out to women on all levels of employment and make sure that they understand the reason for having women in top positions. "Women need to see other women as leaders so that they can envision themselves as leaders."

For women to see themselves as leaders, they have to "own" their accomplishments, according to Wende Jager-Hyman, the executive director of the Woodhull Institute for Ethical Leadership. "It's not a question of taking on the attributes of men; it's recognizing what you *yourself* have done and taking credit for it."[8] Women should not take on the attributes of male leadership, say researchers who believe that men and women lead differently. Dr. Judy Rosner, author of the pioneering article "Ways Women Lead," believes women and men do have different leadership styles—men are more linear, direct, and top-down in their leadership; women are more interactive, collaborative, and engaged in the process.[9] Others disagree and regard leadership as gender neutral but freighted with historical realities. If women are deemed as too collaborative, they may be seen as too weak to make difficult decisions, like firing a coworker or reproaching a fellow lay leader who does not follow up on responsibilities.

Leadership consultant Shifra Bronznick tries to cut between these gender issues and says, "The real question is: 'Under what conditions can more women—and men—lead differently more of the time?' ... Leadership is a verb, not a job title. It's about exercising leadership. We are mired in myths that obscure our perspectives about what leadership really looks like."[10]

The female president of a large Jewish nonprofit on the East Coast claims that the higher she rose in her organization, the more resistance she experienced. "I never saw myself as a feminist, just someone who cut her teeth in a man's world, so I learned to play tougher. I always tell professional women to do their homework about salaries and find out what everyone else is getting paid." Another female professional said the "differences in pay are consistent and persuasive. It's galling." In conversation with a lay leader about an open senior staff position, she was shocked to hear a man report without self-embarrassment, "They'll never take a woman for that job. It has nothing to do with competency. It has to do with politics."

If navigating politics is a perceived challenge for women, then women have to confront this issue head-on. In the words of an influential female lay leader: "Women need to do the same thing men always do. We need to network with each other more and promote each other. If we don't, who will?" She says that women have not always been good at promoting each other: "Women are harder on women than on men. They are more threatened by each other and so they don't always hire other women or support them in place."

As lay leaders, one female chairperson said that she feels that more women have crises of confidence than do men. Subsequently, they have to be mentored more aggressively. This same woman claims that Jewish nonprofit boards have not made the same push for women's leadership as other nonprofits because of assumptions that men make about women and women make about themselves:

> The signs that women will not be promoted in their lay leadership can be very subtle. There is a perception that women are more easily controlled and agree more, instead of viewing this as a difference in management styles. I think women have a more participatory style of leadership and men have more of a command-and-control style. Comments dismissing women are rarely direct. I always tell women not to be afraid. Align yourself with people who will support you, and then stand your ground.

We learn from our biblical heroines that moving from the background to the center requires both a self-propelled push and the support of others that is not gender biased. Some women, like the biblical Miriam, will place themselves in the foreground of history. These are the women we watch. Others need encouragement and mentoring. These are the women we watch over. Leadership is not a condition of personhood that some are granted and others denied. Leadership is a choice that begins with words and actions, that requires the sculpting of language and ideas and the combating of indifference. Women have that choice. Before others decide on their worthiness or their capabilities, women must decide for themselves if they want to lead. Miriam never asked anyone if she could approach an Egyptian princess or if she could sing and play the timbrels at the parting of the Reed Sea. She decided.

—✖︎—

9

JEWISH LEADERSHIP AND CONFLICT RESOLUTION

The leader should patiently bear the burden of the community, as did Moses in the wilderness.

MAIMONIDES

We always serve the best meals during our leadership session on conflict management. Everyone needs a full stomach to tackle crisis because it can leave you feeling empty. Our first reflective question is always the same: Where do you handle conflict best: at home, at work, or in your volunteer capacity? The room is nearly always divided in thirds. A sprinkling of people say their volunteer commitments bring out the best in them because they are more motivated to find solutions for issues they care about deeply. Not receiving a salary relieves them of much of the pressure that comes from a sense of obligation. They can be more open and communicative and feel that their fellow volunteers are usually like-minded, minimizing the potential for conflict. Typically, we hear observations like, "I don't have a lot of authority in my job, and my kids have moved out of the house. I feel that I can really make decisions and be the boss in my volunteer 'job.' I never feel that at work."

When it comes to managing conflict at home, the opinions are passionate. "I am never objective at home." "I am way too emotional and can't control myself the way I should when I'm arguing with my wife or kids." Alternatively, there are people who feel that conflicts at home are much more important and take precedence when it comes to problem solving. "I am so much more invested at home that I care more about the outcome. At work, I can walk away from the conflict and know that it isn't personal. So I care less. I manage conflict best at home because I have to wake up with the same people everyday."

Work-related conflicts arouse the same degree of heated opinions. "At work, I feel safer, more in control. I'm given more authority and respect, and that influences the way I handle difficult people and situations. I wish I could get my kids to work through an issue the way I can help the people I supervise." Sometimes, unhappiness at work makes conflict management that much more tense. "I put on a poker face at my job and act as if I don't care, because I can't lose this job. I'm too old to get hired elsewhere, and there are a lot of layoffs in my industry. I remind myself of that every time I want to complain. Just remember who pays the bills. That always shuts me up."

In these comments lies a hidden cornerstone of conflict management, if not resolution. Whether at work, at home, or on a volunteer board, people want to feel control and authority. They want to be listened to and have the power to exercise decision making. Conflict generally makes people feel a loss of control. Leaders are used to controlling situations and find that the gray area of debate can be very unsettling. Conflict challenges the management abilities of any skilled leader, and no leader can excel unless he or she has the ability to manage conflict effectively. In the words of the Irish poet Robert Lynd: "No doubt there are other important things in life besides conflict, but there are not many things so inevitably interesting."

Severe conflict can break the strongest of wills and derail the best of intentions. Moses, our revered Jewish leader, found himself unable to withstand the complaints of the children of Israel in the desert. In Numbers 11:14, he cries up to God, "I cannot carry all this people by myself, for it is too much for me. If You would deal thus with me, kill me rather, I beg You, and let me see no more of my wretchedness!" Moses claims that he would rather die than deal with the continual dissatisfaction of his people. He cannot cope with it alone. The incessant complaining of the Israelites leaves him feeling lonely and isolated. Nevertheless, his tenacity in the face of conflict gives him the strength to overcome this dark time.

How do we develop the tools to deal with conflict in our non-profit work: a listening ear, an iron will, and an enhanced ability to distinguish legitimate needs from cultures of complaint? How can we distinguish between healthy conflict rooted in diverse opinions and conflict that is destructive and harmful? Moses had this gift, and we can mine his narratives for guidance.

GROWTH THROUGH CONFLICT

Our starting point is attitude. What is our attitude toward conflict? Are we afraid of it, intimidated by it, or strengthened through it? Many people think that if voices of dissent and debate would just quiet down, leaders could accomplish what they really need to. What they sometimes ignore is that it is precisely within the cacophony of tension that their greatest opportunities lie.

Leadership is not about waiting for conflict to die down before initiating change. It is about embracing the conflict and carving out paths to success. Dissent is natural and healthy. Think of social or political environments where dissent and conflict are not invited, are shunned, or are actively suppressed. Those environments stifle the growth of individuals and institutions.

Conflict also presents us with opportunities to become better decision makers, mediators, and negotiators. It hones our ability to make good judgments. In the words of Leslie Wexner, one of the Jewish community's premier philanthropists:

> Good leaders make more good decisions than bad ones.... Good leaders really care about their followers and constituents.

They lead from a values proposition and then sustain the quality of their decisions. If you lead a values-based organization, you can't compromise those values. It's as simple as that. When you do compromise, you begin to trade on your equity and undermine the value of your organization.[1]

Decision making often emerges out of conflict; we make decisions to manage contradicting voices and opinions. Good leaders use their values base and judgment to build consensus from disparate views.

Respectful conflict also frees us from harboring secret tensions, resentment, or grudges. People will often say that they do not like to argue, but at the same time they refuse to budge from their position. They allow a perceived insult to fester without questioning it or approaching the source directly. People in this position can become filled with hatred and a desire for vengeance and act on hidden agendas. Respectful conflict releases us from these inner demons and allows us to operate as leaders with more freedom, transparency, and confidence. We become not only better leaders as a result of conflict; we become better people.

As Jews, we don't shy away from conflict; our sacred texts are filled with the literature of conflict. They serve as a repository of wisdom that encourages us to learn and expand our minds through tension. The basis of the Talmud is argumentation; no thought or law goes unquestioned. In the Talmud, the Sages argued with each other and even argued with the dead. The fact that a Rabbinic authority may have died centuries earlier does not prevent his voice from being loudly heard and questioned in print in a current debate. We do not run away from confronting difficult questions and the sometimes difficult people who ask them. There is a charming Yiddish expression that sums up this sentiment: "No one has ever died from a question."

The Hebrew Bible itself is full of conflicts: family and national squabbles, religious debates, and theological challenges. As individuals, as tribes, and as a nation, we seem to be a people in constant torment and turmoil. We fight with each other, and more strikingly, we fight with God. Arguing with God, in particular, is characteristic of great biblical heroes. We might think that God is not a fair sparring partner in a debate with mere flesh and blood, but psychoanalyst and social philosopher Erich Fromm suggests it is just this aspect of our relationship to the divine that creates true partnership:

> With the conclusion of the covenant, God ceases to be the absolute ruler. He and man have become partners in a treaty. God is transformed from an "absolute" into a "constitutional" monarch. He is bound, as man is bound, to the conditions of the constitution. God has lost his freedom to be arbitrary and man has gained the freedom of being able to challenge God in the name of God's own promises, or the principles laid down in the covenant.[2]

It is precisely because we are in a pact or covenant that we can demand parity from God. Conflict, in this sense, suggests closeness. We often argue most compellingly with those we care most passionately about, over ideas about which we care most deeply. We don't usually argue with a stranger or care deeply about ideas that are distant or irrelevant. Thus, it is only natural for the created to challenge the Creator.

The Jewish literary heritage is replete with laments and dirges, complaints and arguments, all protesting God's mistreatment of God's people. In every period of the people's suffering, a cry of outrage and injustice rose alongside the words of those who continually prayed: *U'mipnei hata'einu,* "On account of our sins we are punished."[3]

We take responsibility for that which befalls us, but at the same time, we hold God to account. Arguing seems to be one of our finest Jewish traditions. From this we might suggest a good starting point for establishing a new perspective on conflict: conflict means we care. We only argue about issues that really matter to us. Every conflict presents a chance to be creative, to think outside of convention, to consider what makes people angry and turn it around. Good leadership is about understanding and navigating this complex universe. What gives our world complexity and color is the diversity of opinions we have to manage. Conflict should be viewed as an opportunity for leaders to manage diverse voices with patience and as part of a democratic tradition.

Moses, in partnership with God, became a great navigator of diversity. He was the compass that revealed the physical and spiritual directions that the conflict would take. He turned ordinary, urgent needs into sublime moments of interaction, validating dissatisfaction where necessary and distancing himself from cultures of complaint that were not productive or fruitful. Those of us who follow Moses's legacy of leadership take consolation in his moments of despair, find companionship in his solitude, and wisdom in his solid judgments.

We also learn that Moses made mistakes, that he ran out of patience and solutions; the Bible does not hide Moses's shortcomings or his frailties from us. He is ready to give up on more than one occasion. But he doesn't. And that is the point. Despite decades of conflict, he has the staying power to reach Mount Nebo and gaze at the Holy Land. Leaders are human and vulnerable. They will suffer solitude. They will want to give up and might even articulate this resignation with harsh language and despair. What makes them leaders is that they keep going, despite adversity—or perhaps because of it.

CONTROLLING THE HEAT

One of the dangers of leadership is allowing conflict to smolder by not dealing with it as soon as it sparks. Tension can be controlled, or it can be allowed to run wild. Leaders who let conflict run amok or try to hold it back with inappropriate force usually end up surrendering their leadership in some way. Take the first hundred days of a presidency. We know presidents will stumble, but what's most important to us is how they respond to it. We want to know that they can manage a challenging question, a difficult personality, a sticky situation. We want to know how they will control circumstances that seem to be beyond their control. Many potential leaders don't realize that you *can* control tension. But to control conflict you have to be a masterful facilitator. Ron Heifetz and Marty Linsky offer us this advice in *Leadership on the Line*:

> Changing the status quo generates tension and produces heat by surfacing hidden conflicts and challenging organizational cultures. It's a deep and natural impulse to seek order and calm, and organizations and communities can tolerate only so much distress before recoiling. If you try to stimulate deep change within an organization, you have to control the temperature. There are really two tasks here. The first is to raise the heat enough that people sit up, pay attention, and deal with the real themes and challenges facing them. Without some distress, there is no incentive for them to change anything. The second is to lower the temperature when necessary to reduce a counterproductive level of tension.[4]

Controlling the temperature is not only about lowering the heat. It's also about generating heat when necessary. Because so many people dislike confrontation or do not know how to argue respectfully, they prefer not to argue at all. The problem is that the feelings of anger or resentment generated by the conflict do not dissipate; they merely surface elsewhere. In the context of nonprofit work on boards, it may mean the difference between a conversation in the boardroom and a conversation in the parking lot. In the boardroom, a veneer of civility generally prevails. There's an orderly, typed meeting agenda and a polite show of hands meant to engage the entire group. This creates a false sense of harmony instead of genuine unity.

In the parking lot, clusters of people review what *really* should have been said, and the *real* power brokers unite—the meeting after the meeting. "Parking lot" agendas can severely impede a board's ability to work optimally, but they happen because the real issues or the real resistance is not directly dealt with at the meeting. The job of a leader is to ferret out the hot-button issues and find respectful, creative ways to bring the parking lot into the boardroom. This may raise the temperature to a point of discomfort. But we should encourage debate and dissent when it is purposively motivated, as it says in *Pirkei Avot* (Ethics of the Fathers): "Any controversy with a noble purpose will result in abiding value, but any controversy that has no noble value will not have abiding value" (5:20). When we invite this level of conflict, everyone in the room becomes aware that if the conflict is meaningful for the organization, it has to be addressed by the entire group.

Peter Senge, a popular leadership guru, places a great deal of importance on testing mental models. He argues that many of the best ideas leaders have are never put into practice because leaders cannot navigate the conflict generated by their own innovations and the established conventions of an institution. Senge believes that we have to teach our leaders to balance "inquiry and advocacy" well and teach our boards how to test innovations productively.[5] In other words, leaders have to invite conflict by creating safe spaces to test their ideas. Invitations to test the worthiness or credibility of an idea are another way of raising the heat. But if you leave the temperature on high, you're likely to get burned. You have to find reasonable ways to lower the heat after raising it to make the atmosphere productive. Heifetz and Linsky make the following five recommendations for lowering the temperature of any conflict:

1. Address the technical aspects of the problem.
2. Establish a structure for the problem-solving process by breaking the problem into parts and creating time frames, decision rules, and clear assignments.
3. Temporarily reclaim responsibility for the tough issues.
4. Employ work avoidance mechanisms.
5. Slow down the process of challenging norms and expectations.[6]

The list makes clear that ways to temper the tension often center on practical responses to conflict. To move this list from the abstract to the concrete, let's use the example of a board meeting of a Jewish day school that is running a budget deficit. The usual parking lot conversations have transpired about who is responsible, why the organization is in debt, and how to extricate the school from its ailing situation. The president of the board finally invites those discussions into the boardroom. Accusations and statements of anger abound. To lower the temperature, the president decides to bring in an outside facilitator. The facilitator maps out the problems by using a blackboard and devising three categories: Why? Who? and How? He listens carefully and makes sure no one is interrupted. He has created a structure to contain the anger safely and analyze it.

Then the president takes over and reclaims responsibility for this tough issue by acknowledging the importance of confronting the brutal facts of the school's budget. She establishes the importance of brainstorming as a group. She then writes "What?" on the board, meaning "What should we do about this?" and writes down every suggestion. She creates small group break-out sessions and divides the options on the board, asking each group to discuss the feasibility of each option. After allowing sufficient time to generate conversation, she invites everyone back into the group to list the top three options. She makes a timeline that indicates a realistic time frame for accomplishing goals. She also puts "work-avoidance mechanisms" into place. Work avoidance is a negative expression used here to indicate the normal reins we put on projects that for some reason we cannot or do not want to finish. By putting aside some options, the sum total of all the possibilities looks more realistic or achievable. The structures she has created, the presence of an outside facilitator, and the realistic limiting of options and placement of them in a time frame slows down the process of "challenging norms," as mentioned above.

When people leave the meeting, they feel tired but they also feel liberated. They feel that there is a safe way to generate and confront conflict and also to create structures around the conflict that help map the way out. Linsky and Heifetz call this process the orchestration of conflict, which implies control, mastery, and even beauty. There is something beautiful about building consensus out of tension. We know that if we have managed conflict successfully, we have created an environment that is rich with debate. Such atmospheres feel charged, interesting, and dynamic. They offer people a greater sense of ownership and participation. The process can be unruly, but it reinforces our faith in the possibility of diverse opinions leading to a coherent outcome.

UNDERSTANDING THE NATURE OF CONFLICT

Since not all conflict is the same, it is important to be a good diagnostician. Identifying the nature of a conflict brings us one step closer to identifying solutions. There is a difference between a legitimate complaint, a legitimate complaint framed in an unfair way, and a culture of complaint. Using this template to frame conflict is very helpful for me. I've seen it work for others as well. Sometimes, we respond in a knee-jerk fashion to complainers because we either want to be accommodating and make people happy or because we simply want to move beyond the problem at hand and concentrate on other, possibly more important issues. But take the time to diagnose the nature of the complaint, and a better solution may emerge naturally that produces longer-lasting results.

Let's use Jewish texts—arguments waged against Moses, Aaron, and God during the Israelites' wilderness journey—to consider the nature of conflict. This trying time in our biblical history yielded much wisdom that still holds true today. During their forty years of wandering, the Israelites lost an anchor: an identifiable place to live. The loss of geographic stability caused an understandable dislocation of identity that gnawed at the very heart of their faith commitment. Early on in Exodus, they mourn the loss of Egypt even though they knew it as a place of oppression. They doubt the bounty of a Promised Land that seems so far away. And in between oppression and redemption stretches the vast desert that gives birth to dissatisfaction. It is not hard to understand that ancient Israelite disappointment is rooted in insecurity; they know what they left but have no real idea about where they are going.

LEGITIMATE COMPLAINTS

The complaining begins not long into the wilderness journey. In Exodus chapter 15, the Bible records the joyous Song of the Sea that Moses addresses to and sings with his people. But once they reach the safe bank, the happiness quickly turns to lament. Only one verse after Moses and Miriam conclude their song, we encounter the first complaint:

> Then Moses caused Israel to set out from the Sea of Reeds. They went on into the wilderness of Shur; they traveled three days in the wilderness and found no water. They came to Marah, but they could not drink the water of Marah because it was bitter; that is why it was named Marah. And the people grumbled against Moses, saying, "What shall we drink?" So he cried out to the LORD, and the LORD showed him a piece of wood; he threw it into the water, and the water became sweet.
>
> (Exodus 15:22–25)

Ironic as it sounds, the children of Israel are saved by water only to complain about the lack of water three days later. The waters of redemption fast retreat in their minds as their daily, prosaic needs come to the forefront. The complaint about water will plague and punctuate the entire journey. However, there are different responses to the complaints, and it is here that we need to examine an important lesson about conflict and leadership: Carefully evaluate the nature and fairness of a complaint. Not all complaints are the same.

Moses does not initially chastise the people for their protestations (as he does later), even though they follow on the heels of salvation. Water in the desert is an urgent need, and urgent needs can get in the way of larger perspectives. It is easy to forget the walls of water that separated for Israel's safe passage when their dry throats call out in desperation. It is hard to find God when you cannot find water. Moses fed the children of Israel on promises, but when they become thirsty he has to show them that the all-powerful God who

127

performed miracle after miracle to get them out of Egypt could perform the relatively simple miracle of providing for them out of Egypt. It is a fair complaint and one that has to be answered immediately to bolster faith in Moses's leadership and in God's ability to provide.

Bible professor Nahum Sarna assesses the Israelite complaint both sympathetically and realistically:

> These misfortunes reflect the harsh realities of life in the wilderness.... Israel's need is very real and the popular discontent is quite understandable. These experiences illustrate both the precarious nature of Israel's survival and God's providential care of His people.... It appears that "faith in the LORD and His servant Moses" to which [Exodus] 14:31 bears witness, began to weaken under the strains of life in the wilderness.[7]

Travelers must be assured at the beginning of any difficult journey that their guide knows the way and can provide for them. If followers instinctively feel that their safety is compromised or that promises made will not be fulfilled, they will articulate their fears. They may want to return home. Home may not always be safe—and certainly the oppression of Egypt was not desirable—but at least at home we know the dangers at hand. When we step into the wilderness, we invite risks. Our intuitive doubts may be understandable, but we sometimes need to live with a degree of insecurity to reach our end goal. Leaders can make the mistake of promising a no-risk endeavor that does not match reality. And here is yet another leadership lesson from the wilderness: Make followers aware of the possible risks. Conflict comes as much from ignorance of the dangers as it does from real unhappiness.

CONFLICT AS A TEST OF RELATIONSHIP

In the next chapter of Exodus, Israelite confidence in Moses erodes again. New challenges emerge that are about material needs, such as water or bread, and about the relationship between God, the Israelites, and Moses, their weary intermediary. A month and a half into their journey, we learn:

> The whole Israelite community grumbled against Moses and Aaron. The Israelites said to them, "If only we had died by the hand of the LORD in the land of Egypt, when we sat by the fleshpots, when we ate our fill of bread! For you have brought us out into this wilderness to starve this whole congregation to death."
>
> (Exodus 16:2–3)

The grumbling takes a grave turn. With the subtle inclusion of the word "whole," we understand that Moses and Aaron are not merely addressing a discontented few but the overwhelming dissatisfaction of the group. Anger displayed in the plural always presents a greater challenge to a leader. It becomes hard to distinguish voices of hesitation or dissent from the majority opinion and it presents what appears to be an intractable situation. When we look carefully at the way the complaint is framed, however, we sense that the Israelites may not be telling the entire truth.

Would they really have wanted to die in Egypt? As oppressed slaves, did they really have their fill of bread? Did Moses and Aaron really bring them to the wilderness "to starve the whole congregation to death"? (Exodus 16:3).

The exaggerated complaint provides a window into the minds of these weary travelers. If Moses can show these perceptions to be false, he can then regain trust. When the nature and fairness of the complaint are evaluated, we see that the genuine desire for bread is not framed legitimately. No one took them out of Egypt to die in the wilderness. God narrows the grumbling down to one essential complaint: the need for bread. In this "diagnosis," God separates out a legitimate complaint from an illegitimate way of complaining.

Now the Israelites have their fill of bread, as they claim they had in Egypt. God tells Moses, "I will rain down bread for you from the sky, and the people shall go out and gather each day that day's portion—that I may thus test them, to see whether they follow My instructions or not" (Exodus 16:4). God gives them more bread than they ever had. But God also gives it to them on condition of their faith and commitment. It is to test their commitment to God. Ironically, the bread is also a test for God. The ancient Israelites doubted that God could provide adequately for them in the desert. This is formalized in a later biblical text, the book of Psalms. There we read:

> To test Israel was in their mind when they demanded food for themselves. They spoke against God saying, "Can God spread a feast in the wilderness?" True, He struck the rock and waters flowed, streams gushed forth; but can He provide bread?
>
> (Psalm 78:18–20)

What we have in the earliest stages of the divine-human relationship in the wilderness is a test of faith. God doubts whether the Israelites will be true to the commandments, and the Israelites doubt God's ability to provide. God grumbles about this errant people, and they grumble about their self-sacrifice and physical needs. From here we see another function and response to complaints: conflict is often about testing the limits of a relationship. Establishing trust early on and rising to the test instead of avoiding it can mitigate tension. It is only natural that in the formative years of a relationship, partners test each other's trust and competence and complain when expectations are not met.

If we understand these harsh interactions as parts of a protracted test on both sides, what are we to learn from it? Aaron Wildavksy, who wrote a political analysis of the Moses narratives, creates a framework for understanding these wilderness years:

> There are two tests: God testing man and man testing God. The people are said to have tested God in their numerous demands for water and for meat without visible prospects of

provision. A parallel is provided by the situations in which God tests man by thirst and by hunger.... Testing, it appears, is reflexive: reciprocal, mutual and interactive, a relationship rather than a definition of subordinate status where only God tests and man alone is tested. It is not just man's capacity to act according to his ideals but the ability of these ideals to live among men that is being tested. The process is one of mutual adaptation between what is and what ought to be.[8]

God tests us not because God does not know the outcome. God tests us to provide opportunities for human decision making.

CULTURES OF COMPLAINT

Thus far, we have explored two different scenarios of wilderness conflict: one where the complaint was legitimate and the response was forthright and helpful, and the second where the complaint was exaggerated and out of place but the response was still positive and forthcoming. The last type of conflict occurs when the complaint is unfair and the response is equally harsh. Turning to Numbers chapter 11, we find just such a conflict. The chapter begins with a familiar refrain:

> The people took to complaining bitterly before the LORD. The LORD heard and was incensed: a fire of the LORD broke out against them, ravishing the outskirts of the camp. The people cried out to Moses. Moses prayed to the LORD, and the fire died down.... The riffraff in their midst felt a gluttonous craving; and then the Israelites wept and said, "If only we had meat to eat! We remember the fish we used to eat in Egypt for free, the cucumbers, the melons, the leeks, the onions, and the garlic. Now our gullets are shriveled. There is nothing at all! Nothing but this manna to look to!"
> (Numbers 11:1–2, 11:4–6)

Understanding the nature of conflict in this narrative requires us to do a more in-depth textual analysis. Perhaps the text is subtly suggesting that there is no substance. The content of the complaint is no longer the issue. We have moved from isolated incidents of dissatisfaction to a culture of complaint. In such a culture, everything becomes fodder for unhappiness. The dissatisfaction of one person feeds off another until an exasperating level of tension is reached. Nahmanides, a medieval Spanish commentator, addressed this act of "grumbling":

> It [the text] states that they were as murmurers, meaning that they spoke in the bitterness of the soul as do people who suffer pain, and this was evil in the sight of the Eternal, since they should have followed him *"with joyfulness and with gladness of the heart by reason of the abundance of all good things"* [Deuteronomy 26:11] which He gave them, but they behaved like people acting under duress and compulsion, murmuring and complaining about their condition.[9]

The children of Israel lose perspective. Murmuring and grumbling are different from lodging a specific complaint. It is a general state of unhappiness characterized by whining, moaning, kvetching, or any other word describing the misery of people who cannot see the blessings in their lives. In this case, they fail to recognize the "abundance of all good things" that God gave them.

Rather than being able to handle specific issues and defuse the tension, the leader facing a culture of complaint sometimes feels himself at sea. He cannot use his skills to accomplish set tasks. He cannot solve every problem, because there is no limit to the problems in such a culture. Solve one and a bewildering assortment of others is laid at his feet. In such circumstances, a leader can find himself paralyzed and unable to act. Alternatively, a leader may lose control and express real anger. This may not be the most productive or mature response, but it is a display of genuine human frustration that may force his antagonists to take notice.

God responds to the culture of complaint in this last text by lashing out at the children of Israel. He can no longer justify or withstand the ingratitude, the sense of entitlement, and the immaturity of the Israelites. God is incensed, the text states, and strikes the outskirts of the camp with fire. As usual, the people cry out to Moses for intervention. He dutifully prays and the fire is quelled, but—as we all know—in a culture of complaint, another fire awaits and, predictably, appears. In this case, it is not a literal fire but another flare-up of indignation.

God's anger does little to squelch the next round of complaints. They are as prolific as before. Those living on the margins of the camp complain again about the lack of meat. This inspires others in the camp to join their protest. It is here that Moses begins to buckle under the mounting stress.

> Moses heard the people weeping, every clan apart, each person at the entrance of his tent. The LORD was very angry, and Moses was distressed. And Moses said to the LORD, "Why have You dealt ill with Your servant, and why have I not enjoyed Your favor that You have laid the burden of all this people upon me? Did I conceive all this people, did I bear them that You should say to me, 'Carry them in your bosom as a nurse carries an infant,' to the land that You have promised on oath to their fathers? Where am I to get meat to give to all this people, when they whine before me and say, 'Give us meat to eat!' I cannot carry all this people by myself, for it is too much for me. If You would deal thus with me, kill me rather, I beg You, and let me see no more of my wretchedness!"
>
> (Numbers 11:10–15)

Moses conjures an image of the nursing mother—perfect for capturing his anxiety. The paradoxical word choice—comparing their request for *meat* to a mother's ability to provide *milk*—indicates Moses's dilemma. He clearly sees that nurturing is a part of his role as leader. However, by evoking the image of a nursing mother, he suggests there are things he simply cannot do. He cannot provide meat. It is as unlikely as a father nursing an infant. The Israelites want to be as dependent as nursing infants. Moses brought them into the desert to become self-reliant.

As the strains of desert life became more noticeable and less easily solvable, the people became more raw and cutting in their assessment of Moses's and God's abilities, and both lose patience with the Israelites. While we cannot solve problems (no matter how much we want to at times) in the fashion of God's wrath or fire, this interchange provides another guiding principle: Minimize cultures of complaint by holding up a mirror to those who complain. Show them an image of themselves.

Too often, leaders feel paralyzed when they are seen as the only ones who can solve a problem or are blamed as its root and sole cause. This completely unbalanced scale of responsibility frees the offender of responsibility for his situation. By delegating and sharing tasks, the leader makes the complainer part of a solution.

A friend once told me that he complained to a conference organizer about an event that he attended. He was shocked when the organizer turned to him with a smile on his face and handed him a clipboard saying, "That is an excellent comment. I am assigning you to work on this very problem." Shocked as he was, when put in the difficult position of handling the responsibility, he was forced to think creatively and quickly. Not only did he take on this new responsibility, he was so impressed with the conference planner's leadership abilities that he willingly took on a larger role working with the planner on organizing future conferences.

Delegating and sharing responsibility to minimize conflict is the strategy God pursues with the dejected Moses. God gathers a group of seventy respected elders to assist Moses and demonstrate that the able leader is not alone. God understands that Moses is complaining as much about his own loneliness as about anyone else's dissatisfaction. Moses is human. Leaders need our support in times of conflict. They need to be nurtured so that they, in turn, can nurture others.

PRACTICAL SOLUTIONS

Conflict can create any number of negative emotions. It can generate a loss of trust, confusion, defensiveness, shame, embarrassment, disbelief, discomfort, self-consciousness, loss of innocence, anger, and isolation for a leader. Leaders who do not feel comfortable with conflict are bound to encounter one or several of these emotions that can push anyone off a leadership track. Not facing conflict can exact its own price in terms of repression and resentment. I often hear a leader tell me that they avoid conflict because they are "nice." "You see, I stay away from conflict. Why be argumentative if you don't have to be? I enjoy being around people and don't like making trouble." This kind of confession immediately tells me that I am standing in the presence of someone who is not a true leader.

Leaders cannot avoid conflict. Do not be fooled by leaders who tell you they are nonconfrontational. This may just be their way of saying that they lack the courage to take a principled stand or make a difficult decision that may make them less popular. Many people who say they are nonconfrontational carry a lot of resentment and indignation because they have not dealt with difficult issues in a direct and forthright way. Claims of being nonconfrontational can be a smoke screen for conflict avoidance.

Conflict can create feelings of isolation. I have found that one of the best ways to fight this emotion is to share conflict with other like-minded leaders. This requires networking. Because conflict shared is conflict halved, I always ask participants in our courses for their advice on conflict management. Over the years, I have heard some outstanding suggestions for managing conflict. Here are some tips from the trenches:

- Validate feelings that are opposed to yours.
- Apologize for bad feelings immediately, even if you did not generate them.
- Don't cover up.
- Take responsibility.

- Comfort and clarify.
- Use speech constructively, not destructively.
- Do not become defensive.
- Listen without judgment.
- Be present.
- Adapt and be flexible.
- Process a complaint without immediately presenting a solution.
- Keep a journal or private place to write your feelings about a conflict.
- Bounce off ideas and speak to those who will keep confidences.
- Vent to someone who wants a positive outcome rather than someone who only exacerbates your feelings and possibly prolongs a bad situation.
- Breathe deeply.
- Release the tension in your shoulders. Your body reacts to conflict. React back.
- Identify the essentials of the conflict and forget the rest.
- Return to the question "What do you need?" Sometimes people just need help figuring out their needs.
- Walk away when you know you are being a liability.
- Ask lots of questions.
- Put your emotions aside.
- Just let go when you realize that you cannot change the obstacles before you.

The biblical image of wilderness creates the perfect metaphor for conflict. Like wilderness, conflict represents the unknowable, the unpredictable, and the unyielding aspects of human nature. Our voyages into the unknown can bring out the worst of our fears, inhibitions, and anger. Alternatively, they can be a time of discovery and adventure. They can help us cement our identities and values. To walk through the wilderness and end in the Promised Land require patience, an accepting attitude to conflict, and an ability to diagnose the nature of a conflict and resolve it by managing the tensions and understanding what the real issues are. It gets quite hot in the desert of leadership. Be prepared.

10

ETHICAL LEADERSHIP

Do what is just and right.
GENESIS 18:19

The British philosopher Bertrand Russell once said, "Nobody ever gossips about people's secret virtues." How true. In both the biblical and Rabbinic tradition, a premium is placed on personal virtue, not just for the leader, but for everyone. Rabbi Abraham Kook, the first chief rabbi of Israel, writes about the relationship of morality and Jewish law as a natural and compelling partnership:

> Morality ... in all the depths of its splendor and power of its strength, must be determined in the soul and will be receptive to those noble influences deriving from the force of the Torah.... The Torah was given to Israel, so that the gates of her light—clearer, more extensive, and holier than all the gates of light of man's natural wisdom and natural moral spirit—will open before us and through us, to the rest of the world.[1]

Kook believed that the Torah demands we be more moral than our natural human inclination dictates and that this profound sense of ethics opens us up to the rest of the world as moral exemplars. If this level of moral behavior is expected by Jewish law of every Jew, then all the more so is it demanded of every Jewish leader.

Focusing on the ethical qualities of Jewish leaders, Rabbi Jonathan Sacks, chief rabbi of the British Commonwealth, says that the ethical qualities a sage should possess are justice, fairness, integrity, patience, a love of peace, an ability to hear both sides of an argument and weigh conflicting situations. He or she does not act out of emotion but on the basis of what is best for all concerned. A zealot, said the rebbe of Kotzk, cannot be a leader. To be a leader, one has to cultivate those traits the Torah ascribes to God: compassion and grace, patience and forgiveness.[2]

These qualities translate well into the traits to look for in Jewish leaders to achieve the highest ethical standards for Jewish organizations. A study of Jewish ethics is beyond the scope of this book. However, a few significant areas of ethics have particular relevance for Jewish leadership. One area of ethical importance is restraint in harmful speech and the use of speech to elevate others and help followers reach their potential. We are commanded in the Torah not to be talebearers of gossip and to refrain from speaking the truth if it can in any way incriminate others or create bad feelings. On Yom Kippur, the majority of personal confessions in the traditional prayer book have to do with use of speech. *Lashon ha-ra*, slanderous speech, can be disruptive, unproductive and deeply harmful.

Effective Jewish leaders not only maintain high standards of personal speech themselves, they facilitate meetings and conversations that reflect these Jewish ideals. This helps people keep in touch with the sacred responsibilities of leadership and helps the group from sinking into the quicksand of gossip. Leaders are often privy to confidential information. They are trustees. It is tempting to let this private information slip out and become an object of discussion. Leaders as stewards have to make sure that they use and help others use speech that affirms the sacred.

Rabbi Joseph Telushkin, the author of many books on Jewish ethics, devotes one book to this subject alone, *Words That Hurt,*

Words That Heal. He offers this helpful way of keeping conversations above the fray:

> What is *most* interesting to *most* of us about other people is their character flaws and private scandals. Therefore, before you spread information or views that will lower the regard in which an acquaintance is held, ask yourself three questions: Is it true? Is it necessary? Is it fair?[3]

These three brief questions can help leaders decide when matters they hold in trust should be shared and when they should not.

Ethical speech is only one small piece of a larger moral compass that we expect Jewish leaders to possess. A contemporary Jewish thinker, Walter Wurzburger, writes in *Ethics of Responsibility*, "Ethics is prescriptive rather than descriptive. It deals with the 'ought,' not with the 'is.'"[4] Wurzburger reminds us that this prescription is not about creating impossibly high standards that cannot realistically be met and will only lead to disappointment. However, this perspective forces us to ask what happens when people do not act in good faith and there is a blur of ethics that borders on the scandalous or challenges the Jewish values at the heart of an organization.

ETHICAL GOVERNANCE

There is no greater test of leadership than a leader's behavior in times of moral crisis. In even the most superficial review of leaders throughout history, we find that a leader's worth is almost always measured by his or her ability to manage crisis, scandal, or a breach of ethics. The opposite is also true. We have had great political and religious leaders who, because of a smirch of character, are never able to overcome the scandal they generated, thus negating their other accomplishments in the public's eye.

Like individual leaders, virtually every organization encounters scandal of some kind in its history. There may be an instance of deliberate fiscal mismanagement, sexual harassment, or abuse. These are extreme situations not likely to happen under the watchful eye of good leadership. But we would be naive to believe that they never happen. Even the best of institutions can suffer a situation that breaches ethically acceptable norms of conduct. The issue for us is not how it happens as much as how it is handled.

Every nonprofit benefits from a stated code of ethics and a standing committee equipped to handle a breach of ethics. A structure must be consciously put in place to let all members of a board and a community know what to do and who to turn to in the event of such an occurrence. Schools, synagogues, and other institutions have building codes and fire drills. In the case of a physical emergency, we expect that our leaders have thought ahead and know how to direct us. If that is true for physical emergencies, it should be all the more true for emotional, financial, and spiritual crises.

To create a structure for ethical governance in your organization, you need turn no further than to your computer. Many synagogue denominations have nationally produced ethical guides or codes that are made available to their membership. Most of these guides utilize Jewish texts as the basis or core of those values. If you do not have such structures in place, consider using some time at a future board meeting to hash out the issues, identify an appropriate mechanism for "ethical complaints," and determine a way for your members to be made aware of this process. This may be in the form of a subcommittee of your board and can be a meaningful role for ex officio presidents, who will already have had experience dealing with complex leadership situations.

The existence of such a group should be well advertised in an organization's literature so that any member has an avenue for a confidential, nonpunitive conversation about these sensitive issues. No parent of a day-school child, no congregant, no volunteer in a social service agency should be left to ponder how they should handle a breach of ethics alone.

Having spoken to numerous leaders and former leaders of nonprofits that have experienced morally compromising situations, I believe that weathering this kind of crisis is one of the loneliest times a leader can face. Having your integrity or the integrity of your institution called into question can make a community look ugly and make the leader feel like a pariah. Making sure that the complaint issued is genuine and grounded in reality is not an easy or reassuring process. Because situations like this can turn people away from you and the good work your nonprofit does, it is critical that you handle these situations gently, compassionately, and swiftly. Reminding your board, congregation, or constituency about the laws of slander, about the importance of giving the benefit of the doubt, and that the situation is being dealt with both confidentially and as transparently as possible will strengthen faith in your leadership. Failure to take any of these steps may lead, not surprisingly, to complete disengagement from your organization.

PRIVATE VERSUS PUBLIC MORALITY

The preceding discussion dealt with ethical dilemmas within an organizational culture. But what about ethical issues raised about a specific Jewish leader? One of the most fascinating questions about the ethics of leadership, especially leadership within a faith or religious community, is the role of public versus private morality and its contribution to the authentic self of leadership. Today, under intense media scrutiny, we have an almost complete blurring of the two. Moral blemishes in private are placed under a microscope and flashed on screens worldwide, as if to say, "Can you trust this person if he or she does X?" It is a fair question on one level and a loaded question on another. We naturally assume that private sin easily translates into public betrayal; spousal infidelity or neglectful parenting means that an organization will one day be betrayed or neglected by the very same person. Any slip into indiscretion is presumed to reflect a pattern of behavior that applies to multiple leadership situations.

It is not surprising then to learn that two leadership experts, Jim Kouzes and Barry Posner, found that out of the four characteristics most sought in leaders—integrity, a sense of the vision, the ability to inspire, and competence—integrity was the most admired quality.[5] Put together, these four qualities are associated with someone who has high personal moral expectations and who, as a leader, will turn these expectations of self into a modus operandi for an institution.

> Character generates moral authority, a powerful form of influence within an organization. As with shared vision and values, these leaders are principle-centered, believing in and demonstrating loving-kindness, dignity and respect for everyone, honesty and integrity, fairness and forgiveness, service about self, excellence and humility. They are particularly noted as being ethical, perhaps even "noble." Character enables the authentic leader to engage moral authority to elevate and pull followers toward the shared vision. Authentic leaders also live a congruent life of spiritual synchronicity that enhances their influence even further.[6]

Unquestionably, in an age of cynicism, holding character up as a necessary aspect of leadership seems natural. James O'Toole, in his important leadership book *Leading Change: Overcoming the Ideology of Comfort and the Tyranny of Custom*, discusses the importance of leaders having respect for followers, and in his words, effective leaders "always keep faith with their people: they must never lie to their followers nor break the laws they are charged with upholding."[7] Having said this, he questions the current wisdom of "private behavior predicts public behavior" as a disqualifier for leadership positions. Looking at world history and our own Hebrew Bible reveals the force of O'Toole's words: "A review of any list of great leaders will reveal that almost all were flawed human beings with notable private failings…. If we insist on perfection of character, we are unlikely to find many exemplary leaders, and our analysis will end in despair."[8]

On a more radical note, a Bible theme running through story after story is that flawed individuals can make great leaders. Because they may be jealous, self-absorbed, or make decisions by fiat, they are able to navigate politics or understand the public that much better. They can move the world because they are of the world. Although Rabbinic tradition includes numerous admonitions about avoiding politics for a life of silence, scholarship, and near saintliness, the Bible is filled with stories that show little of this self-imposed isolation. One of the enduring appeals of biblical texts is their portrayal of the rawness of the human condition; we are almost forced to see our ancient leaders as flawed, even tragic, in text after text that, in offering a leader's life, presents the reader with a character who exhibits nobility as well as human frailty. The subtlety is unavoidable, the message more complex than we often want it to be.

The distinction between private and public morality is displayed powerfully in the early chapters of Genesis, after the floodwaters of the Noah narratives recede. Noah plants a vineyard, grows grapes, and produces wine. "And he drank of the wine and was drunken, and he uncovered himself in the interior of his tent" (Genesis 9:21).

The pressures on this man are, no doubt, very great. He is charged with the building of an ark, the saving of representatives of the animal kingdom and his family, and, finally, with the reconstruction of a new world. These are daunting tasks that might lead anyone to drink.

So Noah takes comfort in drink, and while criticized in Rabbinic commentaries, in the biblical text this indiscretion is not regarded negatively. Could it be that this failing does not deserve public reproach because it was conducted "in the interior of his tent"? It is his son Ham who changes the nature of this private act. "And Ham, the father of Canaan, saw the nakedness of his father— and related it to his two brothers outside" (Genesis 9:22).

Ham gloats over the failings of his father and takes this juicy piece of gossip public, telling his two brothers. Nahmanides, an early thirteenth-century Spanish commentator, makes an important distinction between the inside of Noah's tent and the outside, where Ham imparts his news. The text suggests that there is a difference between private behavior and public indiscretion. In this narrative, it is Ham who is criticized, both by his father upon waking and by the biblical text itself, which leaves his father's curse of subordination as a hallmark of Ham's future, as well as that of his children.

We could move on to talk about Moses's role as husband and father, which is hardly mentioned in the biblical text and when it is, receives scathing Rabbinic commentary. According to Maimonides, a medieval Spanish philosopher, physician, and legalist, Moses was on call for God, and his family life was of secondary concern.[9] King David, the most discussed figure in this arena, was an outstanding military leader and psalmist, but his personal life was in shambles. He called for the murder of several family members, had a son who raped his half sister and then was killed by his half brother, and was personally responsible for the death of Bathsheba's husband, Uriah, because he impregnated Uriah's wife. The baby of that illicit union died of illness. None of David's intense prayers saved him. The list of family tragedy goes on. It is no wonder that King David on his deathbed was so cold that nothing could warm him, not even the young virgin placed in his bed. David died a hero in public and is our most lauded king, but his private life was a moral quagmire that left him cold.

These biblical texts notwithstanding, no one is suggesting that private immorality is desirous or praiseworthy or is to be intentionally ignored. There is not even a hint that leaders may neglect their families because the business of leadership is so pressing and urgent. Quite the opposite. We learn that leadership, from the earliest chapters in Genesis, is interwoven into a family's master story, and the marriages and family units in Genesis—while problematic on many levels—are still strong family units. The Hebrew Bible is imparting a more subtle message: When we move unfairly from a leader's public service to his inner life, we are no longer capable judges of behavior. In the public domain, a leader must exemplify the highest moral standards and be always mindful of his public responsibilities to those he serves.

Franklin Delano Roosevelt said, in one of his famous presidential fireside chats, "I never forget that I live in a house owned by all the American people, and that I have been given their trust."[10] In this respect, O'Toole—the leadership writer—argues that "the gauge of the greatness of leaders is their public record measured over their entire lifetimes."[11] In other words, values-based leadership is not of the moment or an election-year priority; it is a condition of great leadership measured across a life.

In terms of public record, who is the judge of morality? We are. It is in this arena that not only can we judge moral standards, but we must. Maimonides groups leaders who bring the public to error with heretics and traitors; they sacrifice their place in the wolrd to come.[12] It is our obligation as an educated public to scrutinize the public moral record of a leader and, if there is a misdemeanor, to use our ability as a voting public to take a strong stance.

It is also our responsibility to leave a leader's private life private. There will be, no doubt, many who disagree with me and think that anything a leader does, public or private, deserves to be in the public eye. After all, leaders seek positions of power, and they must know that the public will devour all gossip and also hold the leader up to a different private standard than their own. Leaders are role models at all times. This means that leaders can never fail; they must be saintly in their personal and private lives.

This cultural phenomenon of leaders as moral targets is only decades long but has cost us dearly. In fact, it probably emerged not out of any collective moral will but out of sensationalist journalism that keeps the paparazzi in business. We do not learn the personal moral failings of leaders in our desire to create a better organization or country; we learn of them so that we can bring our leaders down several notches, gloat over failings, and sustain a gossip industry. This inability to let leaders conduct private lives distinct from public ones is perhaps the one most salient reason so few great people assume leadership positions today. A past personal indiscretion may be found out by opponents hungry for scandal, or the simple fear of moral condemnation produces a claustrophobic stranglehold that keeps potential leaders from fulfilling their potential.

Think back to American presidents or former Israeli prime ministers who were heroes—the stuff of childhood posters and dreams. Many of them had checkered pasts or behaved inappropriately in their private lives even while in office. We just did not know it at the time. The media did not have as much access as it has today. Today we know where the American president was spotted having dinner and what the Israeli prime minister did on his last vacation and how many pounds celebrities gained over the summer. We know way too much about that which is not consequential to their leadership. Fair judgment should be restricted to their record in office. As O'Toole notes, "If we insist on perfection of character, we are unlikely to find many exemplary leaders, and our analysis will end in despair."[13]

Compare O'Toole's words with the neo-Orthodox commentator of eighteenth-century Germany Rabbi Samson Raphael Hirsch. Rabbi Hirsch comments on the passage in Genesis where Abraham calls his wife his sister to protect himself from being murdered by foreigners after they took him and his wife captive. It is an open admission of flawed leadership, and it is there for a didactic reason:

> The Torah never hides from us the faults, errors and weaknesses of our great men. Just by that it gives the stamp of veracity to what it relates. But in truth, by the knowledge which is given us of their faults and weaknesses, our great men are in no wise made lesser but actually greater and more instructive. If they stood before us as the purest models of perfection, we should attribute them as having a different nature, one which has been denied us. Were they without passion, without internal struggles, their virtues would seem to us the outcome of some higher nature, hardly a merit and certainly no model that we could hope to emulate.[14]

When we expect our leaders to be vastly different than ourselves in moral temperament and offer them saintlike status, we cease to have them as role models because they seem almost genetically different from other mortals. Hirsch also adds that the sterling qualities of our biblical heroes and heroines would be made smaller had we not seen examples to the contrary. He cites Moses's modesty, recorded in Numbers chapter 12, which is all the more distinctive because we see him fly into a passion. By displaying heroes with the subtle complexities that mark them as simply human, Hirsch says that Torah teaches us "the result of a great work of self-control and self-ennoblement which we should all copy because we all could copy."[15] Hirsch dismisses apologetics and says of our patriarchs and matriarchs, "They do not require our apologies, nor do such attempts become them. Truth is the seal of our Torah, and truthfulness is the principle of all its true and great commentators and teachers."[16]

"The Torah also shows us no faults without at the same time letting us see the greater or lesser evil consequences," Hirsch adds.[17] In the Hebrew Bible, we watch the consequences of arrogance or evil scheming or a host of other moral deficiencies. We see the stories unravel in their narrative containers and know that in the biblical eye-for-an-eye method of punishment, crimes do not go unpunished. The leader will pay for private indiscretions with private suffering. But that is ultimately a leader's own private problem.

On the flip side, leaders who make easy distinctions between private and public morality are also walking a fine tightrope of danger that may end in disaster. They may convince themselves that behavior in the bedroom will have no impact on behavior in the boardroom. Maybe. Maybe not. If leaders who engage in private debauchery kid themselves into a state of denial, they may not only bring down themselves, they may bring down the organizations they serve. In the words of Larry Bossidy and Ram Charan, two leadership writers on self-discipline and corporate discipline:

> The culture of a company is the behavior of its leaders. Leaders get the behavior they exhibit and tolerate. You

change the culture of a company by changing the behavior of its leaders. You measure change in culture by measuring change in the personal behavior of its leaders and the performance of the business.[18]

Private indiscretions can corrode public moral stances. Personal transgressions can consume us; they eat time. They are distracting. They can confuse. It is in this moral ambiguity that leaders realize that private and public lines are not so easily drawn. O'Toole may be right that it is unfair of followers to judge the private lives of leaders as diminishing their public contributions, but this may be truer retrospectively than at the time they occur. As followers, we have to give leaders room for moral error of a private nature. As leaders, we should understand that others will see us as moral exemplars at all times. We will find our moral selves in the tension between these expectations.

11

CHANGING THE WORLD, CHANGING OURSELVES
A Crash Course on Change Management

It is not only the most difficult thing to know oneself,
but the most inconvenient one, too.

JOSH BILLINGS

Tradition and change are an ever-present polarity for religions and cultures. How dare we change that which is rooted in thousands of years of belief and observance? Why would we want to? How can we ignore the need for relevance? A young Jewish leader analyzed a beautiful Rabbinic text in light of the delicate relationship between the past and present. In the Babylonian Talmud, we read a famous adage about study: "One who repeated his chapter [learning review] a hundred times is not to be compared with one who repeats it one hundred and one times" (*Hagiga* 9b). In a fresh analysis of this statement, Rabbi Menachem Creditor observed that:

> While *invention* is creating something that has never existed before, *innovation* refers to both radical or incremental changes to things and processes. For instance: The "chapter" within our text has been examined and re-examined. How might any possibility for change manage to survive an already arduous review?... While Jewish communities often say that we've "reinvented ourselves," it is perhaps more

exact to point out how we've turned ourselves and our traditions over and over again in an effort to remain true to both inherited tradition and holy growth. Something both new and familiar is empowered to emerge when we accomplish this integration successfully.[1]

In other words, tradition is built on layers of subtle, integrated changes. It is not based on invention as much as on reinvention and synthesis. We are a living part of the change process.

Kurt Lewin, a German psychologist of the early twentieth century, pioneered work in the study of human behavior. He once observed that if you really want to understand something, you must try to change it. Only when we try to change something do we realize its stubborn, rooted existence, be it an institution, an object, or a person. Adaptation, evolution, adjustment, reengineering are all synonyms for change used by corporate America that are creeping into nonprofit work. One of the hardest trials for nonprofit is change or transition. Transition may involve a change of philosophy, product, or leader. But it will also almost always involve resistance.

> Change and resistance go together, hand in glove. Each is natural, pervasive and universal. Resistance is neither avoidable nor bad. It is a fact of organizational life. As such, it must be managed, not avoided. Resistance is feedback, and feedback is information. Poorly managed resistance ... can be costly.... Managing the feedback contained in resistance is critical to effective working partnerships. Like all living systems, organizations thrive when they balance the need for stability and change.[2]

Effective leadership is contingent on the ability to manage change and resistance. Envisioning the future, creating strategic plans, hiring and firing professionals, or moving board members to different positions are staple responsibilities of nonprofit leadership. All of these tasks have change at their core. Warren Bennis, in *On Becoming a Leader*, writes:

> Learning to lead, is, on one level, learning to manage change ... a leader imposes (in the most positive sense of the word) his philosophy on the organization, creating or re-creating its culture. The organization then acts on that philosophy and carries out the mission, and the culture takes on a life of its own, becoming more cause than effect. But unless the leader continues to evolve, to adapt and adjust to external changes, the organization will sooner or later fall apart.[3]

Many people say they believe in change, yet when put to the test, they show they do not truly believe that they or others can really be different. Even if they believe individuals can change, they may not believe institutions are capable of shifting course in a substantive way. In "The Real Reason People Won't Change," Robert Kegan and Lisa Laskow Lahey believe that people are not purposefully subversive or resistant when asked to change their workplace behavior: "Instead, they may be unwittingly caught in a competing commitment—a subconscious, hidden goal that conflicts with their stated commitments."[4] That is, an employee may not admit he is not finishing a report out of a hidden fear he will be given a new task that will upset his work-life balance. To get this individual to change, a manager has to discern the *real* issue and find a solution that addresses the hidden fears connected to change. This psychological quagmire may seem virtually impossible to sort out, especially if you are not a psychologist, but, as the authors remind us:

> You'll be challenging employees' deepest psychological foundations and questioning their longest-held beliefs. Tread delicately and sympathetically through this potentially painful process.... The truth is, all managers *are* psychologists—whether they want to be or not. Helping people overcome their limitations—including the messy, human contradictions that trouble us all—lies at the very heart of effective leadership.[5]

Getting people to function maximally *does* involve holding up a mirror to them and helping them see themselves as they really are. Helping people question the validity of their assumptions, when they developed, and how they are obstacles to growth is at the root of a leader's task. Leaders are here to stretch us with their vision to go beyond where we were prepared to go before. One Fortune 100 CEO actually defined leadership in these very terms: "Leaders take organizations to places they would not otherwise have gone."[6]

> The value add-on of a leader is the ability to redirect the normal course of business by identifying a goal, a model, an approach, something which inertia would not have created, and then—and this is perhaps the most important—to guide and support its actual implementation to get to this "new place."[7]

This stretching process can be a greater challenge in an organized Jewish community built on decades and even centuries of tradition. Resistance is naturally greater the longer the history of any institution, religion, or idea. In the eyes of one contemporary Jewish leader:

> In Jewish life we tend to be sluggish innovators. Many of our institutions were developed decades ago, and while incremental innovations have unfolded, we have seen few organizations that invite fundamental questioning or create a healthy culture of dissent—both fertile ingredients for innovation…. It is difficult to be innovative in organizations that rely heavily upon tradition and where the patterns of the past are elevated as sacred…. We have not kept pace. Our organizational cultures are not agile, open, and probing, but rather self-contained, closed, and stubbornly conservative in response to dissent and change.[8]

Our "sluggish" approach to change may slow us down, but it need not stop us. Change can be purposefully slow, allowing for a process by which time is the measure of whether or not an innovation is fully integrated. I call this "measured change," and it requires an understanding that institutions, rules, and protocols that have been around for a long time usually have stayed with us because they are or were compelling. When we tamper with age-old practices, we must respect their history and ask ourselves: Is this change necessary? Does it preserve the integrity of what came before it? Is there a hidden agenda behind the change that needs to be questioned?

One of the contradictions that leaders often balance is the dialectic tension of patience and impatience, which is linked to the tension of tradition and innovation or preservation and change. For Warren Bennis and Robert Townsend, "One of the most common paradoxes of leadership is that it requires both patience and urgency.... Incorporating both sides of the paradox, to form what you might call 'patient urgency,' is perhaps a good way to lead."[9] Patient urgency is a good leadership approach to change, but its very name indicates its complexity.

CHALLENGING RESISTANCE

Leaders need to believe that change is both possible and desirable. This belief will inoculate them against those who stand in opposition to innovation. Rabbi Jonathan Sacks challenges notions that hold us back:

> We have to be prepared to change. The trouble is, consistently today we hear the argument that human beings cannot change.... The family is breaking down? Inevitable. Civility is on the wane? That is how things are. Too much violence in the media? If that is what people want, that is what they get. None of these is true. Why are they said? Because we have focused on institutions that reinforce rather than change human behavior. Governments reflect votes. Politics follow [sic] opinion polls. The market mirrors consumer choices. Therapies tell us we are OK as we are. There is only one thing missing from this constellation. It is

the language of aspiration, the idea that, whatever we are, we might be different. We *can* grow and develop. We are not simply a bundle of desires. We have immortal longings.[10]

Sacks questions whether past behavior is the operative model for future behavior. It is if we let it be. It is the difference between responding and aspiring. When we respond, we give people what they want. What they often want—despite what they say—is the comfort of habit, which can be its own tyranny. When we aspire to something else, we stretch ourselves to experience something beyond normal cognition. This, in and of itself, can be a source of enormous anxiety.

The anxiety that change produces requires the leader to be both stalwart and sensitive, principled and attentive, driven and soft. The leader has to anticipate anxiety and empathize—be responsive—while also aspiring to something greater or different and bringing others along. Leaders know that is frightening. They also know that change can be exhilarating.

Change is also different for individuals than it is for institutions. Institutions do not change with the same speed that individuals do. We have to have double or triple the patience. But the fact that institutions do not change as rapidly as do people can be a quiet blessing.

TECHNICAL CHANGE VERSUS ADAPTIVE CHANGE

Change in organizations wears many guises. It can be physical, as in a change of building, office space, or renovations. It can be a change of faces, as in a new board, a new staff member, or a new chair or director. It can be emotional, as when a traumatic event causes an organization to rethink its mandate. It is important to understand the nature of the changes that lie before us. Not all change is the same, and not all change can be handled in the same way.

John Kotter, in his business guide *The Heart of Change: Real-Life Stories of How People Change Their Organizations*, suggests that change is less about facts than about feelings, as mentioned earlier. His book centers on one premise that we've already cited but is worth repeating: "People change what they do less because they are given *analysis* that shifts their *thinking* than because they are *shown* a truth that influences their *feelings*."[11] For Kotter, the reasoning that goes into change is essential but ultimately less important than managing the emotional component of change. For him, no matter what change is undertaken—a merger, acquisition, restructuring, globalization—the hardest part of any transition involves changing people's thinking and behavior: "The central challenge is not strategy, not systems, not culture. These elements and many others can be very important, but the core problem without question is behavior—what people think, and the need for significant shifts in what people do."[12] As leaders, we have to pay close and careful attention to the emotional undercurrents that change induces. All change involves loss.

A compelling book, *Leadership and the New Science*, argues that both individual and organizational change start from the same place. "People need to explore an issue sufficiently to decide whether new meaning is available and desirable. They will change only if they believe a new insight, a new idea or a new form helps them become more of who they are."[13] Change not only involves an emotional affirmation of a new direction; in its base sense, change must also align with essential aspects of our identity. When an organization is considering changes, it must continually revisit the enduring question of its mission. "We don't accept an organizational redesign because a leader tells us it is necessary. We choose to accept it if, and only if, we see how this new design enables us to contribute more to what we've defined as meaningful."[14]

For example, imagine that a synagogue board considering a major renovation is also thinking about how it can use part of its space to bring in much-needed revenue. It can either sell a piece of land or create a community center for seniors; the latter will not be cost effective but will strengthen the community. This change represents two very different needs and can only be answered by tapping into the issue of an institution's core identity. Choosing a new principal for a Hebrew school, a potentially significant change, will also hit at the core of that institution's identity. Does the school want someone with strong intellectual credentials or a background in informal education? Fun or serious? Creative or conservative? These traits and qualities do not have to be mutually exclusive, but when they are, boards have to think about their institution's core identity before jumping into what it might become.

Another important aspect of understanding and managing change lies in the difference between technical and adaptive change. Technical changes are those that involve new systems, technologies, or methods for getting something done more efficiently. An example of technical change is a computer software update. An adaptive change involves the transition of a culture. For example, an institution changes its governance structure by reducing the number of board members, promoting a more active engagement for those who remain. These distinctions seem relatively clear, but the reality is more blurred within many institutions.

Ron Heifetz and Marty Linsky, in *Leadership on the Line*, do not mince words: "The single most common source of leadership failure we've been able to identify—in politics, community life, business or the non-profit sector—is that people, especially those in positions of authority, treat adaptive changes like technical problems."[15] It is easier to change a computer system to maximize efficiency than to downsize administrative staff who are not performing to capacity, or rewrite an organization's mission. Adaptive changes generally reflect core values and can be both frightening and risky. Leaders may shift to technical solutions instead of adaptive changes to minimize the risks or problems. But sooner or later, technical changes put in place to mask the need for adaptive change prove insufficient, and core problems resurface. The need for change persists when it is incorrectly diagnosed or poorly managed.

Heifetz and Linsky claim that in times of difficulty, authority figures are looked to to bring change. "In the face of adaptive pressures, people don't want questions; they want answers. They don't want to be told that they will have to sustain losses, rather they want to know how you're going to protect them from the pains of change."[16] So how do we measure the success of change, especially if we sometimes confuse technical with adaptive changes? Management expert Peter Drucker claims that nonprofits are particularly challenged by this question. What is the bottom line, he asks, when there is no bottom line?

> Performance is the ultimate test of any institution. Yet, non-profit institutions tend not to give priority to performance and results. There are few differences between business and nonprofit institutions, but they are important. Perhaps the most important is in the performance area. *In the nonprofit organization, there is no bottom line*. But there is also a temptation to downplay results. There is a temptation to say, "We are serving a good cause; we are doing the Lord's work." Or, "We are doing something to make life a little bit better for people, and that is a result in itself." *That is not enough.* Results can be defined. They can be quantified, at least some of them."[17]

Nonprofits must offer rewarding experiences to boards as well as other volunteers while still achieving impressive results. They must be able to deal with adaptive changes while not losing sight of their essential mission. For Drucker, this means regularly revisiting an organization's mission. Although we discussed missions in chapter 2, let's consider for a moment how mission is tied into change and performance. For Drucker:

> The mission better be focused and narrow. I see too many nonprofits that are trying to do too many things. Believe me, it is difficult enough to do one thing well. The first job of the institution's leader is to think through and define the mission of the institution. Each member of the organization needs to understand, support, and be able to articulate that mission. Every mission statement reflects three things: the

competence of the organization, the outside opportunities and needs, and its commitment to achieving its goal. The task of the nonprofit leader is to try to translate the organization's mission into specifics. So, your first task is *to know what this organization is really trying to do*, why you are working, why you are asking for money, why you are asking for volunteers, what is it you want to achieve. And the *emphasis is on achievement.*[18]

When making changes, we must constantly ask ourselves what kind of emotions and anxieties they will raise, whether what's called for is a technical or adaptive change, and how we will measure the *results* of those changes. Change should always be linked to performance.

JEWISH CHANGE?

When we do not really believe in change, we are essentially questioning an axiomatic cornerstone of our faith. We have two Jewish values that hinge on change and commitment: *teshuva*, which is repentance or personal change, and *tikkun olam*, our commitment to the systemic improvement of the global community. Let's take each of these change concepts and elaborate.

In Rabbinic literature, the idea of personal change is generally captured with the word *teshuva*. *Teshuva* literally means "return." Change in this sense is not becoming someone different as much as it is *returning* to our most authentic self or returning to a God who seems remote and distant. Those journeys may take place simultaneously or independently. In order to expand our ideas of change and how they influence effective leadership, we have to begin by entertaining the complexity of changing ourselves. The mandate to fix a broken world begins with our own brokenness. In the words of one Talmudic Sage, "Fix yourself and then proceed to fix others" (BT *Bava Metzia* 86a).

Rabbi Nahman of Breslov, an early nineteenth-century Hasidic rabbi, urged people to liken the process of change to throwing a ball against a wall, something with elastic qualities that does not stick. We put our physical energies into asserting ourselves outward when we throw a ball. When it hits the wall, we receive the ball back with almost the same degree of force. When we send our thoughts and best intentions out into the world, they may hit walls of obstruction and inflexibility. But those good intentions and desires to change an existing world come back to us and change us in the process. An act of outreach leads, in the most profound sense, to an act of inner growth. We may not convince others of the importance of change, but we have at least reaffirmed our own commitment to a cause in the process.

The word at the heart of this change process is "forgiveness," but we rarely hear it mentioned in a leadership context. We hear the word "change" a great deal in leadership literature, and yet we think of "forgiveness" in purely emotional or psychological terms. However, when we forgive others, we are allowing them the space to change. Hannah Arendt, a Jewish social and political philosopher who came from Germany to the United States in 1941, wrote:

> Without being forgiven, released from the consequences of what we have done, our capacity to act would, as it were, be confined to a single deed from which we could never recover; we would remain the victims of its consequences forever, not unlike the sorcerer's apprentice who lacked the magic formula to break the spell.[19]

If we do not forgive others, we do not allow people to grow beyond the one act or character trait that gets in their way. We get stuck. Something in the past becomes a permanent barrier to change because we are unable to go beyond it. We even do this to ourselves when we do not forgive ourselves for a past transgression or mistake. A Christian theologian writes powerfully of the need to overcome this barrier:

> Forgiveness is a door to peace and happiness. It is a small, narrow door, and cannot be entered without stooping. It is

161

also hard to find. But no matter how long the search, it *can* be found.... When we forgive someone for a mistake or a deliberate hurt, we still recognize it as such, but instead of lashing out or biting back, we attempt to see beyond it, so as to restore our relationship with the person responsible for it. Our forgiveness may not take away our pain—it may not even be acknowledged or accepted—yet the act of offering it will keep us from being sucked into the downward spiral of resentment.... Forgiveness does not mean ignoring what has been done or putting a false label on an evil act. It means, rather, that the evil act no longer remains a barrier to the relationship.[20]

The ability to see beyond the immediate and act to preserve a relationship—either with a person or an institution—lies at the heart of *teshuva*, regardless of whether it's between individuals or between a person and God. The visual image of an impossibly small door that is difficult to find reminds us that change begins with a small opening that, once through, allows us to get to a new place somewhere beyond our hurt. Change does hurt. Leaders who try to change people and circumstances understand the process of finding the small door and revealing a portal to another place.

It is hard to forgive institutions and believe that they are capable of change, but is that not what we are doing when we reinvent an organization? We are forgiving its past and paving a way forward. In an intensely uncomfortable discussion I had with an acquaintance, I listened for the better part of a half hour to her criticize an institution I cared about deeply. She brought up layers of past history, predating my own involvement with the institution by decades. I mentioned quietly that the institution had changed so much since then. She ran right over me with new charges and accusations. Finally, after feeling as if I had been pummeled, I said, more loudly this time, "It's time to move on. We're not in the same place. I'm sorry that you are not able to move beyond the past. I feel every confidence that things are different and are changing all of the time. Institutions can't change if we don't let them."

Sometimes people won't change their impression of an institution because holding onto stale opinions serves some deeper purpose. Perhaps it reminds them of a time when they had more control in the institution or had more friends and colleagues there. It may be part of a broader personal theme of dissatisfaction that explains resistance to change in an individual's general orientation.

But remember, for institutions to be forgiven they sometimes have to apologize. Leaders of institutions have to be able to validate the articulation of past problems and take responsibility for them. They have to acknowledge hurt and pain and demonstrably show that change has occurred.

Rabbi Abraham Isaac Kook, first chief rabbi of the State of Israel, in his book *Lights of Return*, offers a novel interpretation of a statement in the Babylonian Talmud (*Yoma* 86a): "Great is the power of repentance for it brings healing to the world, and even if one individual repents, both he and the entire world are forgiven." Kook understands this to mean that an individual who repents in this manner brings about forgiveness both for himself and the entire world. The moment you change, the world changes with you. When you change yourself, you do not literally change the world. You change the way that you *see* the world. The world changes in your eyes. You also understand that if you have the will and the discipline to change yourself, then you may also feel personally inspired to repair a piece of the world's brokenness.

GLOBAL JEWISH CHANGE

When we speak of brokenness, we often invoke the term *tikkun olam*, literally "repair of the world." This may just be the most overused expression in the Jewish community today. "*Tikkun olam* is associated with the thesis that Jews bear responsibility not only for their own moral, spiritual and material welfare but for the moral, spiritual and material welfare of society at large."[21] It is easy to understand why we use the expression so often in the world of Jewish nonprofits. In the shadow of terrorist threats, global

163

warming, natural disasters, and unprecedented human violence, the need to heal a wounded world is often at the forefront of our thinking.

The words *tikkun olam* were lifted from the closing prayer in Jewish liturgy, the *Aleinu*, which places the demand to repair the world within "God's heavenly kingdom." Human urgency and compassion take place, in the prayer's wording, under a divine, watchful eye. *Tikkun olam* implies a covenantal partnership between God and human beings to take care of each other and the world around us. The idea is also a bedrock of Lurianic kabbalah, a mystical system developed in sixteenth-century Sefad, in the north of Israel. In mystical literature, its meaning is somewhat different. God burst forth upon the earth with tremendous force, shattering everything into pieces. These pieces are called shards, and each contains a glimmer or spark of God. Each time we behave in a sacred way, perform a commandment, elevate ourselves and the world around us, we are metaphorically picking up one of these broken shards and "fixing" the world, bringing it back to its primordial harmony.

Kook shared a beautiful vision of this outpouring of compassion in lyrical terms: "There is a person who sings the song of his own soul ... there is one who sings the song of his people ... there is one whose soul expands until it spreads beyond the limits of Israel and sings the song of humanity."[22]

The problem with the term *tikkun olam* is not its meaning, which resonates deeply within us, but its simplistic use. When we repair a car or a blocked sink, we fix a technical problem. Repairing the world is systemic or adaptive, not technical. There is a notable difference between fixing and healing. We all understand that healing is a complex process, one that is multifaceted and may take years. The world is filled with acts of kindness but not always with acts of change or healing; those should not be mistaken for *tikkun olam*. Kindness and repairing the world are not the same thing. When we collect food for the needy, give old clothes to the poor, or plant trees in Israel, we are not healing the world. We are helping the world. We are not engaging in the systemic changes that ameliorate poverty, even if we may be helping a few families stay warm for the winter. We call this *gemilut hasadim*, or acts of loving-kindness.

We should never minimize the importance of *hesed* just because it is not *tikkun olam*. An example: I am often asked why we should give money to a homeless person who may use it to purchase alcohol or drugs and, thus, remain homeless. You can argue that giving to a homeless person teaches us something about our own levels of compassion and has little to do with helping another. As it says in *Sefer Hasidim*, a medieval book of spiritual wisdom, "The Almighty has willed that there be two hands in the matter of charity: one that gives and one that receives. Be thankful that yours is the hand that gives." Ultimately, we should help, not judge, and if we are really concerned about the use of the quarter or dollar, then we should carry granola bars or sandwiches with us. I have a stock in my glove compartment, but in the winter, I try to buy gloves. I figure that's what a glove compartment is for.

One winter afternoon, my son and I were in the car at a red light, and we saw a homeless man standing at the intersection with his hand open. I quickly asked my son to get a pair of gloves and to open his window before the light changed. The man who received them was grateful, so grateful it was uncomfortable. The light was long, and we watched him put the gloves on lovingly, one finger at a time. Watching him reminded me of the powerful verse in the book of Psalms, "The world stands on acts of loving-kindness" (Psalm 89:3).

There are all types of hunger in the world. But even if we carried thousands of peanut butter sandwiches and gloves with us every day, we would still only be performing acts of *hesed*. We are not making the kind of political changes that would ameliorate hunger in the world. Let us label our compassion correctly so that we understand the real work of the world and strive one day to do it. In order for us to move from helping to healing, we need to take a larger linguistic leap and use terms accurately. A reconsideration of language may expand the way we think of systemic change.

The other problem with *teshuva* and *tikkun olam* is that one deals with personal change and the other global change, but neither deals specifically with change within our Jewish community. For that, the term *brit*, or covenant, may be more helpful. A *brit* does not indicate change as much as community-wide agreement about our collective identity; each member within a covenantal community must make personal accommodation to meet group needs and values. A *brit* or covenant involves a group understanding about who we are and what we stand for.

As discussed earlier, one of the most pressing issues for Jewish leaders today is sustaining and recruiting membership. We have never had more permeable definitions of what it means to join the Jewish community. Does it involve birth, feelings, responsibilities, or obligations? Does it involve institutional affiliation, education, or religious awareness? It is very hard to establish the parameters of a covenantal community when we cannot decide what constitutes membership. Jewish sociologists studying the nature of community and membership realize that the popular trend toward personal spirituality does not necessarily translate into communal responsibilities. Judaism for many people is about "me," not "we." It will take a great deal of change to revisit this notion of *brit* and ask ourselves what makes our community covenantal. Until we have a core and collective sense of what constitutes *klal Yisrael*, the Jewish people, it is hard to work on changes to that entity.

Nevertheless, leaders must proceed with patient urgency both to sustain and to change the people and institutions they work for and to bring to these groupings a sense of confidence that innovation and tradition can live in a happy marriage. Sometimes we need to forgive ourselves, others, or institutions and give them the space they need to change. Sometimes we will face seemingly intractable problems along the way as those around us resist change. Resistance brings with it critical and important information about how people and institutions work. Leaders must then don their detective hats and delve more deeply into resistance and emerge with a better understanding of problems and solutions. Leaders also need to model willingness to make personal changes to give their followers the belief that change can and really does happen.

—◇◇◇—

12

CREATING MEANINGFUL BOARD SERVICE

See every act you do as being of great significance.
RABBI JOSEPH TELUSHKIN

You've read some books and managed a few large projects, and finally you've just been elected or appointed to a nonprofit board. Congratulations. *Mazel tov.* Welcome to the board. Now what? Do you have any idea what will be asked of you or how to measure your success? Are you clear about the expectations and your responsibilities? How well will your board work as a team? How will you work with the professional staff of your organization? How will Jewish values influence your group decision making?

An alternative scenario: You have just been elected as president of a Jewish nonprofit, having served on its board for several years. There are changes you want to make in the composition and policy governance of your board to strengthen the way it functions. Maybe it is too big and needs restructuring, or its members do not feel they are empowered to make decisions. Meetings are tiresome. You have been considering these issues as part of a personal strategic plan that you want to share with your board, and you also want to create consensus. Where do you start?

Board service is a relatively new "invention" in Jewish culture and shows how far we have come in creating leadership structures in organizations that used to be run by singular individuals. It also demonstrates how much we have swallowed the notion that board service is the most significant way to contribute to an institution. It shows what an institutional culture we have become, one that often values convention and protocols above innovation and creativity. Board service practiced well should be a tribute to well-defined protocols that, nevertheless, stimulate honest conversation about the health, future, and direction of an institution and do not hamper innovation. Yet, in most of our organizations, we have not reached that ideal.

In *Pirkei Avot* (Ethics of the Fathers) we find a fascinating passage that highlights some of the tensions we just presented:

> There are four types of donors to charity: One who desires to give but does not want others to give, begrudging the privilege of others. One who desires that others give but will not give himself, begrudging himself. One who wants both himself and others to give is pious. One who will not give and does not want others to give is lawless.
>
> (*Pirkei Avot* 5:16)

Imagine that we were to replace the word "donor" in this passage with the word "board member," since one is donating money and the other is donating time *and* money. Ideal board members fit the "pious" category; they give of themselves and encourage others to support their institutions. Those who do neither are regarded as lawless (in this translation) or wicked. Their wickedness is not only due to their own parsimonious nature but to their refusal to help others get involved.

The other two categories are much murkier and are helpful in understanding some of the key issues board members today face. There are some board members who want to keep leadership to themselves. They want to be the face of an organization, know all of its "secrets," and be in control of all information and decisions. They do not like to share leadership; they use insider language to be in the center and keep others in the dark. In a session I recently conducted on personal and professional aspirations, a young woman unabashedly shared her personal hope with the group: "I want a day when I feel completely in control, down to organizing all the shampoo bottles in my shower." In the extreme, people who need this kind of control and believe that giving time and money is about gaining control will make board service difficult for others. The second individual mentioned in the quote from *Pirkei Avot* (Ethics of the Fathers) is of the opinion that the work should get done but that others will magically do it. Someone has to do the work of nonprofits, but that someone is always someone *else*. Ironically, there are boards with these kinds of members. They want the prestige of a board position and what it might say to others about their own giving level, yet they may offer virtually no service and may not even make good on their pledges. In the words of a commentator on this passage, this individual fails to understand that "it is primarily that wealth which is spent on good works which truly becomes the permanent possession of its giver."[1] This passage from ancient Jewish wisdom highlights the diverse nature of personalities who serve on boards and differing attitudes about board responsibilities.

If you identified with any of the troubling issues above, you are not alone. You may have served on boards for years already and still ask yourself if you have made a reasonable contribution. You may find yourself president of a board without proper guidance or a sense of vision. Alternatively, you may have been an important critic as you were moving up in board roles, but now as the board's president or as a manager in a nonprofit, you are expected to criticize privately and praise publicly. You are unsure you can handle the transition and now understand the counterintuitive expression "to survive a promotion."[2]

Most people who serve on boards of nonprofit organizations—at all levels—are not sure what is expected of them. In the words of leading organizational developers:

> Nearly all ... volunteers want to be effective board members, yet most are uncertain how to do so.... The vast majority of trustees are not systematically prepared for the role prior to their appointment to a governing board.... Nothing in life to that point quite prepares you for this role.... Trustees ... must draw more upon hand-me-down shibboleths than upon a solid body of knowledge about governance and its influence on not-for-profit organizations.[3]

There is a lot to learn, and many guides for board cultivation and development are available. Within the Jewish community specifically, our resources are more scant. One of the most challenging aspects of Jewish nonprofit organizations, in particular, is the creation of meaningful roles on boards. Volunteers rarely feel engaged or may feel that they are not the real decision makers in an organization. They may experience disappointment because the board they are on is only looking for financial supporters and cheerleaders. Critical dilemmas that they bring up are quickly squelched. In the words of a Jewish leader who recently dropped a board commitment: "All they wanted were people who nodded in agreement with everything the president or executive committee came up with. That's not me. That's not what I joined a board for. I joined to make a difference. If they can't handle disagreement, then I have to find somewhere else to go." And he did.

Despite rapid organizational changes and amidst a general diminishment of volunteerism, we find that board development is still a neglected area of research and development within Jewish institutions. We need to identify the defining aspects of board development and policy governance that can make us more productive, more efficient, and more collaborative in the nonprofit work that we do. Although it may seem obvious, we will try to define the responsibilities and duties of a board and the composition of boards that make them most useful. Bear in mind that board members are not necessarily leaders.

COMPOSING A BOARD AND DEFINING ITS RESPONSIBILITIES

What qualities should we look for in board members? Board members are often chosen by virtue of only one of three outstanding characteristics: a family name, a family fortune, or a reputation for hard work. Each of these characteristics is important, but we should expand this limited view in picking an ideal board. Gerald Bubis, the founding director of the Daniels School of Jewish Communal Service and vice president for the Jerusalem Center for Public Affairs, aids us with his list of notable qualities: wealth, work, wisdom, wallop (he uses this term to refer to people with many community connections), people skills, *menschlichkeitism*, and commitment to Jewish values. No board member will encompass all of these qualities, but Bubis challenges us to think broadly about the people who shepherd our institutions. The last two qualities, in particular, add to distinctive Jewish leadership. In terms of *menschlichkeitism*, the Yiddish expression that communicates both humane values and wise judgment, Bubis has this to say:

> This attribute, often elusive, yet, like love, easy to recognize when it exists, assumes good people skills but goes beyond them. Board members who say thank you to staff, are sensitive about agency goals and their achievement in moral ways, who see the organization as a tool for human and Jewish betterment and not an end in itself, possess this attribute. They are often the people turned to for help in resolving conflict situations.[4]

As for commitment to Jewish values, Bubis writes of the importance of having board members who have institutional memory but who are also "grounded in knowledge and living born of Jewish values and beliefs." By this he does not refer to religious affiliation or observance alone, but to a commitment to Jewish literacy and a general fidelity to the Jewish dimension of the organization's mission.

When considering the composition of a board, it may also be instructive to bear in mind the thesis of Malcolm Gladwell's best-selling book *The Tipping Point*.[5] Gladwell believes that it does not take many people to create trends or even catalyze social change. It takes a few key people who embody certain characteristics to generate momentum and get trends to a tipping point. He identifies three personality types who can have enormous influence when working in collusion: the connector, the maven, and the salesperson. The connector is an individual who casts his or her social and professional net widely. Connectors can take interesting ideas and spread them in imaginative ways by virtue of knowing many people in diverse settings. Mavens, on the other hand, master a body of information. They know a great deal about something or have a novel, well-thought-through idea. Salesmen take the idea and get other people to buy into it. Their defining character trait is persuasiveness. They can convince you to support a great idea or cause. Working in conjunction, these three types of people form a powerful team for social change. When creating a board, it is helpful to consider Gladwell's theory, especially if your organization is confronting critical changes and is experiencing resistance.

Other manuals on board composition also suggest a blend of people: those who are strongly committed to the cause, those with a strong fiduciary sense, and those who bring prestige to the non-profit work that you do. For example, an organization that provides support to breast cancer victims may want a breast cancer survivor, a local celebrity, and a certified accountant to join their board. The breast cancer survivor will bring personal experience, credibility, and sensitivity to the table; the celebrity may bring high profile to the cause; and the accountant can interpret financial statements. Other qualities that potential board members bring to the table may include enthusiasm and energy, institutional memory, gender inclusivity, demographic and minority representation, and legal knowledge. While this is an oversimplification of how boards are selected, it should prompt us to think broadly about board composition. Having boards made up of high-profile donors alone can skew the mission and minimize sensitivity to the diversity of individuals that need to be served.

Board choices and responsibilities should not be looked at in isolation from an organization's mission. The absence of strong connections among board members and their knowledge and commitment to a mission can cause confusion and disruption. For example, a social service board of an organization that serves both Jews and non-Jews as part of its mission may be questioned if it does not allow non-Jews to serve on its boards. A synagogue or day-school board that has a denominational affiliation as part of its mission should be careful in putting together a board that understands the limits and boundaries of that denomination in educating board members.

Board members should also be chosen for their accountability and follow-through. Perhaps the complaint that I hear most often in relation to board members is failure to follow through. "I don't know how to motivate our treasurer. He took on such a significant role and just doesn't get the work done. It's so frustrating." Alternatively, you might hear a related complaint from a board member about an organization's president. "She says all the right things at meetings and has tables and charts and looks good. People think she's really getting things done, but let me tell you, there's nothing behind those charts. She is accountable to no one." Even with all of the qualities mentioned above, a board filled with members with little sense of accountability will be very hard to manage and will underperform for its organization time and again. One of the key components to ensuring responsibility and follow through is to make sure that all board members have a clear sense of the organization's mission (that they can personally articulate well) and are given an unambiguous list of responsibilities.

Nonprofit boards oversee the operations of an institution. They provide the stewardship and supervision of its resources and are charged with ensuring that resources are forthcoming. They are responsible for the governance of an institution, which includes an organization's mission, its bylaws, and the appointment of its members and its leadership. They must also protect the values of the nonprofit, evaluate its programs, and deal with issues of conflict as they arise. The sum total of responsibilities of a board is larger than the individual roles of each of its members.

When people are appointed to boards, their responsibilities are not always clearly defined. Fisher Howe, a well-known consultant to nonprofits, suggests seven responsibilities that a board member must assume to function maximally:

1. Attendance
2. Mission
3. Chief executive/leadership
4. Finances
5. Program oversight
6. Fundraising
7. Board effectiveness[6]

These responsibilities are closely tied to the operational requirements for boards generally. The first for Howe is attendance. If joining a board is simply a symbolic act of support for a cause but does not involve any real activity or responsibility, the role will never be meaningful. Some boards are happy to have an important celebrity or lay leader on their stationery and expect little more from them than a name. But this policy should be used judiciously lest it communicate the message that being on a particular board does not involve personal investment. Howe contends that if board members do not attend meetings regularly, their membership should be brought into question.

Howe advises protecting an organization by a regular rotation system to avoid unpleasant or even traumatic dismissals. In addition, presidents of boards sometimes minimize the work involved in order to persuade particular individuals to join. This, too, contributes to a diminishment of meaning in the role and can lead to aggravation when a new board member realizes that to do the job adequately requires more of a time commitment than was originally voiced. Too many board members have piped up in classes that when they were called by the nominations committee of their organization, the conversation went something like this: "We think you'd be terrific on our board…. You're very busy…. Yeah, we're all busy. Don't worry, there's almost no time commitment. You'll be fine." Within a month or two the board opens a search for a new director or considers bankruptcy, and the time commitment feels like a black hole for which you were never adequately prepared. Board members should not only attend meetings regularly, ideally they should come well prepared for the discussion at hand.

The second responsibility of a board member is to help define and maintain the organization's mission. This may involve deliberate discussions about the mission, the kind that take place in strategic planning. It may also involve the more subtle role of helping an organization stay true to its stated mandate. There is so much compassion in the nonprofit world that organizations sometimes stray from their primary purpose in order to be more inclusive in their funding or programming. This can ultimately eat away at the health and vitality of a nonprofit.

The third responsibility of a board member is to appoint a chief executive or dismiss one who is not performing to satisfaction. Included in this is the regular evaluation of the CEO. In synagogue leadership, this may include the synagogue's executive director or the rabbi. For a Jewish day or supplemental school, this may mean the hiring and firing of a headmaster, principal, or senior staff person. These situations can be potentially charged and unpleasant; thus, a board member must have good judgment and be trusted with confidential information. The moment there is a breach of trust on a board, the ability of a board to make delicate decisions is compromised. A commitment to confidentiality is a key to trustworthy board membership.

The fourth role of a board member involves finances or fiduciary responsibilities. While detailed financial accounts are not the purview of every board member, each board member should be aware of how his or her nonprofit was incorporated, its tax status, and its basic budgetary needs. This includes being able to read a budget. Board members regularly have to approve annual budgets and assure adherence to them. They may be responsible for reviewing audits and the oversight of internal and external controls over the budget. In specific organizations, they may be charged with raising or lowering membership dues or tuition. In larger organizations, the board may also have oversight over investments or capital fund.

The fifth role of a board member is program oversight. Board members need to make sure that the programming of an institution accords with its stated mission. Programs often represent the single largest outlay of a nonprofit; consequently, they must be properly evaluated. The sixth role identified by Howe is fundraising. Most often, board commitments also involve a personal financial pledge and/or a commitment to raise money. Most people feel uncomfortable raising funds even though it may be a central responsibility of a board member. In the *Board Member's Guide to Fund-Raising*, Fisher Howe writes that it is "ironic and unfortunate ... that the very people most clearly associated with non-profit institutions—the board members—are so often heard to say, 'I'll do anything but raise money!'"[7] At these times, bear in mind John D. Rockefeller's wise words: "Never think you need to apologize for asking someone to give to a worthy object." Every time you solicit money for your nonprofit, you are creating an incredible opportunity for someone else to give charity and affirming your own commitment to the mission of your organization at the same time. While not every board member has to raise funds regularly, it is realistic to expect that board members will both contribute to the organization they serve and ask others to do the same.

The last responsibility of a board member is to monitor and evaluate board effectiveness. This may involve recruiting new board members or retiring others. It may involve reviewing current governance structures or initiating a change of responsibilities. Board members should be able to look at their group honestly and critically to ensure that, as a public service, they are doing their utmost at all times.

While every board is different, it is helpful to have a general framework for board responsibilities to organize and to structure board retreats, conversations on an organization's mission, or strategic planning for the future. Sometimes referring to a list of responsibilities can remind boards during times of crisis of their initial mandate. If detailing the exact responsibilities of each of these categories was a challenge for you in your board service, speak to the board president for clarification. If this was difficult for you, it may be a challenge for other board members, and it may be time for a group discussion.

Gerald Bubis adds another important dimension to non-profit board responsibilities. He believes that the members of a board are "interpreters to the community" of an organization's mission. They have the job not only of defining their mission internally but also of making sure that the community the organization serves understands its mission. While this may be accomplished through word of mouth, marketing, and advertising, this role is often not articulated as a board function. Board members can be so wrapped up in their internal tasks and responsibilities, they assume the public they serve is well aware of their organization's objectives. This is rarely the case. Not everyone knows what functions a college Hillel serves. Not everyone knows what resources are available for Jewish teens or seniors. Some people may have never stepped into a Jewish day school or may not be familiar with the range of allocations provided by umbrella organizations like the Federation. To add to the confusion, the Jewish community's organizations are often identified by letter abbreviations, making a resource guide look like military encoding. Abbreviations coupled with the insider language and assumptions of every institution can make external communications challenging. Board members have to decode the mystery of Jewish communal life for those either less affiliated or simply not in need of the services provided.

Sometimes board members work well within the very limited walls of one institution. They learn the language of synagogue life, for example, and can identify needs and objectives and mentor potential board members. Real leadership development means eventually breaking out of that circle and expanding our view of what a community needs in full. A past synagogue president may take on a role at a Federation or a JCC. A school board member who joined to ensure the best standards for her own children may have to rethink her role after her child graduates.

The dilemma of one-institution lay leadership is legion within volunteer service. We get involved in institutions that service a particular life stage. We serve on the board of a preschool when our children are nursery age. We move on to an elementary school board when our children move to that level. There's the synagogue board for parents of bar and bat mitzvah age children. You get the picture. The skills we develop in one setting may be critical or unnecessary in another, as we morph from one stage to another. While this kind of movement displays incredible commitment to our children and is only natural, it also can bias us in a role and prevent us from being sufficiently objective. I have heard school board presidents say directly to their boards: "I want you to stop thinking like parents and start thinking like board members." This trajectory can blind-side us to the holistic needs of a community.

To serve our communities best and to develop ourselves, we have to take on new leadership challenges and expand our circle of concerns. To illustrate, a woman in one of our classes was very committed to the Hillel at her former university. She worked hard on its behalf as a volunteer and contributed generously to its annual campaign. She came to our course to be more effective at her chosen institution. During a retreat, she met another participant who was not in her class but was very active in a nonprofit dedicated to sheltering Jewish women from domestic abuse. The women got to talking and shared their passions. In the course of conversation, our Hillel devotee heard the voice of compassion swelling and had not known the extent of domestic abuse within the Jewish community. Having a legal background, she offered her services pro bono to their cause. When she told me about her interchange, she quipped about how easy it is to feel that the mission of your own institution is the only or most important cause. "Where have I been all these years, locked into one charity and not really thinking beyond it? Maybe it was a way to stay in college forever. It's time to open my eyes."

Here self-honesty is an important aspect of growing leadership. We grow as leaders not only when we get more efficient and creative within our own institutions but when we can transcend the boundaries of one mission and the walls of one institution to realize that we are all in service of the community with a capital "C." Vibrant community leaders—both lay and professional—do not lock themselves into one cause. Over a lifetime of leadership roles, they will open themselves up to any number of leadership challenges that allow them to see and hear the multiple faces and voices within every community.

LAY-PROFESSIONAL RELATIONSHIPS

One of the trickiest areas of board work is creating a good working relationship between professionals and volunteers. Both are responsible for policy and operation, building trust and creating financial transparency within nonprofits. Where do we draw the line between the volunteer and professional arenas? In recent years, this problem has become exacerbated because Jewish communal professionals are better trained than ever before, and mega-philanthropists and donors have made many decisions about the Jewish future previously within the aegis of professionals. Our climate of entitlement and self-esteem has not helped either. I hear disappointment about this relationship more often than ever before from both lay leaders and professionals. "The professional who staffs our board makes all of the decisions and just hands me a script. Does she think I cannot handle writing my own speeches? I am a successful businessman." And then for balance I've heard many variations of this from professionals: "I did not get an M.A. in this field to bring coffee to meetings and then be told it's the wrong kind of coffee. Where does *my* expertise fit into this picture?"

Before addressing any of the clashes and opportunities that this relationship presents, it is important to take a historical step back. There was a time when virtually all Jewish nonprofit work was driven by volunteers. In the historical waves of immigration to the United States, groups formed to feed, shelter, and care for a population foreign to the language and cultural norms of life in America. But as these needs grew and became more complex, professionals were increasingly required to handle financial management of funds and create more influential communal infrastructures. A former CEO of a Federation made this observation:

> This past century in America saw the proliferation of literally hundreds of voluntary organizations…. Literally thousands of caring Jews gave of their time and treasure to build a Jewish community with its wide range of services and institutions. The cacophony created by this wide-ranging and varied multiplicity of opportunities needed increasing attention. Sometimes slowly, sometimes quickly, sometimes unevenly and with little forethought, people were hired to provide the services. Volunteers still worked side-by-side, hand-in-hand with those they hired. There were conflicts. Clarification and re-clarification was needed as to when volunteers performed functions unique to them by virtue of their status, purse, or role. Reciprocally, paid staff began to professionalize and evolve more coherent methods of services.[8]

Professionals did not replace volunteers; ideally, they worked closely with volunteers to manage the internal operations of Jewish nonprofits. But the ideal often gave way to the real. The demarcation lines of which responsibilities "belonged" to the board member and which fell under the aegis of the staff member became increasingly blurred and indistinct. This confusion still plagues nonprofit institutions. One of the key challenges to proper board development is the creation and maintenance of healthy relationships between lay boards and paid professionals. This is best accomplished by establishing clarity regarding roles. A few quotes from conversations about lay-professional relations from a recent issue of the Jewish journal *Sh'ma* showcase some of the difficulties:

> "We use 'lay leader' to mean everything from a volunteer to a donor."
>
> "Among volunteers, there is often confusion between someone's donor capacity, his or her family pedigree, and his or her leadership skills."
>
> "While the volunteer might be available at all hours of the night, it does not mean that the professional should be expected to do the same."
>
> "Although volunteer leaders are just as committed as before, they do not necessarily have the time that a past generation of lay leaders had, and therefore rely more heavily on the professional."
>
> "One day the rabbi is relating to a board member, and the next day he or she is burying the person's mother."
>
> "Professionals are expected to do far more than any of us were trained to do and many volunteers are pulling away because they do not feel as invested or empowered as they previously felt."
>
> "Some quite intelligent and sophisticated people seem to park at the door of a nonprofit boardroom the critical thinking they bring to their own affairs."
>
> "Why do people take on lay leadership positions? Why do people take on professional leadership positions? The answers are complex and include personal identity issues, spiritual identity issues, and professional identity issues. It would be helpful to understand why we are sitting around the table and passionate about what we do, and where our potential partners are coming from. When those identities are compromised the cost is incredibly high, not just to the organization, but to the community as a whole."[9]

Shifra Bronznick, a consultant to Jewish nonprofits, has this to say about potential dysfunction in board-staff relations: "In our community, we often find ourselves—volunteers and professionals—in situations that are exactly the reverse of the good-to-great company. We practice teamwork inconsistently, we avoid controversy, and we allow our internal political conflicts to seethe below the surface. Above ground, we indulge in unkind personal interactions or revert to manicured public conversation."[10]

If unclear roles and responsibilities are the source of the problem, then the solution is to spend more time and effort defining and communicating the role of the board and the role of the professionals. It may be instructive to open a board retreat or first meeting with a list of board members and their backgrounds and areas of specialization or interest and a list of professionals and their job descriptions. On paper, it usually looks neater than it may be in a working relationship, but some board members have never seen the job descriptions of the professionals with whom they work. In early meetings, you may want to have board and staff members partner in small groups to create a congenial atmosphere when working on set issues. You might even broach riskier territory by facilitating a safe conversation about tensions.

Lay leaders must be sensitive to the education and experience that professionals have. After all, lay leaders rotate through positions, while professionals often manage the same or a related portfolio for years. Sadly, a young woman who worked for a Jewish nonprofit shared with one of our classes the moment she decided to leave the field: "I was at a breaking point with some lay leaders, and when one of them screamed at me for bringing the wrong kind of cookies to a meeting, I said to myself that I just can't do this anymore." The class—a group of lay leaders and professionals—sat quietly. She still works in the nonprofit sector but not for a Jewish nonprofit. A woman in a different leadership seminar complained that no matter how many times she explained that she was Sabbath observant, the lay leader she worked with would consistently call her on Saturday. "Where are the boundaries?" she asked.

Professionals, on the other hand, can be just as insensitive. Lay leaders begin their volunteer responsibilities often after a long day in the office. When they are called by professionals during their workday, they may feel that their primary commitments are not valued or respected. Professionals can create an inflated sense of self-importance and make many institutional decisions without any lay feedback. We are all familiar with the scene: professionals at an event stand in the back and speak badly of their lay leaders, affect boredom, or distract themselves at meetings with electronic devices. Boardroom etiquette demands that if we are professional enough to call meetings, then we are professional enough to give our full attention to those in attendance. Dr. Eugene Borowitz suggests that professionals use the kabbalistic notion of *tsimtsum*, "contraction," to make room for lay leadership even when the professionals alone might be able to fill the room with good ideas born of a solid education.[11] By contracting one's ego but maintaining one's presence, professionals communicate that they value lay leaders and can work with them to achieve mutually agreed-upon ends.

One of the most difficult roles to clarify in this respect is that of a congregational rabbi. As an earlier quote expressed, the rabbi's role as confidant, nurturer, and repository of Jewish law can make the rabbi an unusual amalgamation of authority figure, psychologist, encyclopedia, friend, and congregant like anyone else. If the rabbi, by virtue of his or her knowledge of Jewish law, always has veto power or the synagogue becomes synonymous with the rabbi's house, then board members may not feel empowered to effect change. One rabbi who wrote of the tensions of the rabbinic role in a congregation suggests that rabbis make many decisions unilaterally without intending to usurp power. It can be hard to strike a balance of authority with an openness to suggestion and innovation.

> The rabbi may ... be a key facilitator, communicator, and/or strategic planner. In matters involving policy or innovation, the balance among unilateral action, advice and consent, and group decision-making varies widely, but there is always

a balance and there are always disagreements regarding where that balance is.[12]

This balance can be more difficult when a board member has issues with Jewish law or tradition and does not accept the rabbi's role as legal adjudicator. Nevertheless, rabbis and strong-willed professionals have to watch vigilantly that they do not overwhelm other professionals and lay leaders. In the words of influential Jewish educator Isa Aron:

> It is often taken for granted that the vision of a congregation is synonymous with the vision of the rabbi. But if the rabbi and educator [or other professional] fully accept the need to evolve a shared vision, they will realize the value of exercising restraint, and ensure that their contributions do not over-whelm those of other team members. Thus, professionals face the challenge of holding back their opinions while remaining fully engaged in the discussion, or else their restraint will be interpreted as indifference. Professionals who miss meetings regularly or read their mail during meetings they attend, are sending a message that the process is not important to them.[13]

Both volunteers and professionals should not communicate that they are too busy or too important to be fully present with the rest of the board.

SETTING MEETING AGENDAS THAT WORK

One of the key areas of the staff-lay partnership occurs in setting meeting agendas and running meetings well. Professionals often create meeting agendas, knowing what topics should be addressed. Lay people or board members generally run the meetings. Making meetings run smoothly, meaningfully, and in a timely fashion remains a challenge for many nonprofits. Trying to discuss too much, making room for every individual contribution, or not having substantive roles or charges for individual board members can give people the impression that meetings are a waste of time. How often have we heard a potentially great board candidate reject board membership: "I feel moved by your cause, but I can't stand going to meetings." "Meetings run on and on and are poorly facilitated." "We never seem to get anything accomplished."

Dave Barry, in *Clawing Your Way to the Top*, compares meetings to funerals, and it seems that funerals might actually be more productive:

> A meeting can be compared to a funeral in the sense that you have a gathering of people who are wearing uncomfortable clothing and would rather be somewhere else. The major differences are that most funerals have a definite purpose (to say nice things about a person) and reach a definite conclusion (this person is put in the ground).... Nothing is ever buried in a meeting. An idea may look dead, but it will always reappear at another meeting later on.[14]

In *Death by Meeting*, leadership consultant and author Patrick Lencioni questions why two-hour movies can have you sitting on the edge of your seat, while two hour meetings can bore you to tears.[15] His conclusion is that meetings need to have the same dynamic that make movies exciting: conflict. You may not win an Oscar, but if you invite conflict and facilitate it well, you will run the kind of meetings that make people want to come back.

The following general guidelines for meetings may be useful. Limited, manageable agendas given out in advance of the meeting allow all board members to see, in clear print and with adequate time, the central issues that require their input. Consequently, they will have the time to gather their own thoughts. Staff and board presidents or chairs working together before a meeting should be able to script some important follow-up roles for individuals. Professionals may also want to give a chair some advance notice if an issue will be particularly controversial or if a particular member of the board is being difficult. This gives the head of the board time to speak with this member and plan a strategic approach to cooperative discussion during the meeting itself.

One of the most effective techniques for running meetings well is to have a board construct three to five brief protocols decided upon by the group that will determine the interaction at all meetings. This is a contract that all agree to before meetings are run. These protocols are usually read before each meeting and are mentioned in the breach. Examples include the following:

- No interruptions.
- No repetitions.
- We will start and end on time.
- No cell phones or electronic devices permitted.
- Do not make an issue personal.
- What is said in this room stays in this room.

On controversial issues, you might want to try a writing exercise. Have all board members at a meeting write a brief answer to a question, since this will create more diversity of views than meetings where a few voices typically dominate. It is also a good way to facilitate potentially explosive conversations, as the act of writing generally tempers views and creates room for dissent more respectfully.

Most importantly, committing to a start time and an end time and sticking with that clock will increase trust in the person running the meeting. Bear in mind that meetings are *the* time when boards convene as a group and interact with professional staff as a group. If you are asking for several hours of a lay leader's time, you need to ensure that meetings are targeted, beneficial, substantive, and timely. If you don't have enough of an agenda to hold monthly meetings, don't be afraid to cancel. No one will ever complain about a cancelled meeting!

SHOWING APPRECIATION

One of the perpetual complaints I hear about board service is how thankless it so often feels. Not only do leaders feel the heat, but when they put out the fires, no one offers a simple thank you. So much is expected and so little is recognized. A woman who gave two years of board service to her synagogue—which amounted to three to five hours a week of volunteer time—told me that she did not even get a thank you note from the synagogue. She was thanked and told her board service was up on her answering machine!

In Hebrew, when we express gratitude we are *makir tov*, we recognize the good that someone else has done. Acknowledging goodness goes far and beyond thanking someone. It is articulating the *hesed*, the kindness, compassion, or effort that someone else has performed on another's behalf. One of the most neglected aspects of engagement in the nonprofit community is showing appreciation, both for volunteers and for professionals. In synagogue communities where many, if not most, committees are dependent on volunteers, it is easy to forget to say thank you as a leader; after all, you may be putting in more time than anyone else. Nevertheless, you will not be properly thanked for your work unless you can model appropriate expressions of appreciation for others.

Sometimes a few people are thanked excessively and others left out; commonly this is the division between those who give the funds and those who do the work. An evenness of appreciation is the hallmark of fair and just leadership. In addition, try not to make the mistake that only volunteers need to be thanked and paid professionals do not expect any appreciation. Remember: The volunteer usually commits several hours a week or month to this cause. A paid professional has committed every working hour to it. A recent cover of a Jewish journal for nonprofits called *Contact* had a classified ad on the cover looking for a Jewish communal professional with a high level of experience, advanced graduate degree, long hours under intense pressure, thick skin, and a sunshine attitude. Compensation: low $20Ks. We can't ask for the moon and then forget to say thank you to our professionals.

Appreciating someone does not mean the purchase of expensive gifts that can cost nonprofits more than they can afford or long lists of thanks at events that prove tiresome for the general audience. Decide at a board meeting or appoint a subcommittee to consider appropriate and consistent ways to thank volunteers and professionals. A lovely custom adopted by some synagogues is to have a "volunteer" Shabbat where volunteers are mentioned by name and asked to stand in public acknowledgment while a prayer from a traditional prayer book is read in their honor. The rabbi may devote a sermon to this topic that also encourages others who do not volunteer to consider volunteering.

At a final board meeting, a leader might go around the room and thank every individual by mentioning one very specific contribution of each board member or write thank you notes at the end of the year. Professionals may be acknowledged publicly at the last board meeting of the year. Never underestimate the power of a thoughtful, well-expressed thank you note.

A professional I once worked with told me that people do not feel thanked unless you thank them seven times. In other words, appreciation must be specific, detailed, repeated, and sincere to make people feel that the efforts they have displayed are really valued.

13

WHO'S NEXT?

Effective Succession Planning

> *True leaders also know that the only deputies worth hiring are the ones good enough to replace them.*
> DAVID HEENAN AND WARREN BENNIS

At every period of leadership transition, the Hebrew Bible is preoccupied with the question of succession. Who will step into the leader's shoes, and how prepared are they for the enormity of the task? Whenever biblical leaders take their leave, the path has already been paved for succession. Often the question of legacy has been tightly woven into infertility or primogeniture: the right leader has not yet been born or is born second in a climate where the first male child was traditionally called the heir. The fact that the firstborn in every Genesis narrative does not become leader signals an important message about Jewish leadership that travels throughout biblical history: we care more about having the right leader than the "correct" leader.

Let's take Abraham as a good early example. He and Sarah struggle with infertility. Near the close of his narrative, in Genesis chapter 21, Abraham sends away his firstborn son, Ishmael, and in chapter 22, he comes close to sacrificing his second-born son, Isaac. The struggle for the right heir continues for the duration of Abraham's life. One of his last acts before he dies is finding a wife for Isaac. Thus, when he is "old and advanced in years" (Genesis 24:1), he not only makes sure that Isaac replaces him but that Isaac himself has an easier time continuing the line.

Leadership is a family business not only in Genesis. Moses does not pass his leadership position to either of his two sons, Gershom or Eliezer. God informs Moses long before he dies that Joshua, one of the spies to Canaan, is next in line. Moses is told several times that he will be replaced by Joshua. The preparation for a new leader in Moses's case takes years of shadowing Moses and seeing from a close vantage point all of the challenges that this desert people present.

In the biblical book of Joshua, we find that this young military leader undergoes many of the same trials as his predecessor. Like Moses, he also parts the waters—this time the Jordan—to help his people cross to freedom. Like Moses, Joshua encounters an angel and removes his shoes to stand on holy ground. Like Moses, Joshua participates in some impressive miracles. Like Moses, Joshua also perseveres through challenges that come when Technicolor miracles disappear.

Although Moses confronts constant questioning of his capabilities, Joshua transitions into Moses's shoes with relative success and encouragement. "No one will stand in your way as long as you live. As I was with Moses, so will I be with you; I will not fail you or forsake you. Be strong and of good courage" (Joshua 1:5–6). The people echo the refrain, "Be strong and of good courage" (Joshua 1:18). Strangely, this chorus of support was never granted to Moses. Why?

It is always easier for a new leader to replace a good leader than a bad one. As daunting as it may seem to fill big shoes, a good leader's replacement does not have to implement change urgently. He or she must instead maintain and sustain a good track record. Bad leaders, however, can create a self-fulfilling expectation of mediocrity that is difficult to break.

In the unique transition of Moses to Joshua, there is another dimension at play. The people finally arrive at the Promised Land. They have waited decades for this moment. Moses pays the price of self-sacrifice, leading the Israelites during some of their darkest hours. Joshua, however, takes responsibility for the Israelites at an apex in their level of satisfaction and the fulfillment of a long yearned-for dream. Think of the difference between a chair of a board who leads a campaign to raise money to construct a new building and oversees its construction and the first board chair who presides when the building is complete. Who struggled more? Who will get more respect?

A PAUSE ON FOLLOWSHIP

Followship plays a key role in good leadership and effective succession planning. As leaders change, expectations often change. The more leaders are tuned into shifts in expectation, the more they will be able to replace themselves or serve as good replacements. There are potentially great leaders born into cynical and hostile generations and mediocre leaders born at the right time and place to bring change. Because so much of good leadership hinges on willing followship, ensuring the success of a new leader is no simple accomplishment. Training may seem almost irrelevant. But it isn't. In order for a leader to be positioned well, he or she must know the constituents and what is expected of them by their constituents.

Someone once explained to me the choice of a poor successor for an institution based on constituent expectations:

> You have to understand that we chose her because our previous president was very strong-willed and opinionated. When we were thinking of the next president, people really wanted a change. They went to the opposite extreme. In our nominating committee meetings, people spoke about the need for a softer, more accommodating approach. In the end, they chose someone who was simply not strong enough. She let other people walk all over her and had little vision for the position. She wanted to make people happy. It's not her fault that she was not successful. We picked her. That's what we wanted at the time. Now, most of us have forgotten that and

just blame her, but if we are being totally honest, it is our fault, just as much if not more than hers.

One of the great dangers of succession planning, as illustrated in this anecdote, is reactionary, rather than objective, selection. We choose, but we lose because we pick someone for what he or she is *not* rather than for what the institution—by the most objective criteria we can muster—needs.

How do we obtain objective or balanced criteria in choosing a successor? Regardless of changing times, two leadership writers presented a study done in the 1980s and again in the 1990s, across multiple continents, of the characteristics most wanted by followers in their leader. In rank order, here are the top ten qualities:

1. Honesty
2. Forward-looking
3. Inspiring
4. Competent
5. Fair-minded
6. Supportive
7. Broad-minded
8. Intelligent
9. Straightforward
10. Dependable[1]

This list may be a helpful template for nominating or hiring committees in prioritizing their needs in a leader.

We may have no trouble writing down our expectations, but how do we measure them? How did the people interviewed in this study gauge, for instance, the honesty of their leaders?

The leader's behavior provided the evidence. In other words, regardless of what leaders say about their own integrity, people wait to be shown; they observe the behavior. Consistency between word and deed is how we judge someone to be honest…. Honesty is also related to values and ethics. We appreciate people who take a stand on important principles…. Confusion over where the leader stands creates stress; not knowing the leader's beliefs contributes to conflict, indecision, and political rivalry. We simply don't trust people who won't tell us their values, ethics and standards.[2]

Nowhere can we see the verity of leaders' words more than in politics. We want to know what a leader stands for and that he or she has kept campaign promises. We do not want to learn after installing someone in office about out-of-office scandals involving finances or relationships. We want transparency. If this is true for politics, it is all the more true for religious or faith-based communities. We expect Jewish communal leaders to model the values their institutions espouse.

Jim Collins observes that great leaders want to be succeeded by people of skill and expertise. "Level-five leaders want to see the company even more successful in the next generation. They are comfortable with the idea that most people won't even know that the roots of that success trace back to their efforts."[3] Such business people are described almost as parents who take pride in seeing their children far exceed their own levels of success. In contrast, Collins had this insight about comparison leaders: "In over three quarters of the comparison companies, we found executives who set their successors up for failure or chose weak successors, or both."[4] It is hard to imagine neglect for the welfare of a company that you may have transformed. It is even harder to imagine a deliberate attempt to see the company fail.

Collins explained it this way: "The comparison leaders, concerned more with their own reputation for personal greatness, often failed to set the company up for success in the next generation. After all, what better testament to your own personal greatness than that the place falls apart after you leave?"[5] Assuming that more often it is benign neglect than deliberate malice that hurts institutions, why do some great leaders fail their institutions when it comes to choosing a successor?

It seems that the greatness in which many leaders are interested is primarily their own. CEOs switch companies, political agendas change, and institutions suffer. Talented leaders cover themselves by worrying about their own personal futures, sometimes at the expense of the larger picture. Collins calls this the "liability of charisma," an expression worth consideration. Charisma, a quality we typically associate with strong leadership, can often serve us quite badly. People may defer their opinions in the face of the charismatic leader and minimize their autonomy or creativity; they may give that leader more trust than he or she deserves. They may mistakenly assume that charisma means competence. Great leaders—and not merely good ones—put an institution in the spotlight, not themselves.

The biblical figure who most embodies this quality of compelling modesty is Moses himself. In Numbers 12:3 we learn that "Moses was a very humble man, more so than any other man on earth." The description appears in a most unusual context. Moses comes under criticism from his brother, Aaron, and his sister, Miriam. They speak badly of him, but because of his humility, he does not respond. God comes to Moses's defense and puts the siblings in their rightful place. Moses, however, always puts the "company" first and himself far behind.

Today's media culture so often values the person above the idea, what is often called "the cult of personality." Great leaders appreciate that ideas, institutions, and others come first. A commitment to putting ideas center stage, rather than putting leaders at the center, is the best way to ensure a long and healthy future, especially once a particular leader has departed.

A BIBLICAL STORY OF SUCCESSION

One of the Bible's most touching scenes of parting occurs not between parent and child or husband and wife, but between mentor and disciple. In the second chapter of 2 Kings, a great leader leaves this earth, his destination unknown. Elijah ascends heaven-bound in a fiery chariot and leaves poor Elisha, his devoted novice, in a stupor. Elisha knows that Elijah's time has come, but this knowledge does not ease the pain of Elijah's departure; it merely enlarges the vacuum that Elisha feels.

Elijah is a towering prophet who boldly challenges idol worshipers and the indolence and insolence of his own people. He is a zealous prophet who embodies one scholarly summation of the prophetic path:

> The prophet hates the approximate, he shuns the middle of the road. Man must live on the summit to avoid the abyss. There is nothing to hold to except God. Carried away by the challenge, the demand to straighten out man's ways, the prophet is strange, one-sided, an unbearable extremist.[6]

This apt description could have been written with Elijah in mind. For prophets, the intense sense of knowing what the future holds is co-mingled with being almost powerless to prepare people adequately for it. The prophet is exquisitely sensitive to injustice and pained by his own inadequacy and that of others. How can Elijah possibly mentor someone to have these subtle and elusive abilities?

Nevertheless, Elisha does learn the prophet's ways and is receptive to Elijah's mentoring. When the critical moment comes for Elijah to be released from the duties of this world, Elijah is ready. Elisha is not. We open 2 Kings chapter 2 as Elijah makes his last round of visits, traveling his old haunts presumably to say his farewells. Elijah asks to be alone on his last day but his novice, Elisha, knows that separation looms on the horizon and prevails upon his master to be allowed to accompany him. This chapter of 2 Kings shows us the emotional interiority of a leader in waiting and also provides some of the key ingredients to a good transition. Elijah knows that he will be taken away in a whirlwind. A whirlwind signifies a dramatic departure from this world. In our minds, it spells chaos and possible destruction. It is quick; it is all-encompassing, and then it is gone. Elijah's departure contains all of these elements.

As their shared time together grows shorter, Elijah asks Elisha what he can give him before he departs from this world. With his very last breath, the leader understands that he has to impart some wisdom to his successor. World leaders today often have several hours of privacy with a successor at a moment of transition to cement a bond and pass on wisdom. This is an important practice, and it is wise to institute it formally.

Elisha boldly asks for two measures of wisdom to match his master's. Elijah sagaciously tells him that he cannot grant wisdom. Wisdom is often a function of hindsight. Elijah tells his disciple that if Elisha is able to see Elijah depart, then the wisdom he asks for will be granted. On a symbolic level, the leader tells his successor that the knowledge required for the job is only truly apparent when the successor takes on the responsibilities himself. Elisha is granted that wisdom.

When Elijah finally goes up, Elisha cries out, "Father, father, chariots of Israel ..." (2 Kings 2:12) as the conversation trails off into the whirlwind's empty vacuum. The sentence remains unfinished, as unfinished as a conversation between two friends that is suddenly interrupted. There are commentators who try to complete the sentence or make sense of it. Elisha's comments on the chariot reflect his last observation of Elijah and show God that he really did see his master being taken up on high. But the unfinished nature of the statement is more poignant. It demonstrates how death, as prepared as we think we are for it, always catches us unaware. Elisha is suddenly startled by the absence of the figure who had taken the place of his parent, as he calls out, "Father, father ..."

As his last literal and symbolic gesture, Elijah throws down his mantle, a cloak. The cloak in the Bible has other symbolic meanings. In Ezekiel chapter 16 and Ruth chapter 3, the cloak spread out over another person is a sign of marriage. Here, the cloak that Elisha picks up after the clouds ascend represents another type of partnership, one that, at times, resembles the intimacy and the challenges of marriage: leadership. The master endows his disciple with his own responsibilities. Elijah covers Elisha with his wisdom, his love, his nurturing, and his hopes. The moment of transition finally occurs.

Elisha has only a piece of his teacher in his hands with which to begin his leadership. He picks up Elijah's mantle and stands on the banks of the Jordan. Taking the mantle that had dropped from Elijah, he strikes the water and says, "Where is the LORD, the God of Elijah?" (2 Kings 2:14). As he strikes the water, it parts to the right and to the left, and Elisha crosses over. When the disciples of the prophets at Jericho see him from a distance, they exclaim, "The spirit of Elijah has settled on Elisha!" (2 Kings 2:15). They run to meet him and bow low before him.

SUCCESSFUL TRANSITIONS

All emerging leaders—green with the newness of the position and not quite large enough to shoulder a new mantle—know that the ceremonies of installation and inauguration are short-lived. The work of leadership will be the real test of acceptance. As our chapter on Elisha proceeds, the other prophets do not understand where Elijah went in his whirlwind. They begin a three-day, futile search for him. Unlike Elisha, they do not see the master depart; their prophetic insight is limited. They try to find the old leader. Elisha warns them not to go. In this interaction, we find a common ingredient in transition: the unwillingness to let go of the past leader. Elisha responds to this challenge the only way that a new leader can respond—through action. Before the chapter ends, Elisha goes into a town where the water is bad and the land infertile. The people of the town beg for help, and Elisha releases a blocked spring. Elisha becomes a leader by leading.

This biblical chapter of transition does not end here. As he makes his way back to Bethel, Elisha is confronted by some little boys who jeer at him. This small and insignificant interchange is only the beginning of many where the prophet is misunderstood or taunted. Such is leadership.

This chapter shows several tests of transition and maturation: Elisha loses Elijah; he proves himself to competitors and establishes his credibility to those who do not know him. Each of these weighty scenes involves distress. Returning to *Leadership on the Line: Staying Alive through the Dangers of Leading*, we read:

> The most difficult work of leadership involves learning to experience distress without numbing yourself. The virtue of a sacred heart lies in the courage to maintain your innocence and wonder, your doubt and curiosity, and your compassion and love through your darkest, most difficult moments. Leading with an open heart means you could be at your lowest point, abandoned by your people and entirely powerless, yet remain receptive to the full range of human emotions without going numb, striking back, or engaging in some other defense.... A sacred heart allows you to feel, hear, and diagnose, even in the midst of your mission, so that you accurately gauge different situations and respond appropriately.... Without keeping your heart open, it becomes difficult, perhaps impossible, to fashion the right response and to succeed or come out whole.[7]

As a prophet, Elisha had a sacred heart. Heifetz and Linsky remind us that each of us has within us a sacred heart that grows and expands through the trials of our leadership. These include our most difficult and lonely hours. They prepare us to understand the darkest hours of those we serve. Nowhere is this full range of leadership emotions experienced more than in the hours of transition. Followers need to let go of past leaders, put faith in new leaders who are untested, and wait in the murky waters of doubt until the transition is complete. New leaders need to part with their mentors on some level, understand the insecurity of their followership, and demonstrate through action that they are worthy.

Nonprofit institutions need to make succession planning one of their top priorities so that the stewardship of their organization will always be in secure and capable hands. It is hard to let go of leaders. Faith in the next candidate notwithstanding, we form deep attachments to current leaders. Even when our leaders are overpowering, overbearing, or difficult, we might find it hard to transition to leadership that holds promise but is ultimately unfamiliar. The leader's old ways may not have been likeable, but we develop coping mechanisms and strategies for dealing with them. In the absence of that familiarity, a new leader signals a change for us all. Departing leaders should try to impart their wisdom and support to their successors. Successful transition begins with Elisha's request for two measures of wisdom. One measure is for a followship that is patient and responsive. The other is for good judgment so that emerging leaders can cross the river of maturity and usher followers to secure ground.

APPENDIX 1

Twenty-five Questions a Jewish Leader Should Ask

1. Define leadership using three adjectives. Now use three verbs.

2. When you think of a great leader, do you think of a person from the world of history, religion, intellectual life, politics, or family? Explain your answer.

3. Name a great Jewish leader and the source of his or her greatness.

4. What makes your leadership style distinctly Jewish?

5. Name the boards you have served on and in what capacity.

6. Now think of one particular board. Why did you join?

7. Did you find your role meaningful? If so, how? If not, why not?

8. If you were president of your board, what changes would you make to the way your board is run?

9. Can you identify a moment when you were "called" to leadership either through an inner, instinctive voice or through the suggestion of another? Describe that moment in a few sentences.

10. What inspires you to lead? What are the ingredients of inspiration?

11. What cause or organization inspires you? How did they contact you, or how did you find them?

12. Have you passed on your feelings of inspiration to anyone else? If so, how? In what other ways can you communicate those feelings?

13. How would you define emotional intelligence? How would you tie that definition into leadership?

14. Describe a board meeting that required a high level of personal maturity on your part and why.

15. Do the Jewish laws related to slander and gossip—*lashon ha-ra*—influence your personal/professional/volunteer involvements?

16. Describe an organizational situation that you believe could have benefited from better ethical governance.

17. Do you handle conflict best in a personal, professional, or volunteer setting? Explain.

18. Do you have a strategy for dealing with complaints? Can you describe it?

19. Do you think it is acceptable for a leader to complain publicly about his or her constituency? Do you find yourself doing this?

20. Describe a recent change in your life and how you responded to it.

21. Paint a picture in words of a final parting with a person who influenced you as a leader.

22. Create an imaginary "leadership will" to pass on to a fictitious "disciple" of yours.

23. How do you cultivate the support of others in a time of leadership crisis?

24. Can you identify a quote that inspires your leadership?

25. What about Jewish leadership brings you joy?

APPENDIX 2

Leadership Exercises

The following exercises can be done individually or in a board setting, alone or to accompany a chapter. They are best done in writing and followed by discussion so that each participant has
sufficient private, reflective time to think through their answers.

EXERCISE 1: THE LEADER AS SHEPHERD

1. Psalm 23, perhaps the most famous psalm, tells us, "The LORD is my
   shepherd." God creates the primary model of leadership. Name as
   many biblical shepherds as you can.

2. Although we have already mentioned a few, think of reasons that
   biblical leadership is so strongly associated with shepherding.

3. King Saul was also a shepherd, but unlike his successor, he shep-
   herded donkeys. What is the leadership metaphor in the change of
   animal?

Exercise 2: Leadership Heroes

Using the "great men" theory of leadership, name and describe a man or woman who represents a pinnacle of leadership. Name five qualities of this person that contribute to his or her leadership influence.

What could you teach people about leadership from using this leadership model? What are the limitations of such a study?

Exercise 3: Identifying Leadership Issues

1. If you could pick one topic of leadership that you feel your board should be discussing right now, what would it be?

2. What resources would you use to present it at a board meeting? Can you suggest a creative way to communicate the subject?

3. What is preventing you from presenting a leadership challenge at your next meeting, and what could you do to overcome those challenges?

Exercise 4: Leadership Influences

1. Define the following three terms (without using any of them in your definitions), and describe how they influence leadership:

   • Power
   • Authority
   • Influence

2. Define the following three terms (without using any of them in your definitions), and describe how they influence leadership:

   • Humility
   • Modesty
   • Empathy

EXERCISE 5: EXPANDING YOUR LEADERSHIP

Imagine the name of your institution and your name beneath it in a small circle. If it helps, draw a circle on a piece of paper. Now imagine or draw a larger circle that encompasses the smaller circle. Put your name in the larger circle and think of a related institution that services more people than your current institution. Draw another, larger circle, and put your name there. What role could you serve within each institution?

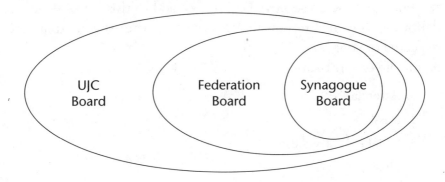

EXERCISE 6: OUR JEWISH JOURNEYS

1. On a separate sheet of paper, draw a timeline like the one you see below. Mark this timeline with important dates and/or moments or events that chart your Jewish journey. Circle the events that were central or transformational.

2. Use this exercise as a trigger to write a paragraph that explains how Judaism influences your life today.

My Jewish journey began ...

EXERCISE 7: IDENTIFYING BOARD RESPONSIBILITIES

Please take a few minutes to think about the following list. For example, if you know the expected attendance of your board is once or twice a month, or you can state your institution's mission in a few sentences, please do so now. Feel free to add to this list of seven or delineate specific responsibilities within the seven that are expected of your board.

Name of your institution:

1. Attendance
2. Mission
3. Chief executive/leadership
4. Finances
5. Program oversight
6. Fundraising
7. Board effectiveness

EXERCISE 8: EXPLAIN AND CLARIFY

Describe your role as an "interpreter to the community" of your organization. Explain your organization in a few sentences.

EXERCISE 9: CRAFTING A MISSION STATEMENT

1. Compose a comprehensive list of nouns, verbs, and adjectives to be shared with the group on individual sheets of paper. Ask people to

circle three words in each list that they think best describes your institution. For example:

- Nouns: education, justice, compassion
- Verbs: engage, care, support
- Adjectives: responsibly, honestly, warmly

2. With this list, ask each person to write down in a hundred words or less, what your institution does—highlighting descriptions that are unique to your institution. You may want to provide examples of mission statements to illustrate. When finished, share the mission statements that people came up with, trying to get people to be expressive but also brief. To pare this down even more, ask people to fill in the blanks:

Our mission is to _____ _____ to, for or with _____.
                 (Verb)   (Noun)   (Adverb)

Your sentence may need filling out to make grammatical sense.

EXERCISE 10: INSPIRED FUNDRAISING AND FRIEND RAISING

1. What is the most money you ever raised and how did you do it?
2. What feelings come to mind before you make a solicitation?
3. How would you approach a friend to ask for money?
4. How can you cultivate a friend when you are asking for funds?

EXERCISE 11: A SOLICITATION STORY

Take a moving experience related to the work your institution does and craft a solicitation story around that experience.

EXERCISE 12: A MOMENT ON MENTORING

Draw two large boxes on a separate piece of paper. In the first box, identify a person who mentored you and the qualities that he or she possessed that pushed you forward. In the second box, describe a person *you* mentored. If you cannot fill in either box, it's time to rethink the role of mentoring in your leadership.

Person who mentored me:

Person I mentored:

EXERCISE 13: A VISION OF LEADERSHIP

1. Describe your nonprofit institution the way an outsider might *see* it.

2. What aspects of your nonprofit institution would you like to *look away* from?

3. How do you *see* yourself responding to what you *see*?

EXERCISE 14: RECRUITMENT

1. Identify three people—either currently affiliated with your organization or not—who are not currently serving in positions of leadership but have leadership potential.

2. How could you inspire them to take on a position of leadership?

3. Can you identify gifted young people who might serve in your communal organization or agency in the future? Name them and consider how you can get them involved.

EXERCISE 15: THE MORAL COMPASS

People, unlike organizations, have so many diverse interests that a mission statement is usually not appropriate to guide our personal work. Instead, a vision statement can help us imagine future achievements without creating limitations. Steven Covey, in *Principle-Centered Leadership*, writes, "In today's world, what is needed is a compass.... The word compass may refer to the reach, extent, limit, or boundary of a space or time.... The compass provides more vision and direction.... [The] compass is a leadership and empowerment tool."[1] **A vision statement is a compass that shows you the direction you need to go while allowing you freedom of exploration.** To help you formulate a vision statement, draw and fill in the quadrants of the compass below, which assert aspects of your personal values, history, and goals:

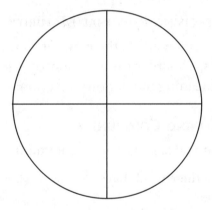

First quadrant: Your English and Hebrew name and history of the names (if known).
Second quadrant: Most important charity or cause of choice (limited to one). Explain your choice in no more than one sentence.

Third quadrant: One professional aspiration in no more than one sentence.

Fourth quadrant: One personal aspiration (choose just one) in no more than one sentence.

Using this compass, write a personal vision statement. A vision statement is as much about dreams and imagination as it is about reality. In a vision statement, we try to create a lofty set of personal objectives. This statement should be no more than a paragraph long and can relate to the specific work you do for a nonprofit organization or can encompass a broad picture of how your personal values are enmeshed with your actions in a general way. You might begin this exercise with the following words:

My life vision is to ...

EXERCISE 16: EXERCISING PERSONAL MATURITY

Think of a dramatic moment in the news, at work, or in your volunteer commitments. Describe the reaction of a leader that helped structure or give meaning to your own reaction:

EXERCISE 17: DEFINING COMMUNITY

List ten words that you associate with community.

1. How many of these words have to do with obligation or responsibility?

2. How many have to do with comfort or support?

3. How many require face-to-face contact?

4. How many require giving rather than taking?

5. Which of these words would you most associate with the Jewish community?

EXERCISE 18: MEETING PROTOCOLS

Devise a list of three to five speech-related protocols that would help your board meetings or leadership interactions run more smoothly. These might relate to the content of speech or method (e.g., interruptions, calling out of turn).

Feel free to use this exercise with your board so that you come up with a mutually agreed-upon list of protocols. Write these out on poster board, and bring them to subsequent meetings so that you can safely remind people who step out of line that you agreed to some speech-related principles as a group.

EXERCISE 19: ETHICAL GOVERNANCE

1. List the name of a person you would turn to in your nonprofit if a serious breach of ethics occurred.

2. Think of a scandal that happened to *another* Jewish institution. How would your institution handle it? If you had been in a position of authority then, how would you have handled it?

EXERCISE 20: ORCHESTRATING CONFLICT

1. On a separate sheet of paper, use one conflict and its resolution to chart your feelings.

Conflict	Your Feelings	Resolution	Your Feelings

2. Describe another conflict (professional or volunteer) that potentially jeopardized your position or someone else's in an organization. Describe its resolution and your feelings.

EXERCISE 21: BOARDROOM BLUES

Draw the boardroom oval and parking lot diagram below on a separate piece of paper. In the oval, write down the main issues of a recent board meeting. In the parking lot drawing, use the spaces to lay out the "real" agenda and jot down some notes. What would happen if you brought the issues in the parking lot—the elephants in the room—to the boardroom table?

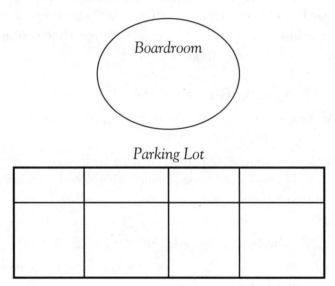

Boardroom

Parking Lot

EXERCISE 22: CONFLICTED EMOTIONS

1. Consider your own flights into the "wilderness," places of the unknown. Describe the feeling of being lost. Whom did you blame? How did you find your way?

2. Describe a moment of alienation, frustration, or loneliness that you experienced as a leader by listing five *adjectives* that expressed your feelings:

3. Now use five *verbs* that helped you get out of that state of alienation or frustration:

EXERCISE 23: FACING CHANGE

1. Write down a significant change that your organization recently underwent or is currently undergoing. Mention in bullet points a few stresses involved in that change.

2. Name a leader who you feel handles or handled change effectively. What works?

3. Do you manage change better in your personal life, your professional life, or your volunteer commitments? Which is most stressful?

EXERCISE 24: JEWISH CHANGE

Draw the circles below on a separate piece of paper. Fill in the circles with acts that you do that represent each of these categories. Use the overlapping spaces between the circles for acts that may be viewed as a bridge between two Jewish values.

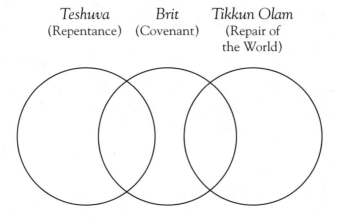

Teshuva   *Brit*   *Tikkun Olam*
(Repentance) (Covenant) (Repair of the World)

EXERCISE 25: THE NEXT LEADER

1. Briefly note your thoughts on the latest leadership transition your nonprofit institution experienced. How did it go? What were some of the challenges? What was your role in this transition, if you had one?

2. Name five qualities that you look for in the leader of your non-profit, and rank their importance, with 1 being least important and 5 being most.

3. Now let's backtrack. Think of your current leaders and grade from 1 to 5 (with 5 being the highest) for each trait. Are they living up to your expectations?

NOTES

INTRODUCTION: LEADING AND MEANING

1. Reprinted in an article by diplomatic editor of *Ha'aretz*, Aluf Benn, "Israel's Gloomy Winter," *World Jewish Digest*, January 2007, 9. Benn cites Grossman to support findings in Israeli polls that found close to 60 percent of the country fearful of Israel's future and insecure about its national leadership.

2. "America's Best Leaders," in *U.S. News and World Report*, November 19, 2007, 42.

3. Ibid.

4. Jonathan Sacks, "Covenant and Conversation," *Beha'alotkha*, summer 2007.

5. Ibid.

6. James Hanley, *A Walk in the Wilderness* (London: Phoenix House, 1950), p. 46.

7. *Batei Midrashot* 234.

8. Numbers Rabbah 21:14, and see *Lekach Tov* on Numbers 11:28 on the importance of Joshua's service.

9. Eleanor Roosevelt, *The Autobiography of Eleanor Roosevelt* (Cambridge: Da Capo Press, 1992) p. 159.

10. James Botkin, Mahdi Elmandjra, and Mirca Malitza, "No Limits to Learning: Bridging the Human Gap," as seen in Warren Bennis, *On Becoming a Leader* (New York: Addison-Wesley Publishing, 1989), p. 74.

11. Moshe Chayim Luzzato, *The Path of the Just*, trans. Shraga Silverstein (New York: Feldheim Publishers, 1966), p. 4.

1. GUILT AND PLEASURE: PUTTING THE *JEWISH* IN JEWISH LEADERSHIP

1. Ruth Andrew Ellenson, *The Modern Jewish Girl's Guide to Guilt* (New York: Plume, 2005), p. 1.

2. Susan Scott, *Fierce Conversations* (New York: Berkley Books, 2002), p. 126.

3. Maimonides, *Mishneh Torah*, "The Book of Judges," 2:6.

4. Ibid., 2:7.

5. Shankar Vedantam, "Why Everyone You Know Thinks the Same as You," *Washington Post*, October 16, 2006, A2.

6. Jim Collins, *Good to Great and the Social Sectors* (New York: HarperCollins, 2005), p. 5.

7. As told in Gordon Zacks, *Defining Moments: Stories of Character, Courage and Leadership* (New York: Beaufort Books, 2006), pp. 38–39.

2. DEFINING LEADERSHIP

1. Marshall Loeb and Stephen Kindel, *Leadership for Dummies* (New York: Wiley Publishing, 1999), p. 9.

2. Jacob Ukeles, "American Jewish Leadership: A Study," American Jewish Committee, Institute of Human Relations (1991), p. v.

3. Steven R. Covey, *Principle-Centered Leadership* (New York: Simon and Schuster, 1991), p. 101.

4. Ibid, p.101.

5. Howard Gardner, *Leading Minds* (New York: Basic Books, 1995), particularly his conclusions, pp. 243–67.

6. Warren Bennis, *On Becoming a Leader* (New York: Addison-Wesley Publishing, 1989), pp. 13–37.

7. Robert Goffee and Gareth Jones, "Leadership: A Small History of a Big Topic," *Harvard Business Review*, September–October 2000, p. 21.

8. Jim Collins, *Good to Great*, p. 31.

9. Larry C. Spears, "Tracing the Growing Impact of Servant-Leadership," in *Insights on Leadership: Service, Stewardship, Spirit and Servant-Leadership*, ed. Larry C. Spears (New York: John Wiley and Sons, 1998), pp. 2–3.

10. Robert K. Greenleaf, *The Servant as Leader* (Indianapolis: Robert Greenleaf Center, 1970), p. 7.

11. Spears, "Tracing the Growing Impact," pp. 4–6.

12. As cited in ibid., p. 3.

3. WHO ARE WE LEADING? AGE, ETHNICITY, AND COMMUNITY

1. For a list of such ideas, see W. B. Gallie, "Essentially Contested Concepts," in *Proceedings of the Aristotelian Society*, 1955.

2. Joel Westheimer, *Among School Teachers: Community, Autonomy and Ideology in Teachers' Work* (New York: Teachers College Press, 1998).

3. Andrew Mason, *Community, Solidarity and Belonging: Levels of Community and Their Normative Significance* (Cambridge: Cambridge University Press).

4. Roberta Rosenberg Farber and Chaim Waxman, "Post-modernity and the Jews: Identity, Identification and Community," in *Jews in America: A Contemporary Reader*, eds. Roberta Rosenberg Farber and Chaim Waxman (Hanover, NH: Brandeis University Press, 1999), p. 398.

5. Steven M. Cohen and Arnold M. Eisen, *The Jew Within: Self, Family and Community in America* (Bloomington: Indiana University Press, 2000). For more on the sovereign self, see the chapter by that name, pp. 13–42 and their conclusions, pp. 182–207.

6. Farber and Waxman, "Post-modernity and the Jews," p. 402.

7. Sylvia Barack Fishman, *Jewish Life and American Culture* (New York: State University of New York Press, 2000), p. 153.

8. Steven Mark Dobbs, Gary Tobin, and Zev Hymowitz, "Selected Excerpts from Listening to the Twenty Something Generation," in *The Development of Professional Leadership in the Jewish Community* (San Francisco: Institute for Jewish and Community Research, 2004).

9. Anna Greenberg, "OMG! How Generation Y Is Redefining Faith in the iPod Era" (New York: Reboot Foundation, 2005) pp. 9–10.

10. Tobin Belzer, "What Do They Want? Synagogues That Speak the Language of Today's Youth," *World Jewish Digest*, November 2006, pp. 23–24.

11. Ibid., p. 25.

12. See P. Taylor and C. Kennedy, *Baby Boomers Approach Age 60: From the Age of Aquarius to the Age of Responsibility* (Washington, DC: Pew Research Center, 2005).

13. United Jewish Communities, *20/20 Vision: Forecasting the Impact of the Baby Boomers on the Jewish Federation System* (2006).

4. VISION AND MENTORING

1. This chapter is based on material from an essay published by the Wexner Heritage Foundation, Leadership Library series, "Samuel and the Call to Leadership," by Erica Brown, vol. 2, no. 2 (April 2000).

2. In Christian scholarship, the term "vocation" is often employed to mean "the call." For more on the Christian view and the use of the call in New Testament texts, see the *Encyclopedia of Religion and Ethics*, ed. James Hastings (New York: Charles Scribner and Sons,1928), pp. 145–46.

3. William James offers an in-depth analysis of the mindset of vocation in *The Varieties of Religious Experience* (New York: New American Library,1958). James describes this process in slightly different terms; he uses the word "conversion," not "calling," to refer to a transformation that takes place in an individual when "religious ideas, previously peripheral in his [or her] consciousness, now take a central place" (p. 162). This process could refer to a host of different religious experiences and helps us better understand the psychology of the divine call.

4. *The Encyclopedia of Religion*, ed. Mircea Eliade (New York: MacMillan, 1987), vol. 15, p. 294.

5. Elizabeth Jeffries, "Work as Calling," in *Insights on Leadership: Service, Spirit and Servant-Leadership*, ed. Larry C. Spears (New York: John Wiley and Sons, 1998), p. 34.

6. See Babylonian Talmud, *Kiddushin* 72b.

7. John W. Gardner, *On Leadership* (New York: Free Press, 1990), pp. 169–70.

8. Chip R. Bell, "Mentoring as Partnership," in *Coaching for Leadership*, eds. Marshall Goldsmith, Laurence Lyons, and Alyssa Freas (San Francisco: Jossey-Bass, 2000), p. 133.

9. Ibid., p. 169.

10. Laurent A. Daloz, *Mentor: Guiding the Journey of Adult Learners* (San Francisco: Jossey-Bass, 1999).

11. Richard Solomon, Neil Davidson, and Elaine Solomon, *Mentoring Teachers in a Professional Learning Community* (Columbia, MD: National Institute for Relationship Training, 2003), p 5.

12. Abraham Joshua Heschel, *The Prophets* (New York: Harper and Row, 1962), p. 16.

13. Ibid., p. 22.

14. John Kotter, "Leading Change: Why Transformation Efforts Fail," *Harvard Business Review*, March–April 1995, p. 63.

15. Ronald Heifetz, *Leadership without Easy Answers* (Cambridge: Harvard University Press, 1994), p. 2.

5. AUTHENTIC LEADERSHIP

1. See Eli Ashkenazi, "Kibbutz to Open Golda Meir's First Home in Israel to Public," *Ha'aretz*, November 29, 2006.

2. William George, *Authentic Leadership* (San Francisco: Jossey-Bass, 2003), p. 12.

3. John Gardner, *Self-Renewal* (New York: Harper Colophon Books, 1964), p. 13.

4. Martin Buber, *The Way of Man: According to the Teaching of Hasidism* (Secaucus, NJ: Citadel Press, 1966), p. 23.

5. Ibid., p. 27.

6. Ibid., p. 28.

7. Ibid., p. 81.

8. William James, *Letters*, ed. T. Flairnoy (Madison, WI: The University of Wisconsin Press, 1966), p. 199.

6. THE OPTIMISTIC LEADER

1. Richard Boyatzis, *Resonant Leadership* (Boston: Harvard Business School Press, 2005), p. 9.

2. Stephen R. Covey, *Principle-Centered Leadership* (New York: Free Press, 2003), p. 34–35.

7. LEADING FOR TRANSFORMATION

1. Harris Collingwood, "Personal Histories: Leaders Remember the Moments and People That Shaped Them," in *Breakthrough Leadership* (Boston: Harvard Business School Press, 2001), p. 23.

2. John Kotter, "What Leaders Really Do," in *What Leaders Really Do* (Boston: Harvard Business Review, 1999), p. 54.

3. John Kotter, *The Heart of Change* (Boston: Harvard Business School Press, 2002), p. 1.

4. Daniel Goleman, Richard Boyatzis, and Annie McKee, *Primal Leadership: Learning to Lead with Emotional Intelligence* (Boston: Harvard Business School Press, 2004), p. 3.

5. Ibid., pp. 8–9. Goleman draws attention to a study, "Emotional Intensity in Groups," a dissertation by Anthony T. Pescosolido submitted to Case Western Reserve University in 2000, and to Howard Gardner, *Leading Minds: An Anatomy of Leadership* (New York: Basic Books, 1995).

6. Barbara Kellerman, *Bad Leadership* (Boston: Harvard Leadership Series, 2004). See also Jean Lipman-Blumen, *The Allure of Toxic Leaders* (Oxford: Oxford University Press, 2004).

7. Goleman, Boyatzis, and McKee, *Primal Leadership*, p. 92.

8. Ibid., p. 94.

9. Ibid., p. 96.

10. Quoted in David Aberbach, *Bialik* (New York: Grove Press, 1988).

8. Nurturing Women's Leadership

1. B. Horowitz, P. Beck, and C. Kadushin, *The Roles of Women and Men on Boards of Major American Jewish Organization: A Research Report* (New York: Center for Social Research and Center for Jewish Studies of the Graduate School and University Center, City University of New York, 1997).

2. See J. Schor and S. Cohen, *Centering on Professionals: The 2001 Study of JCC Personnel in North America* (New York: JCC Association, 2002).

3. S. Cohen, *Gender-Related Distribution of Federation Professional Positions in 2004* (New York: United Jewish Communities and Advancing Women Professionals and the Jewish Community, 2004).

4. Ibid., p. 4.

5. S. Cohen. S. Bronznick, D. Goldenhar, S. Israel, and S. Kelner, *Creating Gender Equity and Organizational Effectiveness in the Jewish Federation System: A Research-and-Action Project* (New York: Advancing Women Professionals and the Jewish Community, 2004), p. 2.

6. Ibid., 6.

7. Paulette Gerkovich, Catalyst, *Women in Corporate US Leadership: 2003* (New York: 2003), sponsored by General Motors Corporation.

8. Quoted in Rahel Musleah, "The Power of One," *Jewish Woman*, Winter, 2006, p. 23.

9. Ibid., p. 22.

10. Ibid.

9. JEWISH LEADERSHIP AND CONFLICT RESOLUTION

1. Leslie Wexner, "An Interview with Our Chairman," *The Leader* (Wexner Heritage Foundation) 3, no. 1 (Winter 2002): 3.

2. Erich Fromm, *You Shall Be Gods* (Greenwich, CT: Fawcett, 1966), p. 23.

3. Anson Laytner, *Arguing with God: A Jewish Tradition* (Northvale, NJ: Jason Aaronson, 1990), p. xv.

4. Ronald Heifetz and Marty Linsky, *Leadership on the Line* (Boston: Harvard Business School Press, 2002), pp. 107–108.

5. Peter M. Senge, "The Leader's New Work: Building Learning Organizations," *Sloane Management Review* 32, no. 1 (Fall 1990): 14.

6. Heifetz and Linsky, *Leadership on the Line*, p. 111.

7. Nahum Sarna, *JPS Commentary to Exodus* (Philadelphia: Jewish Publication Society, 1991), p. 83.

8. Aaron Wildavsky, *The Nursing Father: Moses as a Political Leader* (Tuscaloosa: University of Alabama Press, 1984), p. 125.

9. Nahmanides on Numbers 11:1.

10. ETHICAL LEADERSHIP

1. Abraham Isaac Ha-Cohen Kook, *Orot Ha-Torah* (Jerusalem: Mossad Ha-Rav Kook, 1961), pp. 69–71.

2. Jonathan Sacks, *To Heal a Fractured World* (New York: Schocken, 2005), p. 246.

3. Joseph Telushkin, *Words That Hurt, Words That Heal* (New York: William Morrow, 1996), p. 34.

4. Walter Wurzberger, *Ethics of Responsibility* (Philadelphia: Jewish Publication Society, 1994), p. 113.

5. In Dean Pielstick, "A Model of the Process of Authentic Leading," *Executive Search Consultants for the Nonprofit Sector*, October 2006, p. 2.

6. Ibid., p. 7.

7. James O'Toole, *Leading Change* (San Francisco: Jossey-Bass, 1995), p. 35.

8. Ibid.

9. Maimonides, *Mishneh Torah*, "Laws of the Foundations of the Torah," 7:6.

10. Fireside chat on economic conditions (Washington, DC, April 14, 1938).

11. O'Toole, *Leading Change*, p. 35.

12. Maimonides, *Mishneh Torah*, "Laws of Repentance," 3:10.

13. Ibid., p. 34.

14. Samson Raphael Hirsch, *The Pentateuch: Translation and Commentary*, trans. Isaac Levy (Gateshead, England: Judaic Press, 1976), p. 236.

15. Ibid.

16. Ibid., p. 237.

17. Ibid.

18. Larry Bossidy and Ram Charan, *Execution: The Discipline of Getting Things Done* (New York: Crown Business, 2002), pp. 105–106.

11. CHANGING THE WORLD, CHANGING OURSELVES: A CRASH COURSE ON CHANGE MANAGEMENT

1. Menachem Creidtor, "Let Us Hear," *Sh'ma*, June 2006, p. 16.

2. Barry Dym, "Resistance in Organizations: How to Recognize, Understand and Respond to It," *O.D. Practitioner* 31, no. 1 (1999), p. 6.

3. Bennis, *On Becoming a Leader*, p. 145.

4. Robert Kegan and Lisa Laskow Lahey, *The Real Reason People Won't Change*, (Cambridge: Harvard Business School Publishing Corporation, 2002 HBR OnPoint, 2002), product no. 8121.

5. Ibid.

6. Todd D. Jick, "Vision is 10%, Implementation the Rest," *Business Strategy Review* (London Business School) 12, no. 4:36.

7. Ibid.

8. Larry Moses, "Innovators as Change Agents," *Sh'ma*, June 2006, p. 1.

9. Warren Bennis and Robert Townsend, *Reinventing Leadership* (New York: William Morrow and Company, 1995), pp. 24–25.

10. Jonathan Sacks, *Celebrating Life* (London: Continuum, 2000), p. 182.

11. John Kotter, *The Heart of Change: Real-Life Stories of How People Change Their Organizations* (Boston: Harvard Business School Press, 2002), p. 1.

12. Ibid., p. 2.

13. Margaret J. Wheatley, *Leadership and the New Science: Discovering Order in a Chaotic World* (San Francisco: Berret-Koehler Publishers, 1999), p. 148.

14. Ibid., p. 149.

15. Heifetz and Linsky, *Leadership on the Line*, p. 14.

16. Ibid.

17. Peter F. Drucker, *The Five Most Important Questions You Will Ever Ask about Your Non-Profit Organization* (San Francisco: Jossey-Bass, 1993), participant's workbook, p. 39.

18. Ibid., p. 12.

19. Hannah Arendt, *The Human Condition* (Chicago: University of Chicago Press, 1958), p. 237.

20. Johann Christian Arnold, *Why Forgive?* (Rifton, NY: Plough Publishing House, 2000), p. 1.

21. David Shatz, Chaim I. Waxman, and Nathan J. Diament, "Introduction," in *Tikkun Olam: Social Responsibility in Jewish Thought and Law* (Northvale, NJ: Jason Aronson, 1997), p. 1.

22. Abraham Isaac Ha-Cohen Kook, *Orot Ha-Torah*, p. 149, *Orot Ha-Kodesh* (Jerusalem: Mossad HaRav Kook, 1961), vol. 2, p. 444.

12. CREATING MEANINGFUL BOARD SERVICE

1. Samson Raphael Hirsch, *Chapters of the Fathers*, trans. and commentary by Samson Raphael Hirsch (Jerusalem: Feldheim Publishers, 1979), p. 87.

2. If you or someone you know is struggling with a new promotion, you may find help in Edward Betof and Frederic Harwood's *Just Promoted: How to Survive in Your First 12 Months as a Manager* (New York: McGraw-Hill, 1992).

3. Richard P. Chait, Thomas P. Holland, and Barbara E. Taylor, *The Effective Board of Trustees* (Phoenix: Oryx Press, 1993).

4. Gerald B. Bubis, *The Director Had a Heart Attack and the President Resigned: Board-Staff Relations for the 21st Century* (Jerusalem: Jerusalem Center for Public Affairs, 1999), p. 21.

5. Malcolm Gladwell, *The Tipping Point* (Boston: Little, Brown and Co., 2002).

6. Fisher Howe, *Welcome to the Board: Your Guide to Effective Participation for All Non-Profit Trustees* (San Francisco: Jossey-Bass, 1995), p. 24.

7. Fisher Howe, *The Board Member's Guide to Fund-Raising* (San Francisco: Jossey-Bass, 1991), p. xv.

8. Ibid., pp. 6–7.

9. Excerpts from a conversation guided by Carl Sheingold, "Whither the Professional and Lay Leadership?" *Sh'ma*, April 2004, pp. 1–4.

10. Shifra Bronznick, "Embracing Conflict and Practicing Respect: A New Choreography," *Sh'ma*, April 2004, p. 5.

11. Eugene Horowitz, "*Tsimtsum*: A Mystic Model for Contemporary Leadership," in Stuart Kelman, *What We Know about Jewish Education* (Los Angeles: Torah Aura, 1992).

12. David A. Teutsch, "The Rabbinic Role in Organizational Decision-Making," in Bubis, *Director Had a Heart Attack*, p. 167.

13. Isa Aron, *Becoming a Congregation of Learners* (Woodstock, VT: Jewish Lights, 2002), p. 122.

14. Dave Barry, *Clawing Your Way to the Top* (New York: Rodale Books, 2000).

15. Patrick Lencioni, *Death by Meeting* (San Francisco: Jossey-Bass, 2004).

13. WHO'S NEXT? EFFECTIVE SUCCESSION PLANNING

1. James Kouzes and Barry Posner, *The Leadership Challenge* (San Francisco: Jossey-Bass, 1995), pp. 20–22.

2. Ibid., pp. 22–23.

3. Collins, *Good to Great* (New York: HarperCollins, 2001), p. 26.

4. Ibid.

5. Ibid.

6. Abraham J. Heschel, *The Prophets: An Introduction* (New York: Harper and Row, 1962), p. 16.

7. Heifetz and Linsky, *Leadership on the Line*, pp. 227–28.

APPENDIX 2: LEADERSHIP EXERCISES

1. Stephen R. Covey, *Principled-Centered Leadership* (Glencoe, IL: Free Press, 1992), pp. 96–97.

Suggestions for Further Reading

The following is a non-exhaustive reading list of leadership books that are helpful in thinking through personal and institutional leadership within the Jewish community. Hundreds of leadership books are published annually. Watch your wallet. Very few are really worthwhile, but when a leadership book is valuable it can really change the way that you think and engage.

Arbinger Institute. *Leadership and Self-Deception: Getting Out of the Box.* San Francisco: Berrett-Koehler Publishers, 2002

Aron, Isa. *Becoming a Congregation of Learners: Learning as a Key to Revitalizing Congregational Life.* Woodstock, VT: Jewish Lights, 2002.

Bennis, Warren. *On Becoming a Leader: The Leadership Classic—Updated and Expanded.* New York: Addison-Wesley Publishing, 1989.

Bossidy, Larry, and Ram Charan. *Execution: The Discipline of Getting Things Done.* New York: Crown Business, 2002.

Boyatzis, Richard, and Annie McKee. *Resonant Leadership: Renewing Yourself and Connecting with Others through Mindfulness, Hope and Compassion.* Boston: Harvard Business School Press, 2005.

Bubis, Gerald B. *The Director Had a Heart Attack and the President Resigned: Board-Staff Relations for the 21st Century.* Jerusalem: Jerusalem Center for Public Affairs, 1999.

Cohen, Norman J. *Moses and the Journey to Leadership: Timeless Lessons of Effective Management from the Bible and Today's Leaders.* Woodstock, VT: Jewish Lights, 2008.

Cohen, Steven M., and Arnold M. Eisen. *The Jew Within: Self, Family and Community in America.* Bloomington: Indiana University Press, 2000.

Collins, Jim. *Good to Great: Why Some Companies Make the Leap ... and Others Don't.* New York: HarperCollins, 2001.

———. *Good to Great and the Social Sector: A Monograph to Accompany Good to Great.* New York: Collins, 2005.

Covey, Steven R. *Principle-Centered Leadership.* New York: Simon and Schuster, 1991.

Dym, Barry, and Harry Huston. *Leadership in Nonprofit Organizations: Lessons from the Third Sector.* Thousand Oaks, CA: Sage Publications, 2005.

Farber, Roberta Rosenberg, and Chaim I. Waxman, eds. *Jews in America: A Contemporary Reader.* Hanover, NH: Brandeis University Press, 1999.

Fromm, Erich. *You Shall Be Gods: A Radical Interpretation of the Old Testament and Its Tradition.* Greenwich, CT: Fawcett, 1966.

Gardner, Howard. *Leading Minds.* New York: Basic Books, 1995.

Gladwell, Malcolm. *The Tipping Point: How Little Things Can Make a Big Difference.* Boston: Little, Brown, 2002.

Goldsmith, Marshall, and Laurence Lyons, eds. *Coaching for Leadership: The Practice of Leadership Coaching from the World's Greatest Coaches.* San Francisco: John Wiley & Sons, 2006.

Goleman, Daniel, Richard Boyatzis, and Annie McKee. *Primal Leadership: Learning to Lead with Emotional Intelligence.* Boston: Harvard Business School Press, 2004.

Grace, Kay Sprinkel, and Alan L. Wendroff. *High Impact Philanthropy: How Donors, Boards, and Nonprofit Organizations Can Transform Communities.* New York: Wiley, 2001.

Heifetz, Ronald A. *Leadership without Easy Answers.* Cambridge: President and Fellows of Harvard College, 1994.

Heifetz, Ronald L., and Marty Linsky. *Leadership on the Line: Staying Alive through the Dangers of Leading.* Boston: Harvard Business School Press, 2002.

Heschel, Abraham J. *The Prophets.* New York: HarperCollins Publishers, 2001.

Hoffman, Lawrence A. *Rethinking Synagogues: A New Vocabulary for Congregational Life.* Woodstock, VT: Jewish Lights, 2006.

Howe, Fisher. *The Board Member's Guide to Fund-Raising.* San Francisco: Jossey-Bass Publishers, 1991.

Katzenbach, Jon R., and Douglas K. Smith. *The Wisdom of Teams: Creating the High-Performance Organization.* New York: Harper Business, 1994.

Kellerman, Barbara. *Bad Leadership: What It Is, How It Happens, Why It Matters.* Boston: Harvard Business Review Press, 2004.

Kotter, John P. *On What Leaders Really Do.* Boston: Harvard Business Review Press, 1999.

———. *Leading Change.* John P. Kotter, 1996.

Kotter, John P., and Dan S. Cohen. *The Heart of Change: Real-Life Stories of How People Change Their Organizations.* Boston: Harvard Business Review Press, 2002.

Kouzes, James M., and Barry Z. Posner. *The Leadership Challenge,* 4th ed. San Francisco: Jossey-Bass, 2007.

Kranc, Moshe. *The Hasidic Masters' Guide to Management.* Jerusalem: Devorah Publications, 2004.

Laufer, Nathan. *The Genesis of Leadership: What the Bible Teaches US about Vision, Values and Leading Change.* Woodstock, VT: Jewish Lights, 2008.

Lencioni, Patrick. *Five Dysfunctions of a Team: A Leadership Fable.* San Francisco: Jossey-Bass, 2002.

———. *Death by Meeting: A Leadership Fable ... about Solving the Most Painful Problem in Business.* San Francisco: Jossey-Bass, 2004.

———. *Silos, Politics and Turf Wars: A Leadership Fable about Destroying the Barriers That Turn Colleagues into Competitors.* San Francisco: Jossey-Bass, 2006.

———. *The Three Signs of a Miserable Job: A Fable for Managers (And Their Employees).* San Francisco: Jossey-Bass, 2007.

Pava, Moses. *Leading with Meaning: Using Covenantal Leadership to Build a Better Organization.* New York: Palgrave MacMillan, 2003.

Peters, Thomas J., and Robert H. Waterman, Jr. *In Search of Excellence: Lessons from America's Best-Run Companies.* New York: Warner Books, 1982.

Rath, Tom. *StrengthsFinder 2.0: A New and Upgraded Edition of the Online Test from Gallup's Now, Discover Your Strengths.* New York: Gallup Press, 2007.

Senge, Peter M. "The Leader's New Work: Building Learning Organizations," *Sloane Management Review* 32 (1990): 1.

Shatz, David, Chaim I. Waxman, and Nathan J. Diament, eds. Tikkun Olam: *Social Responsibility in Jewish Thought and Law.* Northvale, NJ: Jason Aronson, 1997.

Spears, Larry C., ed. *Insights on Leadership: Service, Spirit and Servant-Leadership.* New York: Wiley, 1998.

Telushkin, Joseph. *Words That Hurt, Words That Heal: How to Choose Words Wisely and Well.* New York: William Morrow, 1996.

Teutsch, David A. *Spiritual Community: The Power to Restore Hope, Commitment and Joy.* Woodstock, VT: Jewish Lights, 2005.

Wildavsky, Aaron. *The Nursing Father: Moses as a Political Leader*. Tuscaloosa: University of Alabama Press, 1984.

Wolfson, Ron. *The Spirituality of Welcoming: How to Transform Your Congregation into a Sacred Community*. Woodstock, VT: Jewish Lights, 2006.

Bar/Bat Mitzvah

The JGirl's Guide: The Young Jewish Woman's Handbook for Coming of Age
By Penina Adelman, Ali Feldman, and Shulamit Reinharz
This inspirational, interactive guidebook helps pre-teen Jewish girls address the many
issues surrounding coming of age.   6 x 9, 240 pp, Quality PB, 978-1-58023-215-9 **$14.99**
  Also Available: **The JGirl's Teacher's and Parent's Guide**
  8½ x 11, 56 pp, PB, 978-1-58023-225-8 **$8.99**

Bar/Bat Mitzvah Basics: A Practical Family Guide to Coming of Age Together
Edited by Cantor Helen Leneman 6 x 9, 240 pp, Quality PB, 978-1-58023-151-0 **$18.95**
The Bar/Bat Mitzvah Memory Book, 2nd Edition: An Album for Treasuring the
  Spiritual Celebration *By Rabbi Jeffrey K. Salkin and Nina Salkin*
  8 x 10, 48 pp, Deluxe HC, 2-color text, ribbon marker, 978-1-58023-263-0 **$19.99**
For Kids—Putting God on Your Guest List, 2nd Edition: How to Claim the
  Spiritual Meaning of Your Bar or Bat Mitzvah *By Rabbi Jeffrey K. Salkin*
  6 x 9, 144 pp, Quality PB, 978-1-58023-308-8 **$15.99** *For ages 11–13*

Putting God on the Guest List, 3rd Edition: How to Reclaim the Spiritual
  Meaning of Your Child's Bar or Bat Mitzvah *By Rabbi Jeffrey K. Salkin*
  6 x 9, 224 pp, Quality PB, 978-1-58023-222-7 **$16.99**; HC, 978-1-58023-260-9 **$24.99**
  Also Available: **Putting God on the Guest List Teacher's Guide**
  8½ x 11, 48 pp, PB, 978-1-58023-226-5 **$8.99**
Tough Questions Jews Ask: A Young Adult's Guide to Building a Jewish Life
  By Rabbi Edward Feinstein 6 x 9, 160 pp, Quality PB, 978-1-58023-139-8 **$14.99** *For ages 12 & up*
  Also Available: **Tough Questions Jews Ask Teacher's Guide**
  8½ x 11, 72 pp, PB, 978-1-58023-187-9 **$8.95**

Bible Study/Midrash

**Abraham's Bind & Other Bible Tales of Trickery, Folly, Mercy
and Love** *By Michael J. Caduto*
Re-imagines many biblical characters, retelling their stories.
6 x 9, 224 pp, HC, 978-1-59473-186-0 **$19.99** *(A SkyLight Paths book)*
Ancient Secrets: Using the Stories of the Bible to Improve Our Everyday Lives
  By Rabbi Levi Meier, PhD 5½ x 8½, 288 pp, Quality PB, 978-1-58023-064-3 **$16.95**

The Genesis of Leadership: What the Bible Teaches Us about Vision,
Values and Leading Change *By Rabbi Nathan Laufer; Foreword by Senator Joseph I. Lieberman*
Unlike other books on leadership, this one is rooted in the stories of the Bible.
6 x 9, 288 pp, Quality PB, 978-1-58023-352-1 **$18.99**; HC, 978-1-58023-241-8 **$24.99**
Hineini in Our Lives: Learning How to Respond to Others through 14 Biblical Texts and
  Personal Stories *By Norman J. Cohen* 6 x 9, 240 pp, Quality PB, 978-1-58023-274-6 **$16.99**
Moses and the Journey to Leadership: Timeless Lessons of Effective Management from
  the Bible and Today's Leaders *By Dr. Norman J. Cohen*
  6 x 9, 240 pp, Quality PB, 978-1-58023-351-4 **$18.99**; HC, 978-1-58023-227-2 **$21.99**
Self, Struggle & Change: Family Conflict Stories in Genesis and Their Healing Insights for
  Our Lives *By Norman J. Cohen* 6 x 9, 224 pp, Quality PB, 978-1-879045-66-8 **$18.99**
The Triumph of Eve & Other Subversive Bible Tales *By Matt Biers-Ariel*
  5½ x 8½, 192 pp, Quality PB, 978-1-59473-176-1 **$14.99**; HC, 978-1-59473-040-5 **$19.99**
  (A SkyLight Paths book)

The Wisdom of Judaism: An Introduction to the Values of the Talmud
By Rabbi Dov Peretz Elkins
Explores the essence of Judaism.   6 x 9, 192 pp, Quality PB, 978-1-58023-327-9 **$16.99**
  Also Available: **The Wisdom of Judaism Teacher's Guide**
  8½ x 11, 18 pp, PB, 978-1-58023-350-7 **$8.99**

Or phone, fax, mail or e-mail to: **JEWISH LIGHTS** Publishing
Sunset Farm Offices, Route 4 • P.O. Box 237 • Woodstock, Vermont 05091
Tel: (802) 457-4000 • Fax: (802) 457-4004 • www.jewishlights.com
Credit card orders: **(800) 962-4544** (8:30AM–5:30PM ET Monday–Friday)
Generous discounts on quantity orders. SATISFACTION GUARANTEED. Prices subject to change.

Children's Books
by Sandy Eisenberg Sasso

Adam & Eve's First Sunset: God's New Day

Engaging new story explores fear and hope, faith and gratitude in ways that will delight kids and adults—inspiring us to bless each of God's days and nights.

9 x 12, 32 pp, Full-color illus., HC, 978-1-58023-177-0 **$17.95** *For ages 4 & up*

Also Available as a Board Book: **Adam and Eve's New Day**

5 x 5, 24 pp, Full-color illus., Board, 978-1-59473-205-8 **$7.99** *For ages 0–4 (A SkyLight Paths book)*

But God Remembered
Stories of Women from Creation to the Promised Land

Four different stories of women—Lillith, Serach, Bityah, and the Daughters of Z—teach us important values through their faith and actions.

9 x 12, 32 pp, Full-color illus., Quality PB, 978-1-58023-372-9 **$8.99**; HC, 978-1-879045-43-9 **$16.95** *For ages 8 & up*

Cain & Abel: Finding the Fruits of Peace

Shows children that we have the power to deal with anger in positive ways. Provides questions for kids and adults to explore together.

9 x 12, 32 pp, Full-color illus., HC, 978-1-58023-123-7 **$16.95** *For ages 5 & up*

God in Between

If you wanted to find God, where would you look? This magical, mythical tale teaches that God can be found where we are: within all of us and the relationships between us.

9 x 12, 32 pp, Full-color illus., HC, 978-1-879045-86-6 **$16.95** *For ages 4 & up*

God's Paintbrush: Special 10th Anniversary Edition

Wonderfully interactive, invites children of all faiths and backgrounds to encounter God through moments in their own lives. Provides questions adult and child can explore together.

11 x 8½, 32 pp, Full-color illus., HC, 978-1-58023-195-4 **$17.95** *For ages 4 & up*

Also Available: **God's Paintbrush Teacher's Guide**

8½ x 11, 32 pp, PB, 978-1-879045-57-6 **$8.95**

God's Paintbrush Celebration Kit

A Spiritual Activity Kit for Teachers and Students of All Faiths, All Backgrounds

Additional activity sheets available:

8-Student Activity Sheet Pack (40 sheets/5 sessions), 978-1-58023-058-2 **$19.95**

Single-Student Activity Sheet Pack (5 sessions), 978-1-58023-059-9 **$3.95**

In God's Name

Like an ancient myth in its poetic text and vibrant illustrations, this award-winning modern fable about the search for God's name celebrates the diversity and, at the same time, the unity of all people.

9 x 12, 32 pp, Full-color illus., HC, 978-1-879045-26-2 **$16.99** *For ages 4 & up*

Also Available as a Board Book: **What Is God's Name?**

5 x 5, 24 pp, Board, Full-color illus., 978-1-893361-10-2 **$7.99** *For ages 0–4 (A SkyLight Paths book)*

Also Available: **In God's Name video and study guide**

Computer animation, original music, and children's voices. 18 min. **$29.99**

Also Available in Spanish: **El nombre de Dios**

9 x 12, 32 pp, Full-color illus., HC, 978-1-893361-63-8 **$16.95** *(A SkyLight Paths book)*

Noah's Wife: The Story of Naamah

When God tells Noah to bring the animals of the world onto the ark, God also calls on Naamah, Noah's wife, to save each plant on Earth. Based on an ancient text.

9 x 12, 32 pp, Full-color illus., HC, 978-1-58023-134-3 **$16.95** *For ages 4 & up*

Also Available as a Board Book: **Naamah, Noah's Wife**

5 x 5, 24 pp, Full-color illus., Board, 978-1-893361-56-0 **$7.95** *For ages 0–4 (A SkyLight Paths book)*

For Heaven's Sake: Finding God in Unexpected Places

9 x 12, 32 pp, Full-color illus., HC, 978-1-58023-054-4 **$16.95** *For ages 4 & up*

God Said Amen: Finding the Answers to Our Prayers

9 x 12, 32 pp, Full-color illus., HC, 978-1-58023-080-3 **$16.95** *For ages 4 & up*

Current Events/History

A Dream of Zion: American Jews Reflect on Why Israel Matters to Them
Edited by Rabbi Jeffrey K. Salkin Explores what Jewish people in America have to say about Israel. 6 x 9, 304 pp, HC, 978-1-58023-340-8 **$24.99**
  Also Available: **A Dream of Zion Teacher's Guide** 8½ x 11, 18 pp, PB, 978-1-58023-356-9 **$8.99**

The Jewish Connection to Israel, the Promised Land: A Brief Introduction for
  Christians *By Rabbi Eugene Korn, PhD* 5½ x 8½, 192 pp, Quality PB, 978-1-58023-318-7 **$14.99**

The Story of the Jews: A 4,000-Year Adventure—A Graphic History Book
  Written & illustrated by Stan Mack 6 x 9, 288 pp, illus., Quality PB, 978-1-58023-155-8 **$16.99**

Hannah Senesh: Her Life and Diary, the First Complete Edition
  By Hannah Senesh; Foreword by Marge Piercy; Preface by Eitan Senesh
  6 x 9, 368 pp, Quality PB, 978-1-58023-342-2 **$19.99**; 352 pp, HC, 978-1-58023-212-8 **$24.99**

The Ethiopian Jews of Israel: Personal Stories of Life in the Promised
Land *By Len Lyons, PhD; Foreword by Alan Dershowitz; Photographs by Ilan Ossendryver*
Recounts, through photographs and words, stories of Ethiopian Jews.
10½ x 10, 240 pp, 100 full-color photos, HC, 978-1-58023-323-1 **$34.99**

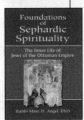

Foundations of Sephardic Spirituality: The Inner Life of Jews of the Ottoman Empire
  By Rabbi Marc D. Angel, PhD 6 x 9, 224 pp, HC, 978-1-58023-243-2 **$24.99**

Judaism and Justice: The Jewish Passion to Repair the World
  By Rabbi Sidney Schwarz 6 x 9, 352 pp, Quality PB, 978-1-58023-353-8 **$19.99**

Ecology/Environment

A Wild Faith: Jewish Ways into Wilderness, Wilderness Ways into Judaism
By Rabbi Mike Comins; Foreword by Nigel Savage
Offers ways to enliven and deepen your spiritual life through wilderness experience.
6 x 9, 240 pp, Quality PB, 978-1-58023-316-3 **$16.99**

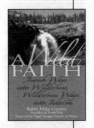

Ecology & the Jewish Spirit: Where Nature & the Sacred Meet
  Edited by Ellen Bernstein 6 x 9, 288 pp, Quality PB, 978-1-58023-082-7 **$18.99**

Torah of the Earth: Exploring 4,000 Years of Ecology in Jewish Thought
  Vol. 1: Biblical Israel: One Land, One People; Rabbinic Judaism: One People, Many Lands
  Vol. 2: Zionism: One Land, Two Peoples; Eco-Judaism: One Earth, Many Peoples
  Edited by Arthur Waskow Vol. 1: 6 x 9, 272 pp, Quality PB, 978-1-58023-086-5 **$19.95**
  Vol. 2: 6 x 9, 336 pp, Quality PB, 978-1-58023-087-2 **$19.95**

The Way Into Judaism and the Environment
  By Jeremy Benstein 6 x 9, 224 pp, HC, 978-1-58023-268-5 **$24.99**

Grief/Healing

Healing and the Jewish Imagination: Spiritual and Practical
Perspectives on Judaism and Health *Edited by Rabbi William Cutter, PhD*
Explores Judaism for comfort in times of illness and perspectives on suffering.
6 x 9, 240 pp, HC, 978-1-58023-314-9 **$24.99**

Grief in Our Seasons: A Mourner's Kaddish Companion *By Rabbi Kerry M. Olitzky*
  4½ x 6½, 448 pp, Quality PB, 978-1-879045-55-2 **$15.95**

Healing of Soul, Healing of Body: Spiritual Leaders Unfold the Strength & Solace
  in Psalms *Edited by Rabbi Simkha Y. Weintraub, CSW*
  6 x 9, 128 pp, 2-color illus. text, Quality PB, 978-1-879045-31-6 **$14.99**

Mourning & Mitzvah, 2nd Edition: A Guided Journal for Walking the Mourner's
  Path through Grief to Healing *By Anne Brener, LCSW*
  7½ x 9, 304 pp, Quality PB, 978-1-58023-113-8 **$19.99**

Tears of Sorrow, Seeds of Hope, 2nd Edition: A Jewish Spiritual Companion for
  Infertility and Pregnancy Loss *By Rabbi Nina Beth Cardin*
  6 x 9, 208 pp, Quality PB, 978-1-58023-233-3 **$18.99**

A Time to Mourn, a Time to Comfort, 2nd Edition: A Guide to Jewish
  Bereavement *By Dr. Ron Wolfson*
  7 x 9, 384 pp, Quality PB, 978-1-58023-253-1 **$19.99**

When a Grandparent Dies: A Kid's Own Remembering Workbook for Dealing
  with Shiva and the Year Beyond *By Nechama Liss-Levinson, PhD*
  8 x 10, 48 pp, 2-color text, HC, 978-1-879045-44-6 **$15.95** *For ages 7–13*

Spirituality/Women's Interest

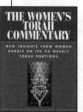

The Quotable Jewish Woman: Wisdom, Inspiration & Humor from the Mind & Heart
Edited and compiled by Elaine Bernstein Partnow
6 x 9, 496 pp, Quality PB, 978-1-58023-236-4 **$19.99**; HC, 978-1-58023-193-0 **$29.99**

The Divine Feminine in Biblical Wisdom Literature: Selections Annotated &
Explained *Translated and Annotated by Rabbi Rami Shapiro*
5½ x 8½, 240 pp, Quality PB, 978-1-59473-109-9 **$16.99** *(A SkyLight Paths book)*

The Women's Haftarah Commentary: New Insights from Women Rabbis on the
54 Weekly Haftarah Portions, the 5 Megillot & Special Shabbatot
Edited by Rabbi Elyse Goldstein 6 x 9, 560 pp, HC, 978-1-58023-133-6 **$39.99**

The Women's Torah Commentary: New Insights from Women Rabbis on the
54 Weekly Torah Portions *Edited by Rabbi Elyse Goldstein*
6 x 9, 496 pp, HC, 978-1-58023-076-6 **$34.95**

The Year Mom Got Religion: One Woman's Midlife Journey into Judaism
By Lee Meyerhoff Hendler 6 x 9, 208 pp, Quality PB, 978-1-58023-070-4 **$15.95**

See Holidays for *The Women's Passover Companion: Women's Reflections
on the Festival of Freedom* and *The Women's Seder Sourcebook: Rituals &
Readings for Use at the Passover Seder*. Also see Bar/Bat Mitzvah for *The
JGirl's Guide: The Young Jewish Woman's Handbook for Coming of Age*.

Spirituality / Crafts
(from SkyLight Paths, our sister imprint)

The Knitting Way: A Guide to Spiritual Self-Discovery
By Linda Skolnick and Janice MacDaniels
Shows how to use the practice of knitting to strengthen our spiritual selves.
7 x 9, 240 pp, Quality PB, 978-1-59473-079-5 **$16.99**

The Quilting Path: A Guide to Spiritual Self-Discovery through Fabric,
Thread and Kabbalah *By Louise Silk*
Explores how to cultivate personal growth through quilt making.
7 x 9, 192 pp, Quality PB, 978-1-59473-206-5 **$16.99**

The Painting Path: Embodying Spiritual Discovery through Yoga, Brush
and Color *By Linda Novick; Foreword by Richard Segalman*
Explores the divine connection you can experience through art.
7 x 9, 208 pp, 8-page full-color insert, Quality PB, 978-1-59473-226-3 **$18.99**

The Scrapbooking Journey: A Hands-On Guide to Spiritual Discovery
By Cory Richardson-Lauve; Foreword by Stacy Julian
Reveals how this craft can become a practice used to deepen and shape your life.
7 x 9, 176 pp, 8-page full-color insert, b/w photos, Quality PB, 978-1-59473-216-4 **$18.99**

Travel

Israel—A Spiritual Travel Guide, 2nd Edition
A Companion for the Modern Jewish Pilgrim
By Rabbi Lawrence A. Hoffman 4¾ x 10, 256 pp, Quality PB, illus., 978-1-58023-261-6 **$18.99**
Also Available: **The Israel Mission Leader's Guide** 978-1-58023-085-8 **$4.95**

12-Step

100 Blessings Every Day: Daily Twelve Step Recovery Affirmations, Exercises for
Personal Growth & Renewal Reflecting Seasons of the Jewish Year
By Rabbi Kerry M. Olitzky; Foreword by Rabbi Neil Gillman
4½ x 6¼, 432 pp, Quality PB, 978-1-879045-30-9 **$16.99**

Recovery from Codependence: A Jewish Twelve Steps Guide to Healing Your Soul
By Rabbi Kerry M. Olitzky 6 x 9, 160 pp, Quality PB, 978-1-879045-32-3 **$13.95**

Twelve Jewish Steps to Recovery: A Personal Guide to Turning from Alcoholism &
Other Addictions—Drugs, Food, Gambling, Sex ...
By Rabbi Kerry M. Olitzky and Stuart A. Copans, MD; Preface by Abraham J. Twerski, MD
6 x 9, 144 pp, Quality PB, 978-1-879045-09-5 **$15.99**

Inspiration

Happiness and the Human Spirit: The Spirituality of Becoming the Best You Can Be *By Abraham J. Twerski, MD*
Shows you that true happiness is attainable once you stop looking outside yourself for the source. 6 x 9, 176 pp, HC, 978-1-58023-343-9 **$19.99**

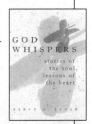

The Bridge to Forgiveness: Stories and Prayers for Finding God and Restoring Wholeness *By Rabbi Karyn D. Kedar*
Examines how forgiveness can be the bridge that connects us to wholeness and peace.
6 x 9, 176 pp, HC, 978-1-58023-324-8 **$19.99**

God's To-Do List: 103 Ways to Be an Angel and Do God's Work on Earth
By Dr. Ron Wolfson 6 x 9, 150 pp, Quality PB, 978-1-58023-301-9 **$16.99**

God in All Moments: Mystical & Practical Spiritual Wisdom from Hasidic Masters
Edited and translated by Or N. Rose with Ebn D. Leader
5½ x 8½, 192 pp, Quality PB, 978-1-58023-186-2 **$16.95**

Our Dance with God: Finding Prayer, Perspective and Meaning in the Stories of Our Lives *By Karyn D. Kedar* 6 x 9, 176 pp, Quality PB, 978-1-58023-202-9 **$16.99**
Also Available: **The Dance of the Dolphin** (HC edition of *Our Dance with God*)
6 x 9, 176 pp, HC, 978-1-58023-154-1 **$19.95**

The Empty Chair: Finding Hope and Joy—Timeless Wisdom from a Hasidic Master,
Rebbe Nachman of Breslov *Adapted by Moshe Mykoff and the Breslov Research Institute*
4 x 6, 128 pp, 2-color text, Deluxe PB w/flaps, 978-1-879045-67-5 **$9.99**

The Gentle Weapon: Prayers for Everyday and Not-So-Everyday Moments—
Timeless Wisdom from the Teachings of the Hasidic Master, Rebbe Nachman of Breslov
Adapted by Moshe Mykoff and S. C. Mizrahi, together with the Breslov Research Institute
4 x 6, 144 pp, 2-color text, Deluxe PB w/flaps, 978-1-58023-022-3 **$9.99**

God Whispers: Stories of the Soul, Lessons of the Heart *By Karyn D. Kedar*
6 x 9, 176 pp, Quality PB, 978-1-58023-088-9 **$15.95**

Restful Reflections: Nighttime Inspiration to Calm the Soul, Based on Jewish Wisdom
By Rabbi Kerry M. Olitzky & Rabbi Lori Forman 4½ x 6½, 448 pp, Quality PB, 978-1-58023-091-9 **$15.95**

Sacred Intentions: Daily Inspiration to Strengthen the Spirit, Based on Jewish Wisdom
By Rabbi Kerry M. Olitzky and Rabbi Lori Forman 4½ x 6½, 448 pp, Quality PB, 978-1-58023-061-2 **$15.95**

Kabbalah/Mysticism/Enneagram

Awakening to Kabbalah: The Guiding Light of Spiritual Fulfillment
By Rav Michael Laitman, PhD 6 x 9, 192 pp, HC, 978-1-58023-264-7 **$21.99**

Seek My Face: A Jewish Mystical Theology *By Arthur Green*
6 x 9, 304 pp, Quality PB, 978-1-58023-130-5 **$19.95**

Zohar: Annotated & Explained
Translation and annotation by Daniel C. Matt; Foreword by Andrew Harvey
5½ x 8½, 176 pp, Quality PB, 978-1-893361-51-5 **$15.99** (A SkyLight Paths book)

Ehyeh: A Kabbalah for Tomorrow
By Arthur Green 6 x 9, 224 pp, Quality PB, 978-1-58023-213-5 **$16.99**

The Flame of the Heart: Prayers of a Chasidic Mystic *By Reb Noson of Breslov. Translated by
David Sears with the Breslov Research Institute* 5 x 7¼, 160 pp, Quality PB, 978-1-58023-246-3 **$15.99**

The Gift of Kabbalah: Discovering the Secrets of Heaven, Renewing Your Life on Earth
By Tamar Frankiel, PhD 6 x 9, 256 pp, Quality PB, 978-1-58023-141-1 **$16.95;**
HC, 978-1-58023-108-4 **$21.95**

Kabbalah: A Brief Introduction for Christians
By Tamar Frankiel, PhD 5½ x 8½, 208 pp, Quality PB, 978-1-58023-303-3 **$16.99**

**The Lost Princess and Other Kabbalistic Tales of Rebbe Nachman of Breslov
The Seven Beggars and Other Kabbalistic Tales of Rebbe Nachman of Breslov**
Translated by Rabbi Aryeh Kaplan; Preface by Rabbi Chaim Kramer
Lost Princess: 6 x 9, 400 pp, Quality PB, 978-1-58023-217-3 **$18.99**
Seven Beggars: 6 x 9, 192 pp, Quality PB, 978-1-58023-250-0 **$16.99**

See also *The Way Into Jewish Mystical Tradition* in Spirituality / The Way Into... Series

Holidays/Holy Days

Rosh Hashanah Readings: Inspiration, Information and Contemplation
Yom Kippur Readings: Inspiration, Information and Contemplation
Edited by Rabbi Dov Peretz Elkins with Section Introductions from Arthur Green's These Are the Words
An extraordinary collection of readings, prayers and insights that enable the modern worshiper to enter into the spirit of the High Holy Days in a personal and powerful way, permitting the meaning of the Jewish New Year to enter the heart.
RHR: 6 x 9, 400 pp, HC, 978-1-58023-239-5 **$24.99**
YKR: 6 x 9, 368 pp, HC, 978-1-58023-271-5 **$24.99**

Jewish Holidays: A Brief Introduction for Christians
By Rabbi Kerry M. Olitzky and Rabbi Daniel Judson
5½ x 8½, 144 pp, Quality PB, 978-1-58023-302-6 **$16.99**

Reclaiming Judaism as a Spiritual Practice: Holy Days and Shabbat
By Rabbi Goldie Milgram
7 x 9, 272 pp, Quality PB, 978-1-58023-205-0 **$19.99**

7th Heaven: Celebrating Shabbat with Rebbe Nachman of Breslov
By Moshe Mykoff with the Breslov Research Institute
5⅛ x 8¼, 224 pp, Deluxe PB w/flaps, 978-1-58023-175-6 **$18.95**

Shabbat, 2nd Edition: The Family Guide to Preparing for and Celebrating the Sabbath
By Dr. Ron Wolfson 7 x 9, 320 pp, illus., Quality PB, 978-1-58023-164-0 **$19.99**

Hanukkah, 2nd Edition: The Family Guide to Spiritual Celebration
By Dr. Ron Wolfson. Edited by Joel Lurie Grishaver.
7 x 9, 240 pp, illus., Quality PB, 978-1-58023-122-0 **$18.95**

The Jewish Family Fun Book, 2nd Edition: Holiday Projects, Everyday Activities, and Travel Ideas with Jewish Themes *By Danielle Dardashti and Roni Sarig. Illus. by Avi Katz.*
6 x 9, 304 pp, 70+ b/w illus. & diagrams, Quality PB, 978-1-58023-333-0 **$18.99**

The Jewish Lights Book of Fun Classroom Activities: Simple and Seasonal Projects for Teachers and Students *By Danielle Dardashti and Roni Sarig*
6 x 9, 240 pp, Quality PB, 978-1-58023-206-7 **$19.99**

Passover

My People's Passover Haggadah
Traditional Texts, Modern Commentaries
Edited by Rabbi Lawrence A. Hoffman, PhD, and David Arnow, PhD
A diverse and exciting collection of commentaries on the traditional Passover Haggadah—in two volumes!
Vol. 1: 7 x 10, 304 pp, HC, 978-1-58023-354-5 **$24.99**
Vol. 2: 7 x 10, 320 pp, HC, 978-1-58023-346-0 **$24.99**

Leading the Passover Journey
The Seder's Meaning Revealed, the Haggadah's Story Retold
By Rabbi Nathan Laufer
Uncovers the hidden meaning of the Seder's rituals and customs.
6 x 9, 224 pp, HC, 978-1-58023-211-1 **$24.99**

The Women's Passover Companion: Women's Reflections on the Festival of Freedom
Edited by Rabbi Sharon Cohen Anisfeld, Tara Mohr, and Catherine Spector
6 x 9, 352 pp, Quality PB, 978-1-58023-231-9 **$19.99**

The Women's Seder Sourcebook: Rituals & Readings for Use at the Passover Seder
Edited by Rabbi Sharon Cohen Anisfeld, Tara Mohr, and Catherine Spector
6 x 9, 384 pp, Quality PB, 978-1-58023-232-6 **$19.99**

Creating Lively Passover Seders: A Sourcebook of Engaging Tales, Texts & Activities
By David Arnow, PhD 7 x 9, 416 pp, Quality PB, 978-1-58023-184-8 **$24.99**

Passover, 2nd Edition: The Family Guide to Spiritual Celebration
By Dr. Ron Wolfson with Joel Lurie Grishaver 7 x 9, 352 pp, Quality PB, 978-1-58023-174-9 **$19.95**

Life Cycle
Marriage / Parenting / Family / Aging

The New Jewish Baby Album: Creating and Celebrating the Beginning of a Spiritual Life—A Jewish Lights Companion
By the Editors at Jewish Lights. Foreword by Anita Diamant. Preface by Rabbi Sandy Eisenberg Sasso.
A spiritual keepsake that will be treasured for generations. More than just a memory book, *shows you how—and why it's important*—to create a Jewish home and a Jewish life. 8 x 10, 64 pp, Deluxe Padded HC, Full-color illus., 978-1-58023-138-1 **$19.95**

The Jewish Pregnancy Book: A Resource for the Soul, Body & Mind during Pregnancy, Birth & the First Three Months
By Sandy Falk, MD, and Rabbi Daniel Judson, with Steven A. Rapp
Includes medical information, prayers and rituals for each stage of pregnancy, from a liberal Jewish perspective. 7 x 10, 208 pp, Quality PB, b/w photos, 978-1-58023-178-7 **$16.95**

Celebrating Your New Jewish Daughter: Creating Jewish Ways to Welcome Baby Girls into the Covenant—New and Traditional Ceremonies *By Debra Nussbaum Cohen; Foreword by Rabbi Sandy Eisenberg Sasso* 6 x 9, 272 pp, Quality PB, 978-1-58023-090-2 **$18.95**

The New Jewish Baby Book, 2nd Edition: Names, Ceremonies & Customs—A Guide for Today's Families *By Anita Diamant* 6 x 9, 336 pp, Quality PB, 978-1-58023-251-7 **$19.99**

Parenting as a Spiritual Journey: Deepening Ordinary and Extraordinary Events into Sacred Occasions *By Rabbi Nancy Fuchs-Kreimer* 6 x 9, 224 pp, Quality PB, 978-1-58023-016-2 **$16.95**

Parenting Jewish Teens: A Guide for the Perplexed
By Joanne Doades
Explores the questions and issues that shape the world in which today's Jewish teenagers live.
6 x 9, 200 pp, Quality PB, 978-1-58023-305-7 **$16.99**

Judaism for Two: A Spiritual Guide for Strengthening and Celebrating Your Loving Relationship *By Rabbi Nancy Fuchs-Kreimer and Rabbi Nancy H. Wiener; Foreword by Rabbi Elliot N. Dorff* Addresses the ways Jewish teachings can enhance and strengthen committed relationships. 6 x 9, 224 pp, Quality PB, 978-1-58023-254-8 **$16.99**

Embracing the Covenant: Converts to Judaism Talk About Why & How
By Rabbi Allan Berkowitz and Patti Moskovitz 6 x 9, 192 pp, Quality PB, 978-1-879045-50-7 **$16.95**

The Guide to Jewish Interfaith Family Life: An InterfaithFamily.com Handbook
Edited by Ronnie Friedland and Edmund Case 6 x 9, 384 pp, Quality PB, 978-1-58023-153-4 **$18.95**

Introducing My Faith and My Community
The Jewish Outreach Institute Guide for the Christian in a Jewish Interfaith Relationship
By Rabbi Kerry M. Olitzky 6 x 9, 176 pp, Quality PB, 978-1-58023-192-3 **$16.99**

Making a Successful Jewish Interfaith Marriage: The Jewish Outreach Institute Guide to Opportunities, Challenges and Resources *By Rabbi Kerry M. Olitzky with Joan Peterson Littman* 6 x 9, 176 pp, Quality PB, 978-1-58023-170-1 **$16.95**

The Creative Jewish Wedding Book: A Hands-On Guide to New & Old Traditions, Ceremonies & Celebrations *By Gabrielle Kaplan-Mayer* 9 x 9, 288 pp, b/w photos, Quality PB, 978-1-58023-194-7 **$19.99**

Divorce Is a Mitzvah: A Practical Guide to Finding Wholeness and Holiness When Your Marriage Dies *By Rabbi Perry Netter; Afterword by Rabbi Laura Geller.* 6 x 9, 224 pp, Quality PB, 978-1-58023-172-5 **$16.95**

A Heart of Wisdom: Making the Jewish Journey from Midlife through the Elder Years *Edited by Susan Berrin; Foreword by Harold Kushner* 6 x 9, 384 pp, Quality PB, 978-1-58023-051-3 **$18.95**

So That Your Values Live On: Ethical Wills and How to Prepare Them *Edited by Jack Riemer and Nathaniel Stampfer* 6 x 9, 272 pp, Quality PB, 978-1-879045-34-7 **$18.99**

Meditation

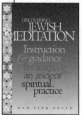

The Handbook of Jewish Meditation Practices
A Guide for Enriching the Sabbath and Other Days of Your Life
By Rabbi David A. Cooper Easy-to-learn meditation techniques.
6 x 9, 208 pp, Quality PB, 978-1-58023-102-2 **$16.95**

Discovering Jewish Meditation: Instruction & Guidance for Learning an Ancient
Spiritual Practice By Nan Fink Gefen
6 x 9, 208 pp, Quality PB, 978-1-58023-067-4 **$16.95**

A Heart of Stillness: A Complete Guide to Learning the Art of Meditation
By David A. Cooper 5½ x 8½, 272 pp, Quality PB, 978-1-893361-03-4 **$16.95** (A SkyLight Paths book)

Meditation from the Heart of Judaism: Today's Teachers Share Their Practices,
Techniques, and Faith Edited by Avram Davis
6 x 9, 256 pp, Quality PB, 978-1-58023-049-0 **$16.95**

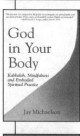

Silence, Simplicity & Solitude: A Complete Guide to Spiritual Retreat at Home
By David A. Cooper 5½ x 8½, 336 pp, Quality PB, 978-1-893361-04-1 **$16.95**
(A SkyLight Paths book)

Ritual/Sacred Practice

The Jewish Dream Book: The Key to Opening the Inner Meaning of
Your Dreams By Vanessa L. Ochs with Elizabeth Ochs; Full-color illus. by Kristina Swarner
Instructions for how modern people can perform ancient Jewish dream practices
and dream interpretations drawn from the Jewish wisdom tradition.
8 x 8, 128 pp, Full-color illus., Deluxe PB w/flaps, 978-1-58023-132-9 **$16.95**

God in Your Body: Kabbalah, Mindfulness and Embodied Spiritual Practice
By Jay Michaelson
The first comprehensive treatment of the body in Jewish spiritual practice and an
essential guide to the sacred.
6 x 9, 288 pp, Quality PB, 978-1-58023-304-0 **$18.99**

The Book of Jewish Sacred Practices: CLAL's Guide to Everyday & Holiday
Rituals & Blessings Edited by Rabbi Irwin Kula and Vanessa L. Ochs, PhD
6 x 9, 368 pp, Quality PB, 978-1-58023-152-7 **$18.95**

Jewish Ritual: A Brief Introduction for Christians
By Rabbi Kerry M. Olitzky and Rabbi Daniel Judson
5½ x 8½, 144 pp, Quality PB, 978-1-58023-210-4 **$14.99**

The Rituals & Practices of a Jewish Life: A Handbook for Personal Spiritual
Renewal Edited by Rabbi Kerry M. Olitzky and Rabbi Daniel Judson
6 x 9, 272 pp, illus., Quality PB, 978-1-58023-169-5 **$18.95**

The Sacred Art of Lovingkindness: Preparing to Practice
By Rabbi Rami Shapiro 5½ x 8½, 176 pp, Quality PB, 978-1-59473-151-8 **$16.99**
(A SkyLight Paths book)

Science Fiction/Mystery & Detective Fiction

Mystery Midrash: An Anthology of Jewish Mystery & Detective Fiction
Edited by Lawrence W. Raphael; Preface by Joel Siegel
6 x 9, 304 pp, Quality PB, 978-1-58023-055-1 **$16.95**

Criminal Kabbalah: An Intriguing Anthology of Jewish Mystery & Detective Fiction
Edited by Lawrence W. Raphael; Foreword by Laurie R. King
6 x 9, 256 pp, Quality PB, 978-1-58023-109-1 **$16.95**

Wandering Stars: An Anthology of Jewish Fantasy & Science Fiction
Edited by Jack Dann; Introduction by Isaac Asimov
6 x 9, 272 pp, Quality PB, 978-1-58023-005-6 **$18.99**

More Wandering Stars: An Anthology of Outstanding Stories of Jewish Fantasy and
Science Fiction Edited by Jack Dann; Introduction by Isaac Asimov
6 x 9, 192 pp, Quality PB, 978-1-58023-063-6 **$16.95**

Spirituality

Journeys to a Jewish Life: Inspiring Stories from the Spiritual Journeys of American Jews *By Paula Amann*
Examines the soul treks of Jews lost and found. 6 x 9, 208 pp, HC, 978-1-58023-317-0 **$19.99**

The Adventures of Rabbi Harvey: A Graphic Novel of Jewish Wisdom and Wit in the Wild West *By Steve Sheinkin*
Jewish and American folktales combine in this witty and original graphic novel collection. Creatively retold and set on the western frontier of the 1870s.
6 x 9, 144 pp, Full-color illus., Quality PB, 978-1-58023-310-1 **$16.99**
Also Available: **The Adventures of Rabbi Harvey Teacher's Guide**
8½ x 11, 32 pp, PB, 978-1-58023-326-2 **$8.99**

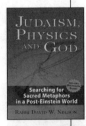

Ethics of the Sages: *Pirke Avot—Annotated & Explained*
Translation and Annotation by Rabbi Rami Shapiro
5½ x 8½, 192 pp, Quality PB, 978-1-59473-207-2 **$16.99** *(A SkyLight Paths book)*

A Book of Life: Embracing Judaism as a Spiritual Practice
By Michael Strassfeld 6 x 9, 528 pp, Quality PB, 978-1-58023-247-0 **$19.99**

Meaning and Mitzvah: Daily Practices for Reclaiming Judaism through Prayer, God, Torah, Hebrew, Mitzvot and Peoplehood *By Rabbi Goldie Milgram*
7 x 9, 336 pp, Quality PB, 978-1-58023-256-2 **$19.99**

The Soul of the Story: Meetings with Remarkable People
By Rabbi David Zeller 6 x 9, 288 pp, HC, 978-1-58023-272-2 **$21.99**

Aleph-Bet Yoga: Embodying the Hebrew Letters for Physical and Spiritual Well-Being
By Steven A. Rapp. Foreword by Tamar Frankiel, PhD and Judy Greenfeld. Preface by Hart Lazer.
7 x 10, 128 pp, b/w photos, Quality PB, Layflat binding, 978-1-58023-162-6 **$16.95**

Does the Soul Survive? A Jewish Journey to Belief in Afterlife, Past Lives & Living with Purpose *By Rabbi Elie Kaplan Spitz; Foreword by Brian L. Weiss, MD*
6 x 9, 288 pp, Quality PB, 978-1-58023-165-7 **$16.99**

First Steps to a New Jewish Spirit: Reb Zalman's Guide to Recapturing the Intimacy & Ecstasy in Your Relationship with God *By Rabbi Zalman M. Schachter-Shalomi with Donald Gropman* 6 x 9, 144 pp, Quality PB, 978-1-58023-182-4 **$16.95**

God in Our Relationships: Spirituality between People from the Teachings of Martin Buber *By Rabbi Dennis S. Ross* 5½ x 8½, 160 pp, Quality PB, 978-1-58023-147-3 **$16.95**

Judaism, Physics and God: Searching for Sacred Metaphors in a Post-Einstein World
By Rabbi David W. Nelson 6 x 9, 368 pp, Quality PB, inc. reader's discussion guide, 978-1-58023-306-4 **$18.99**; HC, 352 pp, 978-1-58023-252-4 **$24.99**

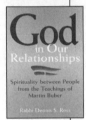

The Jewish Lights Spirituality Handbook: A Guide to Understanding, Exploring & Living a Spiritual Life *Edited by Stuart M. Matlins*
What exactly is "Jewish" about spirituality? How do I make it a part of my life? Fifty of today's foremost spiritual leaders share their ideas and experience with us.
6 x 9, 456 pp, Quality PB, 978-1-58023-093-3 **$19.99**

Bringing the Psalms to Life: How to Understand and Use the Book of Psalms
By Daniel F. Polish 6 x 9, 208 pp, Quality PB, 978-1-58023-157-2 **$16.95**;
HC, 978-1-58023-077-3 **$21.95**

God & the Big Bang: Discovering Harmony between Science & Spirituality
By Daniel C. Matt 6 x 9, 216 pp, Quality PB, 978-1-879045-89-7 **$16.99**

Minding the Temple of the Soul: Balancing Body, Mind, and Spirit through Traditional Jewish Prayer, Movement, and Meditation *By Tamar Frankiel, PhD, and Judy Greenfeld*
7 x 10, 184 pp, illus., Quality PB, 978-1-879045-64-4 **$16.95**
Audiotape of the Blessings and Meditations: 60 min. **$9.95**
Videotape of the Movements and Meditations: 46 min. **$20.00**

One God Clapping: The Spiritual Path of a Zen Rabbi *By Alan Lew with Sherril Jaffe*
5½ x 8½, 336 pp, Quality PB, 978-1-58023-115-2 **$16.95**

There Is No Messiah ... and You're It: The Stunning Transformation of Judaism's Most Provocative Idea *By Rabbi Robert N. Levine, DD*
6 x 9, 192 pp, Quality PB, 978-1-58023-255-5 **$16.99**

These Are the Words: A Vocabulary of Jewish Spiritual Life
By Arthur Green 6 x 9, 304 pp, Quality PB, 978-1-58023-107-7 **$18.95**

Theology/Philosophy

A Touch of the Sacred: A Theologian's Informal Guide to Jewish Belief
By Dr. Eugene B. Borowitz and Frances W. Schwartz Explores the musings from the leading theologian of liberal Judaism. 6 x 9, 256 pp, HC, 978-1-58023-337-8 **$21.99**

Talking about God: Exploring the Meaning of Religious Life with Kierkegaard, Buber, Tillich and Heschel *By Daniel F. Polish, PhD*
Examines the meaning of the human religious experience with the greatest theologians of modern times. 6 x 9, 160 pp, HC, 978-1-59473-230-0 **$21.99** *(A SkyLight Paths book)*

Jews & Judaism in the 21st Century: Human Responsibility, the Presence of God, and the Future of the Covenant
Edited by Rabbi Edward Feinstein; Foreword by Paula E. Hyman
Five celebrated leaders in Judaism examine contemporary Jewish life.
6 x 9, 192 pp, HC, 978-1-58023-315-6 **$24.99**

Christians and Jews in Dialogue: Learning in the Presence of the Other
By Mary C. Boys and Sara S. Lee; Foreword by Dr. Dorothy Bass
6 x 9, 240 pp, HC, 978-1-59473-144-0 **$21.99** *(A SkyLight Paths book)*

The Death of Death: Resurrection and Immortality in Jewish Thought
By Neil Gillman 6 x 9, 336 pp, Quality PB, 978-1-58023-081-0 **$18.95**

Ethics of the Sages: Pirke Avot—Annotated & Explained
Translation & Annotation by Rabbi Rami Shapiro
5½ x 8½, 208 pp, Quality PB, 978-1-59473-207-2 **$16.99** *(A SkyLight Paths book)*

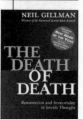

Hasidic Tales: Annotated & Explained
By Rabbi Rami Shapiro; Foreword by Andrew Harvey
5½ x 8½, 240 pp, Quality PB, 978-1-893361-86-7 **$16.95** *(A SkyLight Paths Book)*

A Heart of Many Rooms: Celebrating the Many Voices within Judaism
By David Hartman 6 x 9, 352 pp, Quality PB, 978-1-58023-156-5 **$19.95**

The Hebrew Prophets: Selections Annotated & Explained
Translation & Annotation by Rabbi Rami Shapiro; Foreword by Zalman M. Schachter-Shalomi
5½ x 8½, 224 pp, Quality PB, 978-1-59473-037-5 **$16.99** *(A SkyLight Paths book)*

A Jewish Understanding of the New Testament
By Rabbi Samuel Sandmel; Preface by Rabbi David Sandmel
5½ x 8½, 368 pp, Quality PB, 978-1-59473-048-1 **$19.99** *(A SkyLight Paths book)*

Keeping Faith with the Psalms: Deepen Your Relationship with God Using the Book of Psalms *By Daniel F. Polish* 6 x 9, 320 pp, Quality PB, 978-1-58023-300-2 **$18.99**

A Living Covenant: The Innovative Spirit in Traditional Judaism
By David Hartman 6 x 9, 368 pp, Quality PB, 978-1-58023-011-7 **$20.00**

Love and Terror in the God Encounter
The Theological Legacy of Rabbi Joseph B. Soloveitchik
By David Hartman 6 x 9, 240 pp, Quality PB, 978-1-58023-176-3 **$19.95**

The Personhood of God: Biblical Theology, Human Faith and the Divine Image
By Dr. Yochanan Muffs; Foreword by Dr. David Hartman 6 x 9, 240 pp, HC, 978-1-58023-265-4 **$24.99**

Traces of God: Seeing God in Torah, History and Everyday Life
By Neil Gillman 6 x 9, 240 pp, HC, 978-1-58023-249-4 **$21.99**

We Jews and Jesus: Exploring Theological Differences for Mutual Understanding
By Rabbi Samuel Sandmel; Preface by Rabbi David Sandmel
6 x 9, 176 pp, Quality PB, 978-1-59473-208-9 **$16.99** *(A SkyLight Paths book)*

Your Word Is Fire: The Hasidic Masters on Contemplative Prayer
Edited and translated by Arthur Green and Barry W. Holtz
6 x 9, 160 pp, Quality PB, 978-1-879045-25-5 **$15.95**

I Am Jewish
Personal Reflections Inspired by the Last Words of Daniel Pearl
Almost 150 Jews—both famous and not—from all walks of life, from all around the world, write about many aspects of their Judaism.
Edited by Judea and Ruth Pearl
6 x 9, 304 pp, Deluxe PB w/flaps, 978-1-58023-259-3 **$18.99**
Download a free copy of the *I Am Jewish Teacher's Guide* **at our website:**
www.jewishlights.com

Theology/Philosophy/*The Way Into...* Series

The Way Into... series offers an accessible and highly usable "guided tour" of the Jewish faith, people, history and beliefs—in total, an introduction to Judaism that will enable you to understand and interact with the sacred texts of the Jewish tradition. Each volume is written by a leading contemporary scholar and teacher, and explores one key aspect of Judaism. *The Way Into...* series enables all readers to achieve a real sense of Jewish cultural literacy through guided study.

The Way Into Encountering God in Judaism
By Neil Gillman
For everyone who wants to understand how Jews have encountered God throughout history and today.
6 x 9, 240 pp, Quality PB, 978-1-58023-199-2 **$18.99**; HC, 978-1-58023-025-4 **$21.95**
Also Available: **The Jewish Approach to God:** A Brief Introduction for Christians
By Neil Gillman
5½ x 8½, 192 pp, Quality PB, 978-1-58023-190-9 **$16.95**

The Way Into Jewish Mystical Tradition
By Lawrence Kushner
Allows readers to interact directly with the sacred mystical text of the Jewish tradition. An accessible introduction to the concepts of Jewish mysticism, their religious and spiritual significance and how they relate to life today.
6 x 9, 224 pp, Quality PB, 978-1-58023-200-5 **$18.99**; HC, 978-1-58023-029-2 **$21.95**

The Way Into Jewish Prayer
By Lawrence A. Hoffman
Opens the door to 3,000 years of Jewish prayer, making available all anyone needs to feel at home in the Jewish way of communicating with God.
6 x 9, 208 pp, Quality PB, 978-1-58023-201-2 **$18.99**

Also Available: **The Way Into Jewish Prayer Teacher's Guide**
By Rabbi Jennifer Ossakow Goldsmith
8½ x 11, 42 pp, PB, 978-1-58023-345-3 **$8.99**
Visit our website to download a free copy.

The Way Into Judaism and the Environment
By Jeremy Benstein
Explores the ways in which Judaism contributes to contemporary social-environmental issues, the extent to which Judaism is part of the problem and how it can be part of the solution.
6 x 9, 288 pp, HC, 978-1-58023-268-5 **$24.99**

The Way Into *Tikkun Olam* (Repairing the World)
By Elliot N. Dorff
An accessible introduction to the Jewish concept of the individual's responsibility to care for others and repair the world.
6 x 9, 320 pp, HC, 978-1-58023-269-2 **$24.99**; 304 pp, Quality PB, 978-1-58023-328-6 **$18.99**

The Way Into Torah
By Norman J. Cohen
Helps guide in the exploration of the origins and development of Torah, explains why it should be studied and how to do it.
6 x 9, 176 pp, Quality PB, 978-1-58023-198-5 **$16.99**

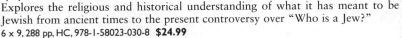

The Way Into the Varieties of Jewishness
By Sylvia Barack Fishman, PhD
Explores the religious and historical understanding of what it has meant to be Jewish from ancient times to the present controversy over "Who is a Jew?"
6 x 9, 288 pp, HC, 978-1-58023-030-8 **$24.99**

Spirituality/Lawrence Kushner

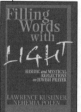

Filling Words with Light: Hasidic and Mystical Reflections on Jewish Prayer
By Lawrence Kushner and Nehemia Polen
5½ x 8½, 176 pp, Quality PB, 978-1-58023-238-8 **$16.99**; HC, 978-1-58023-216-6 **$21.99**

The Book of Letters: A Mystical Hebrew Alphabet
Popular HC Edition, 6 x 9, 80 pp, 2-color text, 978-1-879045-00-2 **$24.95**
Collector's Limited Edition, 9 x 12, 80 pp, gold foil embossed pages, w/limited edition silkscreened print, 978-1-879045-04-0 **$349.00**

The Book of Miracles: A Young Person's Guide to Jewish Spiritual Awareness
6 x 9, 96 pp, 2-color illus., HC, 978-1-879045-78-1 **$16.95** *For ages 9 and up*

The Book of Words: Talking Spiritual Life, Living Spiritual Talk
6 x 9, 160 pp, Quality PB, 978-1-58023-020-9 **$16.95**

Eyes Remade for Wonder: A Lawrence Kushner Reader *Introduction by Thomas Moore*
6 x 9, 240 pp, Quality PB, 978-1-58023-042-1 **$18.95**

God Was in This Place & I, i Did Not Know: Finding Self, Spirituality and Ultimate Meaning 6 x 9, 192 pp, Quality PB, 978-1-879045-33-0 **$16.95**

Honey from the Rock: An Introduction to Jewish Mysticism
6 x 9, 176 pp, Quality PB, 978-1-58023-073-5 **$16.95**

Invisible Lines of Connection: Sacred Stories of the Ordinary
5½ x 8½, 160 pp, Quality PB, 978-1-879045-98-9 **$15.95**

Jewish Spirituality—A Brief Introduction for Christians
5½ x 8½, 112 pp, Quality PB, 978-1-58023-150-3 **$12.95**

The River of Light: Jewish Mystical Awareness
6 x 9, 192 pp, Quality PB, 978-1-58023-096-4 **$16.95**

The Way Into Jewish Mystical Tradition
6 x 9, 224 pp, Quality PB, 978-1-58023-200-5 **$18.99**; HC, 978-1-58023-029-2 **$21.95**

Spirituality/Prayer

My People's Passover Haggadah: Traditional Texts, Modern Commentaries
Edited by Rabbi Lawrence A. Hoffman, PhD, and David Arnow, PhD Diverse commentaries on the traditional Passover Haggadah—in two volumes! Vol. 1: 7 x 10, 304 pp, HC 978-1-58023-354-5 **$24.99** Vol. 2: 7 x 10, 320 pp, HC, 978-1-58023-346-0 **$24.99**

Witnesses to the One: The Spiritual History of the *Sh'ma* *By Rabbi Joseph B. Meszler; Foreword by Rabbi Elyse Goldstein* 6 x 9, 176 pp, HC, 978-1-58023-309-5 **$19.99**

My People's Prayer Book Series

Traditional Prayers, Modern Commentaries *Edited by Rabbi Lawrence A. Hoffman*
Provides diverse and exciting commentary to the traditional liturgy, helping modern men and women find new wisdom in Jewish prayer, and bring liturgy into their lives. Each book includes Hebrew text, modern translation, and commentaries from all perspectives of the Jewish world.

Vol. 1—The *Sh'ma* and Its Blessings
7 x 10, 168 pp, HC, 978-1-879045-79-8 **$24.99**
Vol. 2—The *Amidah*
7 x 10, 240 pp, HC, 978-1-879045-80-4 **$24.95**
Vol. 3—*P'sukei D'zimrah* (Morning Psalms)
7 x 10, 240 pp, HC, 978-1-879045-81-1 **$24.95**
Vol. 4—*Seder K'riat Hatorah* (The Torah Service)
7 x 10, 264 pp, HC, 978-1-879045-82-8 **$23.95**
Vol. 5—*Birkhot Hashachar* (Morning Blessings)
7 x 10, 240 pp, HC, 978-1-879045-83-5 **$24.95**
Vol. 6—*Tachanun* and Concluding Prayers
7 x 10, 240 pp, HC, 978-1-879045-84-2 **$24.95**
Vol. 7—Shabbat at Home
7 x 10, 240 pp, HC, 978-1-879045-85-9 **$24.95**
Vol. 8—*Kabbalat Shabbat* (Welcoming Shabbat in the Synagogue)
7 x 10, 240 pp, HC, 978-1-58023-121-3 **$24.99**
Vol. 9—Welcoming the Night: *Minchah* and *Ma'ariv* (Afternoon and Evening Prayer) 7 x 10, 272 pp, HC, 978-1-58023-262-3 **$24.99**
Vol. 10—Shabbat Morning: *Shacharit* and *Musaf* (Morning and Additional Services) 7 x 10, 240 pp, HC, 978-1-58023-240-1 **$24.99**

Congregation Resources

The Art of Public Prayer, 2nd Edition: Not for Clergy Only *By Lawrence A. Hoffman*
6 x 9, 272 pp, Quality PB, 978-1-893361-06-5 **$19.99** *(A SkyLight Paths book)*

Becoming a Congregation of Learners: Learning as a Key to Revitalizing
Congregational Life *By Isa Aron, PhD; Foreword by Rabbi Lawrence A. Hoffman*
6 x 9, 304 pp, Quality PB, 978-1-58023-089-6 **$19.95**

Finding a Spiritual Home: How a New Generation of Jews Can Transform the
American Synagogue *By Rabbi Sidney Schwarz*
6 x 9, 352 pp, Quality PB, 978-1-58023-185-5 **$19.95**

Jewish Pastoral Care, 2nd Edition: A Practical Handbook from Traditional &
Contemporary Sources *Edited by Rabbi Dayle A. Friedman*
6 x 9, 528 pp, HC, 978-1-58023-221-0 **$40.00**

Jewish Spiritual Direction: An Innovative Guide from Traditional and Contemporary
Sources *Edited by Rabbi Howard A. Addison and Barbara Eve Breitman*
6 x 9, 368 pp, HC, 978-1-58023-230-2 **$30.00**

The Self-Renewing Congregation: Organizational Strategies for Revitalizing
Congregational Life *By Isa Aron, PhD; Foreword by Dr. Ron Wolfson*
6 x 9, 304 pp, Quality PB, 978-1-58023-166-4 **$19.95**

Spiritual Community: The Power to Restore Hope, Commitment and Joy
By Rabbi David A. Teutsch, PhD 5½ x 8½, 144 pp, HC, 978-1-58023-270-8 **$19.99**

The Spirituality of Welcoming: How to Transform Your Congregation into a
Sacred Community *By Dr. Ron Wolfson* 6 x 9, 224 pp, Quality PB, 978-1-58023-244-9 **$19.99**

Rethinking Synagogues: A New Vocabulary for Congregational Life
By Rabbi Lawrence A. Hoffman 6 x 9, 240 pp, Quality PB, 978-1-58023-248-7 **$19.99**

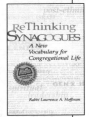

Children's Books

What You Will See Inside a Synagogue
By Rabbi Lawrence A. Hoffman and Dr. Ron Wolfson; Full-color photos by Bill Aron
A colorful, fun-to-read introduction that explains the ways and whys of Jewish
worship and religious life. 8½ x 10½, 32 pp, Full-color photos, Quality PB, 978-1-59473-256-0 **$8.99**
For ages 6 & up (A SkyLight Paths book)

The Kids' Fun Book of Jewish Time
By Emily Sper 9 x 7½, 24 pp, Full-color illus., HC, 978-1-58023-311-8 **$16.99**

In God's Hands
By Lawrence Kushner and Gary Schmidt 9 x 12, 32 pp, HC, 978-1-58023-224-1 **$16.99**

Because Nothing Looks Like God
By Lawrence and Karen Kushner
Introduces children to the possibilities of spiritual life.
11 x 8½, 32 pp, Full-color illus., HC, 978-1-58023-092-6 **$17.99** *For ages 4 & up*
Also Available: **Because Nothing Looks Like God Teacher's Guide**
8½ x 11, 22 pp, PB, 978-1-58023-140-4 **$6.95** *For ages 5–8*

Board Book Companions to *Because Nothing Looks Like God*
5 x 5, 24 pp, Full-color illus., SkyLight Paths Board Books *For ages 0–4*

What Does God Look Like? 978-1-893361-23-2 **$7.99**

How Does God Make Things Happen? 978-1-893361-24-9 **$7.95**

Where Is God? 978-1-893361-17-1 **$7.99**

The Book of Miracles: A Young Person's Guide to Jewish Spiritual Awareness
By Lawrence Kushner. All-new illustrations by the author
6 x 9, 96 pp, 2-color illus., HC, 978-1-879045-78-1 **$16.95** *For ages 9 and up*

In Our Image: God's First Creatures
By Nancy Sohn Swartz 9 x 12, 32 pp, Full-color illus., HC, 978-1-879045-99-6 **$16.95** *For ages 4 & up*
Also Available as a Board Book: **How Did the Animals Help God?**
5 x 5, 24 pp, Board, Full-color illus., 978-1-59473-044-3 **$7.99** *For ages 0–4 (A SkyLight Paths book)*

What Makes Someone a Jew?
By Lauren Seidman
Reflects the changing face of American Judaism.
10 x 8½, 32 pp, Full-color photos, Quality PB Original, 978-1-58023-321-7 **$8.99** *For ages 3–6*

About Jewish Lights

People of all faiths and backgrounds yearn for books that attract, engage, educate, and spiritually inspire.

Our principal goal is to stimulate thought and help all people learn about who the Jewish People are, where they come from, and what the future can be made to hold. While people of our diverse Jewish heritage are the primary audience, our books speak to people in the Christian world as well and will broaden their understanding of Judaism and the roots of their own faith.

We bring to you authors who are at the forefront of spiritual thought and experience. While each has something different to say, they all say it in a voice that you can hear.

Our books are designed to welcome you and then to engage, stimulate, and inspire. We judge our success not only by whether or not our books are beautiful and commercially successful, but by whether or not they make a difference in your life.

For your information and convenience, at the back of this book we have provided a list of other Jewish Lights books you might find interesting and useful. They cover all the categories of your life:

Bar/Bat Mitzvah	Life Cycle
Bible Study / Midrash	Meditation
Children's Books	Parenting
Congregation Resources	Prayer
Current Events / History	Ritual / Sacred Practice
Ecology/ Environment	Spirituality
Fiction: Mystery, Science Fiction	Theology / Philosophy
Grief / Healing	Travel
Holidays / Holy Days	12-Step
Inspiration	Women's Interest
Kabbalah / Mysticism / Enneagram	

Stuart M. Matlins, Publisher

Or phone, fax, mail or e-mail to: **JEWISH LIGHTS Publishing**
Sunset Farm Offices, Route 4 • P.O. Box 237 • Woodstock, Vermont 05091
Tel: (802) 457-4000 • Fax: (802) 457-4004 • www.jewishlights.com
Credit card orders: **(800) 962-4544** (8:30AM–5:30PM ET Monday–Friday)
Generous discounts on quantity orders. SATISFACTION GUARANTEED. Prices subject to change.

For more information about each book, visit our website at www.jewishlights.com